A Japanese 'Val' dive-bomber beginning to pull out of its dive over a US
carrier c.1942. (U.S. National Archives)

DIVE BOMBERS
IN ACTION

Peter C. Smith

BLANDFORD PRESS
London New York Sydney

◄
Cockpit layout of an A-31 Northrop-built Vultee
Vengeance dive-bomber showing the ample
space common in American aircraft of this
period. (Northrop)

For Eileen and Ernie
with thanks for everything
and I mean everything!

The Author would like to offer his sincere thanks to the following for their stories, their helpfulness, their patience and their kindness during the preparation of this book: George W. Allen; Squadron Leader Lennart Berns; Burton S. Block; Captain E. M. Brown; M. Jean Cuny; Chas Dellow; the late Admiral Sir Michael Denny; Larry Dye; E. Christopher Deanesly; James L. R. Flynn; L. F. Foster; Wing Commander Arthur M. Gill; Kenneth Gray; Captain Tom Harrington; Douglas Johnstone; Lord Kilbracken (for permission to quote from his book *Bring Back my Stringbag*; Colonel Nils Kindberg; Admiral Francis Laine; the late Hans-Joachim Lehmann; Valentine Maluga (for translating many Russian documents and papers for me so patiently); Admiral William I. Martin; Paul L. Muir; Bud McInnes; Cyril McPherson; Hugh V. Morgan; Paul L. Muir; Major Frank Neubert; Major R. J. C. O'Loan; my good friend, Robert Olds, for permission to quote from his book *Helldiver Squadron*; Nicola Patella; Bob Piper; Donald Ritchie; the late Hans-Ulrich Rudel; Mark A. Savage; Kurt Scheffel; Peter Schwartzkopf; Heinz Sellhorn; J. R. Spiers; Gerd Stamp; James M. Swan; Roland W. Tapp; Major Ennio Tarantola; Tommy Thompson; Allan H. Thomson; Ron Walesby; John Blair Watson, Jnr.; Rolf Westerberg; Dr Erik Wilkenson; Stanley Worth.

This story is their story.

Peter C. Smith, Riseley, Bedford.

First published in Great Britain in 1988 by Blandford Press, Artillery House, Artillery Row, London SW1P 1RT.

Distributed in the USA by Sterling Publishing Co. Inc., 2 Park Avenue, New York, NY 10016.

Distributed in Australia by Capricorn Link (Australia) Pty. Ltd., P.O Box 665, Lane Cove, New South Wales 2066, Australia.

The illustrations in this book have been collected from many sources, and vary in quality owing to the variety of circumstances under which they were taken and preserved. As a result, certain of the illustrations are not of the standard to be expected from the best of today's equipment, materials and techniques. They are nevertheless included for their inherent information value, to provide an authentic visual coverage of the subject.

Designed and edited by DAG Publications Ltd. Designed by David Gibbons; edited by Michael Boxall; typeset by Typesetters (Birmingham) Ltd., camerawork by M&E Reproductions, North Fambridge, Essex; printed and bound in Great Britain by The Bath Press, Avon.

British Library Cataloguing in Publication Data:
Smith, Peter, C. (Peter Charles), 1940–
Dive-bombers in action.
Dive-bomber aeroplanes, to 1985
I. Title
623.74′63′09

ISBN 0-7137-1957-5

Contents

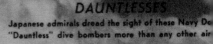
DAUNTLESSES
Japanese admirals dread the sight of these Navy Do
"Dauntless" dive bombers more than any other air

▲
Douglas Dauntless dive-bombers wearing the normal US Navy Pacific 'dark-blue' colour scheme for aircraft. Note enlarged and simplified National markings. Note how the original solid red disc in the centre of the star has been eliminated to prevent confusion with the red 'meatball' of the Japanese marking. (US National Archives)

◀
Back-seat man. Always the man who had to 'sit-and-take-it', the rear-gunner had the same philosophical viewpoint no matter what nation he served with. Here a US Marine Corps Dauntless gunner flexes his armament prior to another mission from a Bougainville airstrip. (Meg Campbell)

PART ONE
THEORY AND PRACTICE:
Evolution to 1939

A STUDY of the role of the dive-bomber in action during the Second World War makes a fascinating voyage of discovery into the pages of neglected air history. So much has been written on all other aspects of the air war, and so little deep research has been conducted into dive-bombing itself, that fresh and surprising facts will reward any researcher who cares to delve into the forgotten and often overlooked archives of this aspect of air fighting.

So much that is dismissive has been written about dive-bombers and dive-bombing, both during the war in an attempt to detract from its effectiveness, and since by historians who settle for the simple and shallow view, that it is hard to break through the myth and propaganda to establish the facts. One thing is certain: the story of the dive-bombers is exciting and action-packed, revealing courage and daring to equal that of any fighter pilots' exploits during the same conflict.

This book concentrates mainly on the battles and achievements of the dive-bombers and their crews. It is not a technical book and makes no pretence to be so, but the background and the technical and practical applications of this method of bombing cannot be ignored, and a brief résumé of the dive-bomber story up to the outbreak of war is included. Finally, the ideas behind the aircraft, the experimental work, trials and tests, the improvisations – with their spectacular successes and ghastly failures – are also given their due measure in this book. But in the main it is a record of gallantry and skill in battle by pilots whose whole rationale was to throw themselves full-tilt at the enemy and meet all he had to offer face-to-face. What more exciting and daring method of warfare could there have been than this aerial equivalent of a cavalry charge!

The man who conducted the very first true dive-bomber combat mission, Harry Brown of 84 Squadron (second from the left) on the Western Front in 1918. He was the smallest pilot in his unit and therefore chosen to fly the mission carrying a bomb and diving vertically on German supply barges on a canal in northern France. Twenty-two years later the Germans were to reply in kind, but on a rather larger scale! (RAF Museum)

1. Early History to 1919

ALMOST as soon as man was able to build aerial machines and fly he began converting them to instruments for the furtherance of war. Reconnaissance was the immediate and most obvious role, but this soon developed into armed patrolling with small bombs. Here 'targets of opportunity' could be attacked and these were usually distinctive and individual features, an enemy staff car, a train laden with munitions or troops, a troublesome gun battery.

It quickly became apparent that accurate bomb dropping from any great height while the aircraft itself was travelling horizontally was a difficult task. The forward movement of the aircraft, the curvature of the bomb's path in flight, the time delay which allowed the target to take cover or avoiding action and the natural hazards of cross-winds and air currents with their effects upon primitive machine and bomb alike, were factors that reduced the chances of actually hitting such small targets at all. Moreover, the small size and destructive power of the early airborne missiles meant that even a close miss was ineffectual. A direct hit was needed.

The solution was equally obvious: direct the aircraft at the target by means of a dive. This, in turn, solved several problems. The rapid reduction in height of the attacking aircraft lessened the time lapse between bomb release and impact. This in turn reduced the target's

chance of taking avoiding action, and the reduction in descent time of the missile reduced the chances of cross-winds and air currents to interfere with the flight path to the target. Another valuable spin-off in the early days was that defending gunners had less time to align the plunging aircraft in their gun sights.

And so dive-bombing commenced and gradually became a highly valued method of attack. Although there had been previous isolated examples of ordnance being dropped from flying machines while diving, the first full flowering of the technique, as indeed with most other early aspects of aerial warfare, was made manifest during the war of 1914–18.

In the early days, the actual angle at which the aircraft dived was never measured precisely; anything from forty degrees to the vertical was acceptable according to the whim of the pilot and the conditions prevailing. What soon became apparent was that the greater the angle of attack, the greater was the degree of accuracy obtained. As there were no instruments to gauge the dive angle, many attacks described as 'vertical dives' in pilots' log-books and memoirs were not so, for it is accepted that in any steep dive the natural tendency of the pilot is to over-estimate how close to the vertical he is. Indeed many later pilots described a common phenomenon when dive-bombing of feeling to

Among the earliest of American dive-bomber pilots were those of the United States Marine Corps, here seen manning their planes during operations in Nicaragua in 1927. (US Marine Corps Official)

be 'over the vertical', even if their instruments said otherwise.

The estimation of height during a rapid descent was another factor left entirely to the pilot's discretion. With no altimeter, or only a primitive piece of equipment, the rapid loss of height could be dangerous in the extreme. The natural tendency was to press on down as close as possible to the target to ensure its destruction. This led to an over-concentration on the aiming-point by inexperienced pilots with the result that their dives became truly 'terminal' in that they failed to pull out in time. Even if the 'pull-out' factor was adjudged correctly, the height at which the dive commenced, the wind and weather, the resistance put up by the target and the pilot's expertise were all random factors, which would be met more by 'feel' than by scientific analysis.

The stresses imposed by high-speed diving followed by sudden pull-out to normal flight affected man and machine alike. The notorious 'G' factor caused pilots to lose consciousness for a few vital seconds ('black-out') or to experience blurred vision and sluggishness ('grey-out'). The fragile aircraft of the early years tended to shed their wings and other vital structural components. This was gradually to lead to more suitable aircraft fully stressed to take account of such factors. Thus began the move which took dive-bombing from the province of any small aircraft into the realms of a highly specialized machine, designed and built purely for the job.

Despite these hazards the results more than justified the risks in that the percentage of targets hit and destroyed against aircraft lost became more and more favourable. The other much-favoured method of attacking ground targets was the 'strafing' concept of low-level approach, and this was to lead to a crippling casualty rate as anti-aircraft defences increased. So the diving attack was both more accurate and, relatively, more cost-effective.

The Royal Flying Corps of Great Britain was the service that did the most to carry the dive-bombing method into combat, Lieutenant Harry Brown of No. 84 Squadron making the first recognized such attack when he sank a munitions barge by dive-bombing on the Western Front in 1917. The RFC conducted full and detailed trials of all aspects of dive-bombing and made the first scientific study of this new form of flying. Extensive trials were held with a wide variety of experience and novice pilots at the Orfordness Bombing Range in Suffolk during the years 1918–19, and much valuable data was formulated. Among the conclusions reached was the significant one that dive-bombing was a skill or an art and that, as with fighter pilots, natural flair and ability counted a great deal. In other words dive-bomber men were born not made, although with careful training it was a skill that could be learned and a fair degree of expertise reached.

More significant, as regards the future of dive-bombing they concluded that it was too dangerous a method to continue with, although they conceded its accuracy. Dive-bombing while using an Aldis telescope sight led to fatalities, and the accuracy achieved was no more than that achieved by 'eye sighting'. Again this was to have repercussions later when the Air Ministry refused to develop a proper sight for Naval dive-bombers. But the whole concept of dive-bombing was thrown aside in the immediate aftermath of the war for reasons as much political as scientific.

It was the introduction by the Germans of the strategical and terror methods of aerial attack on civilian targets, typified by the Gotha raids on London in the summer of 1917, which induced the British Admiralty to develop a counter. This resulted in the long-range bomber capable of striking at Berlin from British airfields, and the concept was eagerly embraced by the newly formed Royal Air Force in 1918 as it gave them a strong *raison d'être*. Under the influence of Lord Trenchard this doctrine spread, influencing even former enthusiasts of the dive-bomber concept such as the American, Billy Mitchell, and finding 'prophets' such as the Italian, Douhet, in every nation.

The resulting growth of the 'Strategical' rather than 'Tactical' school of thought with regard to the proper em-

One of the early experimental dive-bomber adaptations which the Flygvapnet (Royal Swedish Air Force) used to practise and perfect its dive-bomber techniques were licensed-built Hawker Harts. Here a formation of five of these machines, known as the ASJA B4, are seen in formation in 1936. (Flygvapnet)

The old order passes. A Curtiss SBC-4, the last of the biplane dive-bombers. This one belonged to the US 15th Naval District and, as the grey paintwork and national insignia layout show, was photographed in late 1941.
(US National Archives)

ployment of air power led to the scornful dismissal of any type of air attack that smacked of subservience to the other services or detracted from the false vision of air power winning future wars unaided. So close air support, whether at sea with the Navy or in land battles, was not encouraged. This general neglect and prejudice encompassed the doctrine of dive-bombing itself, which became the object of particularly virulent and deep-seated scorn in the higher echelons of both the RAF and USAAC, and its many subsequent proofs of accuracy and efficiency failed to eradicate this.

Dive-bombing was the most spectacular form of aerial attack, and it was the most accurate method of airborne delivery of ordnance on to a precise target area in places conventional artillery bombardment could not reach. Unlike other forms of air attack, the dive-bomber could place its bombs exactly and so could conduct its support mission very close to its own friendly forces. Its inherent accuracy thereby made it not only a reliable and effective form of air support, but, just as importantly, a trust-worthy method of delivery. Medium bombers laying a carpet of bombs indiscriminately or fighter-bombers skimming low and dropping bombs where trajectories bounced them into friendly forces did as much to *discourage* Allied ground troops from calling for air strikes as the exactitude of the Junkers Ju 87 delivery positively *encouraged* its use by

the German Army.

In common with all other forms of bombing efficiency, it was the forgotten heroes who ensured that what the air-crews delivered was worth the trip. The groundcrews that kept the aircraft flying rarely receive their due merit in books of this nature. For obvious reasons the men 'at the sharp end' receive the attention, and that is how it should be. But those who sweated in back area landing-fields, whether hand-cranking Stukas in sub-zero temperatures in the Russian wastes; sweating and toiling on humid and dank airstrips hacked out of virgin Pacific jungle to keep Val or Dauntless air-worthy; cursing the sand and heat on lonely desert airfields or toiling in vast hangar decks of vulnerable aircraft-carriers surrounded by bombs, munitions and aviation fuel in a floating target for every enemy aircraft and submarine, the fitters and armourers earned their right to be remembered along with the pilots and navigators. Without their patience and ingenuity the dive-bombers would not have been able to mount their round-the-clock missions to such effect. They had to rise before dawn to get the planes fuelled, checked and armed, and often had to work on after dusk the same day trying to patch up the much-needed bombers for yet more missions the following day.

Shortly before his death the most famous dive-bomber pilot of all, Hans-Ulrich Rudel, wrote to me saying:

'The missions of the German dive-bomber units were widespread and losses were high, but despite this they were ready to fly at any time. With every alert we Stuka flyers fought very close with our troops on the ground as they had to carry the main burden of the fighting. The name "Infantry of the Air" given to us by the soldiers was a recognition that we helped our comrades on the ground and sometimes saved them from impossible situations and terrible fates.

The story of the unique successes of Stuka pilots and gunners all over Europe and North Africa, despite their small numbers and the inferiority of their machines, is also respected by many of our former enemies. Even during the war itself the word "Stuka" meant bravery and readiness. In no other air force and in no other German flying corps were the achievements of single aircrews and squadrons even nearly as high as with the Stuka flyers.

But we must not forget that without the technical ground personnel all this would have been impossible.'[1]

High praise indeed. Often the ground crews had to pay the ultimate price for operating so close to the front line. A breakthrough on the Eastern Front often left the forward airstrips cut off and the faithful back-up teams isolated and doomed to imprisonment, or worse.

2. Between the wars developments

IN the 1920s the only remaining formations where one might have found dive-bombing practised were the Fleet Air Arm of the Royal Navy and the US Army Air Corps. That two such unrelated services should have retained a minimal interest in the technique is remarkable, but that the method survived this barren period at all is due solely to that interest. In the Royal Navy the fleets' aircraft were designed and provided by the RAF, much to the detriment of all types of naval aviation. No dive-bombers as such were built, despite an increasing clamour for them by the Navy as the years went by. During the 1920s fighter aircraft, equipped with very small bombs, did practise diving attacks with sections of aircraft coming in from different points of the compass against target ships. These were the famous 'converging attacks', and, although the bombs carried would have been ineffectual against all but the smallest of warships, the theory and tactics evolved and kept under review by the young Navy pilots convinced them of the inherent value of dive-bombing and so kept the flame flickering dimly in Great Britain.

The US Marine Corp's 4 Air Squadron, led by Captain Harvey B. Mims, carried out a very primitive form of dive-bombing during their counter-insurgency intervention in Haiti in 1919, but although this is often cited as the origins of dive-bombing it was in fact a poor substitute (utilizing a dive angle of only 45 degrees) for the already proven and combat-tested attacks carried out in 1917–18 on the Western Front. The real American innovators proved to be the aviators of Army Air Corps Attack Group 3, led by Lieutenant Lewis H. Brereton, patrolling the Mexican border during the same period. They were flying De Havilland DH4 aircraft fitted with Liberty engines, but even so frequently dived at angles of 60–70 degrees to drop their bombs from improvised underwing bomb racks, and achieved great accuracy.

They freely admitted that they had been taught the technique while serving with RFC units in France in 1918, and one convert was Marine aviator Lieutenant Erasmus Rowell. He later incorporated the method in his own unit, VO-1-M, when he assumed command in 1924. He rapidly refined the technique and proved it in frequent actions during the American intervention in Nicaragua from 1927 to 1929. Marine Corps flyers had already given many demonstrations of dive-bombing at Air Fairs in the United States, and the US Navy became another convert.

Captain Reeves of the USN was a particularly enthusiastic convert as was Admiral F. D. Wagner, and soon Navy pursuit aircraft were carrying increasingly large underwing bomb loads and delivering them in dives of more than 70 degrees from heights above 10,000 feet.

One classic dummy attack on the US Fleet off San Diego was made by VF-2 flying Curtiss F6C aircraft in October 1926 and was so successful that dive-bombing became permanently enshrined in US Navy doctrine from that time.

Increasing funds were devoted to the development of highly specialized dive-bomber aircraft for the Navy and Marine Corps from the late 1920s onward. These developed through several types, the most famous of which was the Curtiss aircraft christened 'Helldiver'. Ample publicity and Hollywood movies ensured that they became well-known the world over, and both British and Japanese naval flyers were equally impressed when they visited the United States. They took their enthusiasm back to their own fleets on their return home.

In Japan the conversion to dive-bombing communicated itself to the highest level, Admiral Yamamoto himself, and thus received financial backing on a par with that which the US Navy was giving dive-bombing. The Japanese rapidly produced a succession of steadily improving designs, like the Aichi D1A Type 94 Carrier Bomber, and built them in large numbers. They also soon acquired great skill in the technique and proved it in battle in China during the 1930s.

The Japanese operations in China proved as valuable to their armed forces in preparation for the major war to come as was the Spanish Civil War in the same period to the German, Italian and Soviet forces. Both campaigns showed the need of precision aircraft, small and expendable enough to operate right up in the front line no matter how rugged the terrain. Here range and defensive armament was not so essential as toughness and accuracy. The attacking of targets in a power-dive was soon adopted by both the Japanese Army and the Navy as the best method of maximizing hits on vital targets. Although the long-range over water flights by Japanese twin-engined bombers pioneered strategical applications, and their terror bombings of Chinese open cities did much to influence other powers, it was the dive-bombing of vital objectives that led to the rapid expansion of Japanese power.

In Great Britain equal interest was inhibited by the fact that the RAF proved reluctant to supply the aircraft, the dive-bombing sights or the pilots to carry out such a policy, but constant Admiralty pressure brought about a reluctant agreement to provide a custom-built dive-bomber for the fleet. This turned out to be the Blackburn Skua (of which more later), but its excellence as a dive-bomber was compromised by the insistence that it operate as a fighter aircraft as well – two totally different roles!

One unexpected side-effect of the publicity afforded to the American dive-bombers was the reinforcement of the already well-established interest in the dive-bomber in Germany. When visiting America, Ernst Udet had been so impressed by the Helldivers that he persuaded Goering to purchase a couple for his own personal evaluation. Although the oft-quoted statement that this led to the Stuka concept is incorrect, it did underline the commitment of the new Luftwaffe to this form of bombing. The economy of dive-bombing and ratio of hits per sortie fitted in perfectly with this mainly ex-Army officered service's concept of the bomber as a close-support arm for a mechanized army.

Actually the Junkers Ju 87 Stuka owed its origins to existing German experimentation much closer to home, and to the research work conducted by a small European neighbour, Sweden, with whom Goering had many industrial connections. The first planned Swedish dive-bombing trials were held in the autumn of 1934 by N.4 Wing at Fröson. These trials influenced the German Junkers team then experimenting with the modified K.47 monoplane fighter aircraft. It is still stoutly maintained by some that Swedish interest in this type of attack dated back to German experiments with the K.47, but official Swedish aviation historians firmly refute this. Colonel Nils Kindberg stated quite unequivocally in a special *Flygvapnet* Memorandum prepared for the author in 1978:

'We can state here that an entirely independent, separate occurrence was noted at that time. A well-known test pilot from the German Junkers works at

◀

A great opportunity wasted. The much-mourned Hawker Henley. Built with classic lines, this dive-bomber was aborted pre-war and thrown away as a target tug while the RAF went to war with the inferior Fairey Battle light bomber which was shot out of the sky over the Maas bridges, achieving nothing. (RAF Museum)

▶

Another view of the classy chassis of the Hawker Henley. Its shared parentage with the Hurricane is obvious, and its shared power-plant was to contribute to its downfall. One of the great 'What Ifs' of the war, the Henley might have become famous if it had been used in its designed role. (RAF Museum)

Dessau and some other personnel from that factory, with a Limnham-assembled, for specialized rocket-bombing Junkers K.47 plane, had obtained permission from the Swedish government to execute rocket-bombing tests at the same air-base at Fröson at the same time. The Swedish team and the German team therefore got the opportunity to observe their respective trials and to exchange some views with each other. The German preference in the premier stages of the Second World War for dive-bombing and the birth of their ominous Stuka plane, the Junkers Ju 87, shortly before that period, was influenced in part by the Swedish Fröson experiments of 1934.'[2]

That would seem clear enough. As early as October 1933 orders were given to set up an experimental dive-bomber group for the fledgling German Air Force, not yet out in the open. The unit selected was a fighter unit, Jagdgeschwader 132, but it was to be re-equipped with the Heinkel He 50 biplane dive-bombers designed specifically for the task. These were to replace its existing Heinkel He 51 fighters, and two years later fifty He 50s were in service conducting trials and training. More modern, custom-built dive-bombers were provided by the Reichswehr's supply officer, Major Freiherr von Richthofen, who was not totally convinced of the value of the method, in the form of the Fieseler Fi 98 and the Henschel 123. The latter proved superior and was adopted. Meanwhile

the Junkers team continued with their own development of the Ju 87, receiving considerable encouragement from Ernst Udet himself.

Among the rival designs were Heinkel's clean monoplane design, the He 118, the Blohm & Voss Ha 137 and the Arado Ar 81, but only the former was a serious contender and after extensive trials held at Rechlin in 1936 the Junkers was adopted as the new 'standard' dive-bomber, mainly due to its strength in the dive configuration. Further experiments with the Junkers Ju 87 continued in 1937 and the dispatch of three of these aircraft to participate in the Spanish Civil War was part and parcel of those experiments, designed to test new equipment and tactics under combat conditions. That nothing final had been determined is made clear by the statement issued that year in which the evaluation staff from Rugen who were monitoring the work conducted by Bomber Group K/88, commented:

'The operational dive-bombing trials that have been in progress since September 1936, with three Junkers Ju A-1s, have remained at an elementary stage owing to difficulties encountered with the equipment.'[3]

Not until the introduction of the Junkers Ju 87B-1 in October 1938, did the dive-bomber trials start to throw up more positive results and 'firmed up' German attitudes to the weapon. At Rechlin, the RLM (German Air Ministry)

conducted their trials and tests of bomb-release equipment, including the swing-crutch to carry the bomb clear of the propeller arc, an idea copied from the Americans, while sighting and aiming experiments were conducted at Tarnewitz.

A Kette (Flight) of three Junkers Ju 87B-1s was sent to Spain in the autumn of 1938 to replace the As and a succession of pilots used these three aircraft in order to be able to spread their combat experience and expertise as widely as possible among the personnel equipping the now rapidly expanding dive-bomber arm. Among young Stuka pilots thus gaining combat experience were many who later were to become dive-bomber aces in the Second World War.

The Junkers Ju 87B-1 was an inverted gull wing monoplane, with a fixed, 'spatted' undercarriage and powered by a single Jumo 221D engine of some 1,210hp. This gave it a speed of 380kph and a range of 800 kilometres. This was ample for a machine intended from the first to operate with the spearheads of the army and be rugged enough to operate from rough, forward airstrips in order to keep up with the advance. A crew of two, pilot and navigator/rear gunner/wireless operator, sat in tandem in a long 'greenhouse' type cockpit which gave excellent all-round vision. Two fixed guns firing forward in the wings and a rear gun mounted on a flexible pivot was its modest armament,

After the abortive failure of the SM85, Italy's aircraft manufacturers made strenuous attempts to produce a workable dive-bomber, by adapting existing fighter types and designing new dive-bombers straight from the drawing-board. The resulting aircraft were often promising, but such was the sorry state of Italy's economy that few if any of these ideas ever got much further than the prototype stage. Here are three views of the Caproni Ca 335, a fighter adaptation with a limited dive-bombing potential. (Nicola Malizia)

Far more workmanlike was the Fiat FC 12 Tuffo. This is the prototype of the new aircraft which featured retractable landing gear and internal bomb bay. (Nicola Malizia)

but close formation tactics could give some mutual protection against the fighters of the day, and it was always intended that fighter cover would be on hand. Usual payload was a single 550lb bomb mounted on the swing-crutch under the centre fuselage. Two 250lb or four 110lb bombs could be carried under the wings outboard of the undercarriage. The slatted dive brakes gave the pilot perfect control and the aircraft balanced naturally when stood on its head. It was, in fact, the perfect dive-bombing machine. Although often declared obsolete, its outstanding merits as an accurate and stable delivery platform of precision ordnance ensured its continued front-line deployment and production until 1944.

In Spain the clutch of Ju 87Bs proved highly successful in attacking pin-point targets such as bridges, command posts and artillery positions, and helped in the formulation of the standard Luftwaffe doctrine for close-support and ground-attack operations. The value of such lessons and their assimilation into standard practice cannot be over-estimated and bore fruit in the Polish, French and Balkan campaigns a few years later. They also achieved some notable hits on ships in harbour during the final siege operations against Barcelona and Valencia and this aspect of their worth was an omen of their future deployment against the Royal Navy. The Germans set up a special dive-bomber unit for operating from the two new aircraft carriers

being built for their own navy. They featured folding wings and flotation bags for ditching as well as tail-hooks for carrier deck landings. Several Naval Office volunteers were consequently trained in dive-bombing. In the event, however, the carriers never materialized and the 'naval' Stukas and their former naval officer pilots took part in the land battles, to good effect and became part of the Luftwaffe.

At the outbreak of war in September 1939, the aircraft available for dive-bombing naturally reflected both the status accorded the technique by each nation and the aeronautical state of the art each had reached. Only sometimes the two did not match. Thus America (Vought SBU Vindicator, Douglas SBD Dauntless, Curtiss SB2C Helldiver, Vultee A34 Vengeance and Brewster SB2A Buccaneer), Germany (Junkers Ju 87 and Ju 88) and Japan (Aichi D3A1 Val, Yokosuka D4Y Comet and Aichi B7A Shooting Star) were the three nations which could combine firm commitment to the art with the technology to back it up. The Soviet Union (Archangelski Ar-2) had the technology to spare, but in 1939 was only just coming round to the dive-bomber concept. Nevertheless, she more than made up for lost time, producing a world-beater (Petlyakov Pe-2 Peshka) at almost the first attempt, a dive-bomber actually faster than the most modern fighter aircraft! Great Britain (Hawker Henley and Blackburn Skua) was unique

in that she had the technology and had produced perfect aircraft for the job, but had then turned her back on them. Only the minority representation of the Fleet Air Arm had an interest in dive-bombing. Moreover, having a specialized dive-bomber and then expecting it to act as a fighter for most of its career tended to negate the good qualities it had in its correct role.

Italy's Regia Aeronautica had also partaken of widespread operations in support of Franco's forces in Spain and they too had learned the value of the dive-bomber's inherent accuracy, utilizing such fighter aircraft as the Breda Ca 65. These were used in the dive-bomber role, most outstandingly during July 1938 when 65 Squadriglia Assalto attacked vital bridges across the River Ebro at Flix. Diving at an angle of 80 degrees, they breached the bridges with direct hits. From such successes came many dive-bomber designs. The most well-known of these was the Savoia Marchetti SM85/86, but Italy although in the forefront of ideas, was behind in the application of technology and lacked the manufacturing base to exploit them. Thus, although she had the right idea with regard to concept and tactics, she consistently failed to produce aircraft in anything other than 'penny packets'.

Poland had a small, high-quality base, but again came too late to the dive-bomber (PZL P38 Wilk), while France (Loire Nieuport LN 401/410) was hope-

lessly over-extended in every direction and her home industry was too fragmented to produce the quantity required. Sweden (SAAB 18) was high in knowledge, technique and practice, and concentrated her small but efficient resources to a large extent on dive-bombing.

Where specialized aircraft did not exist, either through lack of interest, priority or time, each nation pressed into service other types as makeshift dive-bombers, or purchased well-proven types from other nations. In this regard, Italy, Hungary and other lesser Axis partners tended to buy the Junkers Ju 87 'off the shelf' as a tried and tested product, although some like Bulgaria (DAF 10F) and Roumania (IAR 81) home-made dive-bombers were attempted with varying degrees of success or failure. Likewise France, running out of time, had to supplement her few home-grown products with bulk purchase from the USA (Vought V156F and Curtiss SBC4) as, even more belatedly, did Great Britain (Vought-Sikorsky Cheapeake, Curtiss SBC4 Cleveland, Douglas SBD Dauntless, Brewster Bermuda and Vultee Vengeance). Lesser powers such as China (Heinkel He66a CH), Sweden (BJS-built Hawker Hart), Thailand (Curtiss BFC Hawk) soldiered on with obsolete models or, like Finland later (Pe-2), captured enemy aircraft.

A pair of Vought 156F dive-bombers of the French Navy at Mardyck air base in France, February 1940. (Musée de l'Air, Paris)

A Vought 156F of AB-1-12 showing full French Navy markings and bomb load. This export version of the Vought Vindicator also saw service with the Royal Navy as the Chesapeake. (Musée del 'Air, Paris) ▼

Two views of experimental model of the Curtiss SBC2 'Helldiver' with yellow wing markings, etc., undergoing trials. (US National Archives)

3. Theory and Practice

BEFORE proceeding to our main story it might be as well briefly to set out the parameters of dive-bombing as they existed at the outbreak of the war. Each nation varied slightly in its interpretation of what constituted dive-bombing, but the general principles remained valid and the arguments mainly rested on what degree of dive was taken as the matrix. In the RAF the dive angle had to be of 70 degrees or greater, anything less being considered glide bombing. Indeed, in 1938, so opposed was the Air Ministry to this form of attack that they decided to stop using the description 'dive-bombing' and to substitute the term 'losing height bombing'. Perhaps the 'Bomb Berlin' school thought that the method would be lost along with the expression. Unfortunately for them the rest of the world (and the Royal Navy) continued to call dive-bombing just that and the RAF's attempt to will away what they did not wish to acknowledge failed utterly.

The generally accepted definition of dive-bombing was that it was a method of attack whereby the bombs were released during a dive, from a height of between 1,000 and 3,000 feet or upward. The general method of such an attack

featured four phases: approach; initial dive; aiming dive; get-away.

The approach

If possible the approach was made in high cloud cover so as to achieve immunity from fighters and high-angle AA. The target was 'stalked' with care (radar was in its infancy in 1939), but without undue delay in order to ensure surprise; quick peep and back into cloud. A compact formation offered a better defence against fighters, but if none were about the aircraft split up into subformations and re-assembled at the initial diving position.

The initial dive

This was necessary if the approach were carried out from above 6,000 feet in order to reduce the length of the aiming dive. It formed a link between the end of the approach (at the edge of cover or beyond target's gun range) and the aiming dive. Normally the attackers would have assumed line astern or sections in line astern formation, according to circumstances and type. Individual aircraft or sections would open out to intervals of about 500 yards to make things difficult for defending gunners. In

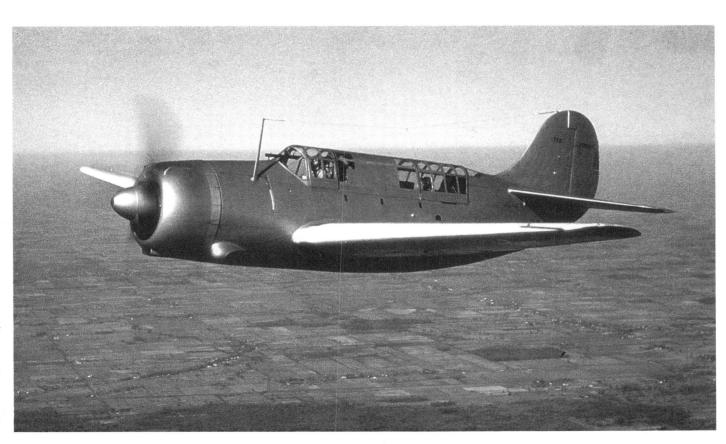

certain circumstances, sections began the initial dive from different directions ('converging attack' scenario), sufficiently dispersed to avoid the zone of close-range fire directed at another section.

The aiming dive

This was begun from a position known colloquially as the 'X' point, which depended on conditions of release, i.e., height, angle of dive and air speed at moment of release. Selection of the 'X' point rested primarily with each pilot's judgement, aided by markings on the leading or trailing edges of wings, or graticules on the cockpit perspex. The tendency to follow the aircraft ahead had to be resisted, although in practice it was common.

On occasion all attacks were made from the same side of the target, e.g., when bombing warships, because only half their AA guns could fire at any one time. The Germans and Japanese quickly found that British warships, which tended to distribute their very limited AA weapons to port and starboard, were vulnerable to attacks from directly astern or ahead, where their guns would not bear.

The get-away

Each pilot also had to get out of AA range, regain cloud cover and re-group on the formation as quickly as possible.[4] The optimum angle of dive was that which would, taking all factors into consideration, obtain the greatest number of hits with the fewest casualties from AA fire. Broadly speaking, this meant the steepest possible angle without losing the control necessary to give accurate aiming, and it varied according to aircraft and pilot expertise. While longitudinal control was usually satisfactory, lateral control gradually became worse as the speed increased, the aircraft became 'set' in the dive and it became far more difficult, if not impossible, to correct the aim except in a longitudinal direction. A Blackburn Skua, with dive flaps down, would not exceed 240 knots in a dive, but lateral control was not good at this speed.

In a steep dive (70 degrees plus), less skill was required to judge the moment of release, because the bombing angle was smaller and the bomb could be released with appreciable 'pull-out', but it was essential that the pilot got 'on' the target at once as otherwise he might find himself unable to, or might find himself skidding or turning at the moment of release, with consequent large errors.

It was always vital to reduce the aircraft's speed at the end of the initial dive. In purpose-built dive bombers this was necessary so that the dive flaps could be lowered safely, in cases where these flaps had not been lowered before the initial dive began. The sudden lowering of dive flaps at high speed would have ripped the wings out of the aircraft. The maximum speed at which this could be done safely in those aircraft fitted with dive brakes (i.e., Skua, Stuka, Dauntless or Val), varied considerably.

Of course it was even more important to prevent the speed in the aiming dive becoming excessive in a makeshift dive-bomber (such as the Spitfire or Mustang) without proper diving flaps, because the stresses could (and in practice, did) produce wide-ranging structural distortion and cause the aircraft to disintegrate in mid-air.

In a shallower dive, of 40 degrees or less (more favoured by the RAF, Soviet Union and the USAAF), which many air forces did not rate as dive-bombing at all, there was less difficulty in keeping steady and taking correct aim, but the aircraft had to be pulled out through a

Air-to-air photograph of a Vultee Vengeance airborne over California in standard RAF paintwork and markings, *circa* 1942. (Northrop)

◄

A Northrop-built V-72 Vengeance, later given the US designation A-31 after Lend-Lease came into force in March 1941, revs up at the manufacturer's airfield at Hawthorne, California. Note air intakes at both top and bottom of the engine cowling, for the Wright Double Cyclone power plant. (Northrop)

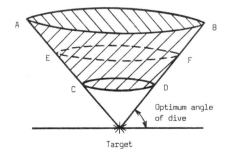

DIAGRAM 1
RAF THEORY OF DIVE BOMBING: OPTIMUM DIVE ANGLE

Optimum angle of dive

Target

large angle before release and this was difficult to judge, and the target was lost sight of under the nose some time before bomb release. If a satisfactory automatic gyro release incorporated in a multi-directional dive-bombing sight was employed (as with German and Swedish designs of the time) this disadvantage was overcome and it was not necessary for the target to be visible at the moment of release.

With regard to the effects of AA fire, the 70-degree dive was less vulnerable than a 50-degree dive since the steeper angle introduced laying and training difficulties for the gunners, and the aircraft was over the vertical from the target slightly sooner. At angles of dive below 50 degrees, aircraft became increasingly more vulnerable (as the Fairey Battles found over the Meuse in 1940).

In a purpose-built dive-bomber, like the Skua, fitted with dive flaps, the optimum angle of dive was a specific angle of descent, but the speed of that descent could be controlled by dive brakes, which meant that then the height of the 'X' point could be varied within considerable limits. It could be situated anywhere on the curved surface of the shaded frustum A.B.C.D. in Diagram 1, whose

centre is located vertically above the target (and which assumes still air and a stationary target).

The lower limit of this shaded frustum, C.D., would have been the absolute minimum height that would allow the aircraft sufficient time to get into the dive, aim and release the bomb, before diving below the safe low height limit. For a makeshift dive-bomber with no dive brakes, the 'X' point would be situated at a higher safety level, somewhere on the perimeter of a circle E.–F. The height of release would also depend upon the angle of dive adopted. Also, the safe period permissible in the dive before the aircraft became too stiff for proper control or its engine revolutions became excessive, would vary from type to type, but would always be greater than for a purpose-built dive-bomber with flaps. Another factor which was crucial to the actual real height represented by E.–F. was the speed of the aircraft at the start of its dive.

When dive-bombing was conducted with a sight (in practice, hardly ever) it was essential that the 'X' point and thus the conditions of release, always remain the same so that the aiming technique was consistent. This also applied in par-

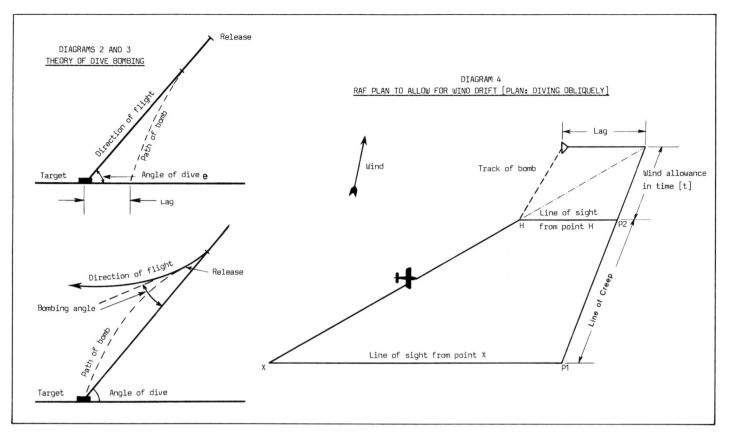

DIAGRAMS 2 AND 3
THEORY OF DIVE BOMBING

Release

Direction of flight

Path of bomb

Target — Angle of dive e

Lag

Direction of flight — Release

Bombing angle

Path of bomb

Target — Angle of dive

DIAGRAM 4
RAF PLAN TO ALLOW FOR WIND DRIFT [PLAN: DIVING OBLIQUELY]

Wind

Lag

Track of bomb

Wind allowance in time [t]

Line of sight from point H

H — from point H — P2

Line of Creep

Line of sight from point X

X — P1

ticular release conditions, such as when using a multi-directional dive-bomb sight. With the adoption of an automatic sight considerable latitude in the release conditions, and therefore the 'X' point, became possible.

An automatic dive-bomb sight was one based on tachymetric principles, which, within certain limits, measured and corrected the aim for the 'relative wind'. We shall return to the various powers' efforts to perfect such a sight in a later chapter. At the outbreak of war Germany was most far advanced down this road, with Sweden a close second. Smith's Industries in Great Britain had one under experimental design, but had been hampered by lack of funding, while in the US all efforts had been put into the Norden gunsight for high-altitude bombing.

Meanwhile most pilots continued to use 'eye-sighting' for their attacks, although a front gun-sight or distinctive projection on the engine cowling were also employed to give the basic 'no-wind' sighting line for the aiming dive, and also gave a measure whereby the pilot could gauge the angular 'aim-off' for relative wind.

When diving at a target at about 50 degrees and at a speed of about 200 knots, the direction of flight or motion was along a line about 5 degrees above the datum line of the aircraft owing to its aerodynamic characteristics. This 5 degrees was the 'datum sighting angle'. It therefore follows, that with no relative wind the pilot would dive with this 'no wind' sighting line of 5 degrees above the datum line on the target.

If he selected some other sighting line of greater or less angular distance above the aircraft's datum line, he would not be actually flying at his aiming point on the target, and the dive would tend to become steeper or shallower, i.e., the aircraft would not track on a straight line towards the target.

If a bomb were released in a dive at a fixed target in no wind, the path of the bomb would have been as shown in Diagram 2.

The distance that the bomb would fall behind the position where the direction of flight line produced met the ground, which was usually referred to as the 'lag', varied with the conditions of release and the ballistics of the bomb. The actual flight path of the bomb after release could be plotted with sufficient accuracy if it were assumed that the bomb would fall away from the direction of flight at the moment of release (projected) at a gravity acceleration (measured vertically) of 30fps^2. Diagram 2 illustrates a 50-degree dive.

To allow for this distance, the aircraft had to be pulled out through the 'bombing angle', before the bomb was released, as indicated in Diagram 3.

The 'bombing angle' varied. Where there was no gyro-release gear fitted it was desirable that the bombing angle be not greater than the angle between the flight path of the aircraft and a line from the pilot's eye to the top of the engine cowling. If it exceeded this angle, the target would be out of sight at the moment of release and the pilot would have difficulty in judging it correctly.

As can be seen, the technical requirements for dive-bombing, coupled with the specially strengthened aircraft and other factors such as the swinging bomb arm for the bomb to clear the propeller arc, made an aircraft quite distinctive from fighters or bombers. And yet highly skilful dive-bombing was to be conducted by all manner of likely and unlikely aircraft and by untrained aircrew. This all brings us back to the original hypothesis that good dive-bomber pilots were born rather than made.

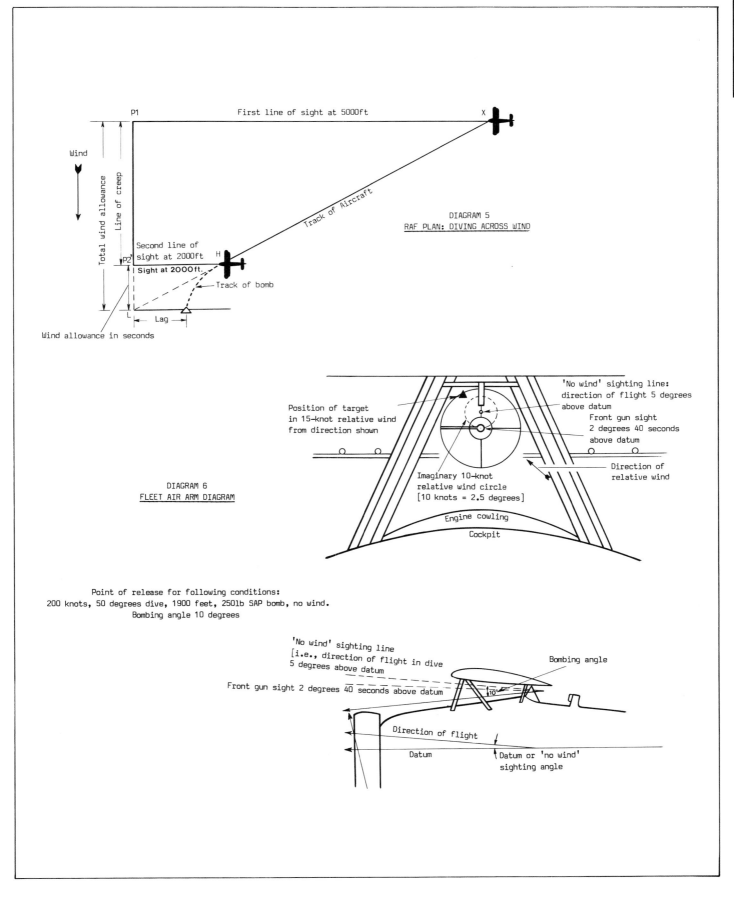

P1

First line of sight at 5000ft

X

Wind

Total wind allowance

Line of creep

Track of Aircraft

DIAGRAM 5
RAF PLAN: DIVING ACROSS WIND

Second line of
sight at 2000ft

H

P2

Sight at 2000ft.

Track of bomb

L

Lag

Wind allowance in seconds

'No wind' sighting line:
direction of flight 5 degrees
above datum

Front gun sight
2 degrees 40 seconds
above datum

Position of target
in 15-knot relative wind
from direction shown

Direction of
relative wind

Imaginary 10-knot
relative wind circle
[10 knots = 2.5 degrees]

DIAGRAM 6
FLEET AIR ARM DIAGRAM

Engine cowling

Cockpit

Point of release for following conditions:
200 knots, 50 degrees dive, 1900 feet, 250lb SAP bomb, no wind.
Bombing angle 10 degrees

'No wind' sighting line
[i.e., direction of flight in dive
5 degrees above datum

Bombing angle

Front gun sight 2 degrees 40 seconds above datum

10

Direction of flight

Datum

Datum or 'no wind'
sighting angle

21

Spanish combat dive-bombing

As for practise in combat conditions, there was by 1939 a limited amount of hard fact to go on. The Japanese in China and the Germans and Italians in Spain had proved the technique to their own satisfaction with regard to fixed land targets and also against ships in port, the latter proving particularly vulnerable. The Americans had the experiences of the Marine Corps flyers from a decade earlier to go on, while the British had to go back another ten years to 1918 to glean the same lessons. The years of war were soon to show up how much these nations, and others, had absorbed from these examples, both in attack and in defence.

One good example of pre-war dive-bombing being almost totally ignored was the series of attacks carried out against the Spanish battleship *España* in June 1937. She had been built originally as a cut-down 'Dreadnought', in 1917, displacing some 15,452 tons and mounting eight 12in guns. These big guns were still valuable for bombarding the Republican armies ashore off Bilbao as they enabled her to stay out of range of shore-based artillery.

An immediate solution was required

and air attacks were directed against her. Attacks by conventional means using French Breguet XIX bombers were totally unsuccessful so a more radical approach was decided upon. There was a fighter squadron defending Bilbao using Soviet I-15 'Rata' fighters. They were led by a young teenaged fighter ace, Lieutenant Miguel Zambudio who had 26 victories credited to him. They used French Gourdou-Leseurre GL-32 aircraft as dive-bombers. The GL-42 Navy dive-bomber derived from this had four prototypes built for the carrier *Béarn* but progressed no farther. These particular aircraft had been purchased by the Basque Government directly from France and were mainly used as defensive fighters when they threw in with the Republican forces. Their airstrip was about ten miles from where the battleship was shooting and the only bombs available were 100kg armour-piercing types. These would have been useless against normal battleships, but *España* had been built with only light (0.6in) deck armour and this could be pierced easily in a dive attack.

Zambudio led his GL-32s in a series of relay attacks, dive-bombing, returning to base, re-arming and attacking again all

through the daylight hours of 6 and 7 April. Between twenty and thirty attacks were made, but the fatal hits were delivered by Zambudio himself who launched two bombs at the end of dive and recovered safely. Both hit the ship. He later recalled that he was severely shaken by the shock waves of the explosions. Looking back he saw the battleship surrounded by smoke and she had stopped firing. He recalled later 'I had possibly hit the *Santa Barbara*' [an ammunition ship alongside]. *España* was later reported to have been sunk. All the French naval experts he consulted about the possibility of 100kg bombs being able to perforate the battleship's 15mm armoured deck were categorical in their response: 'Very easy!' So *España* was possibly the first battleship to be sunk by dive-bombing.[5]

Why was this fact not recognized then? Possibly for three reasons. Nobody could believe that destruction of a major warship by a small aircraft could be so easy. All 'Red' claims were dismissed as false because of their many previous claims which had turned out to be lies and propaganda. Also, *España* had previously been announced as sunk by them. British agencies and newspapers

◄ Extremely rare colour print showing Vultee Vengeance in Brazilian Air Force markings. This machine, AN838, was the first Northrop-built Vengeance I. (Northrop)

► A French Navy Douglas Dauntless landing on an escort carrier illustrates the 'cheesegrater' type holes in the dive brake flaps, a unique feature of the famous SBD. (ECP des Armées, Fort d'Ivry)

▼ Engine warm-up aboard a carrier as a Douglas Dauntless prepares to sortie. (ECP des Armées, Fort d'Ivry)

THREE QUARTER RIGHT REAR VIEW – VULTEE MODEL

(the main information source at the time) did not believe a Vickers-built battleship (even an old one) could be so easily destroyed. Whether Zambudio's attacks were instrumental in her destruction or not cannot be definitely proven for all the official documents relating to this incident were destroyed in the subsequent evacuation of the port, but 'officially' the battleship has always been listed as sunk by mines off Bilbao on 30 April.

All Spanish air forces used dive-bombing during the civil war. One Spanish-manned unit thus employed was commanded by M. Capillas who survived to die about five years ago in France. Before the war he had been a Spanish Navy NCO, piloting seaplanes, and had been trained to attack submarines in glide-bombing attacks. This led to his employment on such missions ashore and gradually he found that the steeper the dive the more accuracy he achieved. He said that the FF1 fighters he flew in this role were 'relatively handy' for dive-bombing and that they suffered extremely light losses because, operating near the front line with short combat duration times, they were extremely difficult to intercept. Thus these missions were both successful and popular. He

was replaced as commander of this unit when he steadfastly refused to strafe a Republican refugee column which had enemy troops intermingled with them during the collapse of the Catalonian front in 1938. At that time his unit was the only Spanish squadron remaining that specialized in dive-bombing after the departure of the last of the Gordou-Lesseur aircraft in 1937.

The Russians also tried their hand, less successfully. On several occasions their twin-engined SB2 bombers carried out glide-bombing, but the maximum angle was only about 30 degrees so it was never true dive-bombing. However, the seeds were sown which awakened their interest in this method of attack which hitherto they had largely ignored.

▲
A rare view of an experimental version of the Vultee Vengeance, fitted with a three-bladed prop for testing the 'Wasp X' engine. (US National Archives)

▶▲
One of the two remaining Vultee Vengeances being restored in Australia. 'DINA MIGHT' is seen here with Wayne Brown her restorer while the Wright Cyclone engine is 'run up' after more than forty years of dereliction. (Wayne Brown)

Three Commonwealth Wirraways of 21 Squadron RAAF at Laverton air base, preparing to take-off for practise flights. (Australian War Memorial)

▲
The prototype Curtiss Helldiver, XSBC-1, which crashed on 9 February 1941, and which subsequently had to be re-built. It featured gun ports on each wing and above the engine cowling. Its bulky body and stubby shape resulted from the need to get two side-by-side on the deck lift of the *Essex*-class aircraft carriers then being built for the US Navy. Note conventional tail and Aldis-sight. (US National Archives)

This Helldiver, airborne from the Naval Air Station at Anacostia in December 1942, was equipped with ABD, IFF and electrics. (US National Archives)
▼

PART TWO
AIRCRAFT AND EXPERIMENTS

PURPOSE-built dive-bombers held sway in a limited number of air fleets in 1939. The principal exponents were Germany, the United States Navy and Marine Corps and the Imperial Japanese Navy. Minute numbers of custom-built dive-bombers also existed in other nations' armouries, the Fleet Air Arm of Great Britain or the Swedish Air Force for example. Under development at this time, however, were a large number of specific dive-bombers. These were building not only for the above nations but also for new converts to the method, France, the United States Army Air Force, the Soviet Union and Italy.

Nations with little or no dive-bombing expertise of their own (France and Italy), or who had turned their backs on it (Great Britain) were forced to purchase abroad (Britain, France and the Nether-lands) mainly from the United States, Italy from Germany and the smaller nations, Spain, Greece, Norway and Thailand, for example, where they could.

By far the greatest provider of dive-bombers, both in terms of numbers and in the diversity of types, was of course the 'Arsenal of Democracy', America, but many types built in the USA mainly served in combat with foreign air forces (Vultee Vengeance, Brewster Bermuda). Other types served equally well with American, French or British pilots (Vought Vindicator/167F/Chesapeake, Douglas Dauntless, Curtiss SB2C Hell-diver).

For the sake of convenience the air-craft are described under nationality headings, but for the reasons given above, some necessarily stray across several chapters while others remain only the plaything of test-pilots.

▶ Stuka Aspects. A Kette of Junkers Ju 87A dive-bombers of St.G.165. Early pioneering work was done with this aircraft and it was also used in the occupation of Czechoslovakia in 1938, but it was replaced by the Ju 87B before outbreak of war. This early version featured the heavy 'trouser' type wheel fairings, later replaced by the lighter 'spats'. (Peter Schwarzkopf)

▶▶ Junkers Ju 87Bs of St.G.77 on the prowl early in the war. Notice the many modifications over the previous photograph and the differences in Luftwaffe markings. (Peter Schwarzkopf)

4. The Stuka becomes established

WHAT had begun as a hesistant programme of Junker develop-ment, had by outbreak of war, been fully embraced. The dive-bomber was now viewed in Germany as a 'back area' tactical support aircraft and more than 340 new Ju 87Bs stood ready for combat by 1 September 1939.

An essential aid developed for the Stuka was the Askania auto-pilot for automatic pull-out from the power-dive. The woman test-pilot, Melitta Schiller, tested this device and it was fitted to the ten pre-production models of the Ju 87A-0. With this, even should the pilot black-out, the bomb-release gear was inter-connected with the dive brakes and elevator settings and normal pull-out was activated. The bomb could be released during the pull-out at a set time after the start of the manoeuvre, the time being computed as a function of the height of release and dive angle, being set on the automatic bomb distributor. The track of the aircraft was aimed at the target using the Revi gunsight, which could be swung in elevation to allow for head winds, and such bombing could be

carried out with accuracy provided the dive was made in the up-wind direction. The time interval between the start of the pull-out and release of the missile could be so computed that the bomb struck the point at which the Stuka was aimed.

The basic technique on which the German system was based was that the dive brakes' hydraulic system also moved and locked in position a tab on the elevator. Movement of the tab was such that the trim was not greatly upset when the dive-brakes were lowered. The tab could be reset to its original setting by a strong spring which operated when a control button was pressed or, more usually, when a previously set contacting altimeter made contact at a predeter-mined height. When the dive brakes were retracted, therefore, the mechanism was automatically reset so that if the dive brakes were used again the cycle could be repeated.

A typical Stuka attack sequence would therefore develop along these lines. At this stage of development it was still left for the pilot to decide which dive angle to use for a particular target or set of

circumstances, and he would also pre-
judge the height of the pull-out which
would also vary according to type of
target or bomb load carried. Armour-
piercing bombs would require more
height to be effective than high-explosive
bombs and so on. The pilot set a time
interval on the time distributor and also
set his contacting altimeter to the height
at which the pull-out was to start. The
Stuka would then be trimmed for the
dive, anything from 50 degrees to near
vertical – 70 degrees being the most
common. The throttle and cooling gills
were then closed and the dive brakes
were lowered, thus moving the compen-
sating tab on the elevator automatically.

The Stuka's pilot could now maintain
his airspeed in the initial shallow, or
initial dive, down to a certain height
which he considered suitable before
commencing the aiming dive. Aim-off to
compensate for wind-speed was allowed for by adjusting the gunsight from
the no-wind condition using a simple
table. Then the main attack dive would
commence.

This was initiated by the pilot moving

the control column forward and lining up
a series of graduated angle markings
etched in red on the cockpit cowling. The
plane was set nose-heavy, and Allied
pilots who flew captured Stukas later
commented that the Junkers Ju 87 felt
'right', at its best, when dived absolutely
vertically. It was a 'natural' dive-bomber
which is why it was the best of its kind.

When the contacting altimeter circuit
closed the bomb distributor was started,
the spring control on the elevator tab
was released and the tab moved quickly
back to its original position, making the
Stuka tail heavy. The plane thus pulled
itself out of the dive and the bomb was
automatically released as this occurred
after the set time interval had elapsed.
The pilot then resumed control of his
aircraft, retracting the dive brakes,
opening the throttle for level flight and
making his get-away.

The German BZA-1 Dive-Bomb Sight
By the outbreak of war this basic technique had been greatly extended and
improved upon. Thus the dive-bombing
devices found aboard a shot-down

Junkers Ju 88 amazed the Farnborough
scientist who examined it at Blyth in 1939.
They incorporated the BZA-1 Dive-Bomb
Sight, which on detailed examination
proved to be far superior to the British
designs still being sketched out and
planned. This gave some indication of
how far behind pre-war neglect had left
the British in this field. A detailed break-
down of just how the BZA-1 worked
aboard a Junkers Ju 88 in 1939 is
therefore of considerable interest as it
shows the 'state of the art' as the Second
World War began.

Before the German dive-bomber crew
took off they would obtain from the
Meteorological Officer of their base
details of the wind force and direction
and the barometric pressure for the
target area. They would also determine
the height of the target above sea level
(height according to map) if it were a
land target. Meanwhile the pilot would
check on the BZA-1 in the tail of the
aircraft while running up his engines or
while taxiing out to the take-off position.
To activate the device he would wait until
his engine revs exceeded 1400 and the

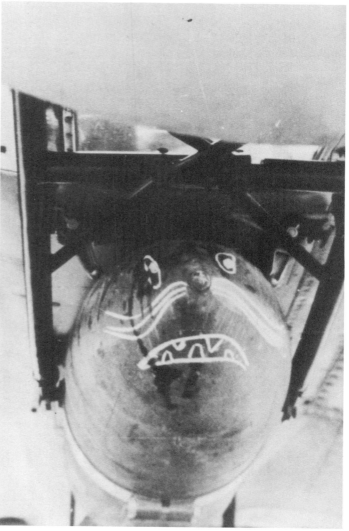

Known as the 'Stuka Father' because of his age, Gunter Schwartzkopf was the most loved and respected leader of St.G.77 at the beginning of the war. He led by example and had a good sense of humour and the common touch which ensured the efficiency of his Stuka units. From 1937 to 1939 he did much to perfect the Junkers Ju 87 as the powerful instrument of army co-operation it had become by the outbreak of war. He led his men into action with great élan during the Polish campaign, but was killed leading the attacks which forced the crossing of the Meuse in May 1940, when his Ju 87 was destroyed by French AA fire. (Peter Schwartzkopf)

A specially chalked up face on a 500lb bomb mounted on the swing-crutch of Gunter Schwarzkopf's Stuka for the first missions into Poland in September 1939. (Peter Schwarzkopf)

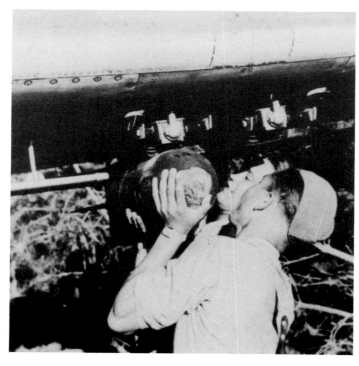

Loading up the underwing secondary bomb armament on a St.G.77 Stuka during the fast-moving operations which crushed the Polish Army in September 1939. The groundcrew were known as the 'Black Men' to the Stuka crews, but here they can be seen here in their summer uniforms as they keep the Stukas flying from the most primitive of airstrips. (Peter Schwartzkopf)

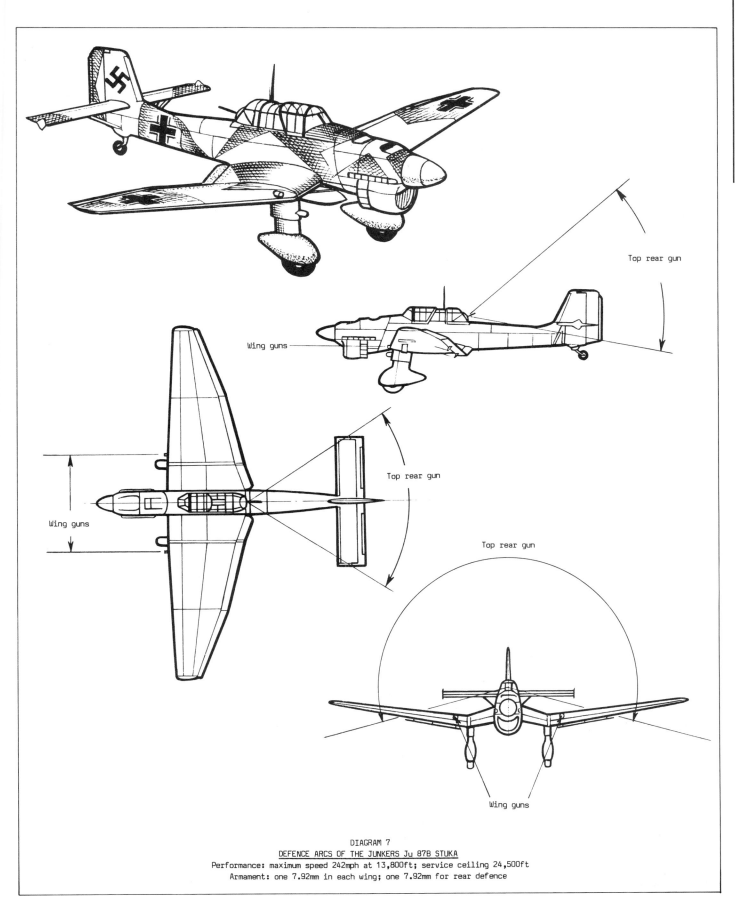

DIAGRAM 7
DEFENCE ARCS OF THE JUNKERS Ju 87B STUKA
Performance: maximum speed 242mph at 13,800ft; service ceiling 24,500ft
Armament: one 7.92mm in each wing; one 7.92mm for rear defence

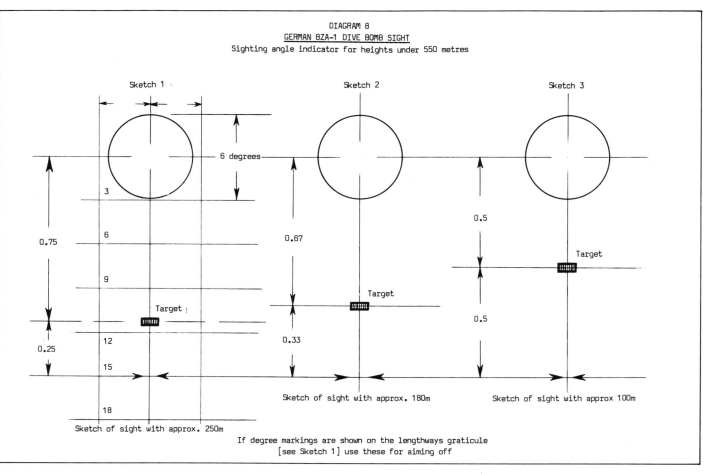

DIAGRAM 8
GERMAN BZA-1 DIVE BOMB SIGHT
Sighting angle indicator for heights under 550 metres

Sketch 1   Sketch 2   Sketch 3

6 degrees

3

0.75   6   0.67

9

                                                         0.5

Target   Target

                           0.67

Target   0.33   0.5

12

15   0.5

18

Sketch of sight with approx. 250m

Sketch of sight with approx. 180m   Sketch of sight with approx 100m

If degree markings are shown on the lengthways graticule
[see Sketch 1] use these for aiming off

generators were charging (thus sparing the battery), and then flick the two automatic switches. These had to be on from take-off to landing of every flight even if no bombs were dropped. The calculator took ten minutes to warm up after these switches were thrown. The air speed dial would be set at 550kph, the height correction setter set at zero, the barometric pressure set at 1000 millibars and the wind speed set at zero meters/second. The Sturvi was swung into position and the tumbler and lighting switch had to be thrown. The test after ten minutes was to run back the sight angle scale (the 'Winkel scale') from plus 25 degrees to about plus 16 degrees. If the scale moved only about half a degree and no further it was deemed out of order. On conclusion of this test the Sturvi was switched off again.

An in-flight test followed a similar procedure, but was only possible at heights below 1,000 metres. Again both switches were thrown on with the setting as before. The inclination of the aircraft was set to about 15 to 20 degrees at a height of about 800 metres before the

Sturvi was switched on. The Winkel scale sighting angle would have run back from plus 25 degrees to about 21 or 22 degrees minimum for a successful test. Anything else and the reading during the actual dive, if it appeared at all, would be unreliable. At conclusion of test the Sturvi was switched off and swung back into the 'rest' position.

When the target was sighted and the approach commenced, the Observer would set the air speed dial to the initial air speed expected and the wind speed dial had to be set accurately according to the current data. The direction and force of the wind had to be checked and the setting corrected as the attack developed. The height correction dial had to have the target height and barometric pressure similarly adjusted if necessary, the RAB (no time delay) was selected and the ZSK switched on. The pilot meanwhile swung the Sturvi out to ready for use position and switched on again.

Once committed to the dive the Observer had to adjust the air speed setting according to the indicator on the height-compensated air-speed indicator

and to do so continually 'smoothly, not jerkily' while the pilot had to fly on to target exactly so that no lateral forces arose (side slips – skidding in RAF parlance – produce considerable lateral bombing errors). To avoid this, lateral correction was made by means of the ailerons not by the rudder.

It was noted that the field of view, in a dive of between 10 and 40 degrees, was restricted to a sight angle of 17 degrees. With a sighting angle of more than 17 to 25 degrees the Indicator was hidden by the cockpit. If a strong headwind was encountered (60–100kph) the downward field of vision was smaller; 'Therefore dive more steeply!'[6] For a release height above 550 metres the indicator had to be made to coincide with the target. At the same time the aircraft had to be diving in a completely even configuration with no skidding or turns.

Once 'bombs off' was sounded the pilot would switch off the Sturvi and replace it in its rest position while the Observer turned off the ZSK. It was further noted that should a number of attack dives be conducted in immediate

sequence 'the aircraft must not be climbed in spirals after a dive and then dived again immediately, as the gyroscope will be set incorrectly.' While climbing, they were instructed to fly for long straight stretches or on a straight course for 5 to 10 minutes before any new dive in order that the gyroscope could recover itself. All very well but one assumes the target would not be passive while this was going on. In the event of AA fire, therefore, the pilot was given the discretion of curving immediately before re-commencing the dive attack; 'The curve should not, if possible, be continued for more than five minutes.'

It was emphasised that an error of 10m/sec on the wind speed dial setting would result in a bombing error of about 84 metres with a dive angle of 60 degrees. Attacks against shipping targets were slightly different.

It must be remembered that this computer and the flight controls were fully integrated. Bomb fuzing in the Luftwaffe was all-electric and 'decidedly superior' to the RAF system. In addition to the BZA-1 there were the graticule markings

etched on a small floor window in front of the pilot to help alignment and distance judgement. Once the dive brakes under each wing were activated the tabs on the elevators operated automatically to push the tail up and throw the machine into a 60-degree dive. This brought the target up to the pilot's front window. It took about twelve seconds going 4,000ft downhill to reach the optimum release height of 820 feet above the previous set pull-out altitude when a warning horn was activated. Easing the stick back the pilot let the target drift into the bottom of his sight and the bomb release initiated the automatic pull-out forcing the elevator trim tab down and the nose up. Meanwhile, as the aircraft pulled out, the automatic bomb release mechanism was allowing the bombs to fall away as predetermined and all the pilot had to do was retract the dive brakes and throttle away.

Such a device and system gave the Junkers Ju 88 an outstanding edge in dive-bombing as innumerable successful missions, from Scapa Flow to Sebastapol, bore eloquent testimony.

▲
The Junkers Ju 88 was one of the most versatile of a the long-range dive-bombers. Known as the 'Wonder Bomber' when it first appeared, its ability to carry a heavy bomb load for great distances and to couple this with great accuracy in the fully automatic dive, made it a formidable opponent, especially in the hands of experienced aircrew like those of the LG 1 units based in Crete. Here two Ju 88s taxi out to take-off from their base at Lannion in France for a mission over the Bay of Biscay in 1942.
(ECP des Armées, Fort d'Ivry)

5. The Imperial Eagles gather in the East

IT has often been remarked that the most surprising thing about the Japanese aircraft which began the Pacific War so devastatingly was *not* their effectiveness but the fact that the Allies appeared to know so little about them. And this ignorance is all the more strange if one remembers that most of the aircraft employed from December 1941 to March 1942, a period of almost continuous defeats for the Allies, had been used in China under scrutiny by neutral observers. Observers *may* have reported back, but scant attention seems to have been paid in London or Washington, judging by the subsequent testimonies of our leaders – who confessed themselves amazed!

Typical of this attitude is a report on Japanese Navy aircraft made by Squadron Leader R. Steele on 13 December 1941 to the Air Ministry and other official bodies. In the immediate aftermath of Pearl Harbor and the sinking of the British capital ships *Prince of Wales* and *Repulse* it might be thought it was a bit

late to start wondering just what the Japanese had in their armoury, but such appears to have been the case. The horse having not only bolted, but kicked to death the stall-holders in the process and to be half-way round the course, a report was called for and duly delivered. It is interesting to see how the principal Japanese Navy dive-bomber, the Aichi D3A1, was rated, especially when one remembers that at this date, this dive-bomber's greatest victories against the British were still five months in the future.

The report commenced with stunning under-emphasis:

'Events in the Far East suggest that Japanese naval aircraft may be worthy of closer study than has yet been undertaken.'[6] It then described the Aichi Type 99 dive-bomber as follows:

'The superficial resemblance of this type to the two versions (sic) of the T97 torpedo-bomber is misleading as the machine was designed primarily as a dive-bomber. It has been reported that

◀◀
The Japanese Army air force did not use dive-bombers to a very great extent, but its experiences in China prompted it to ask for a rugged, reliable close-support aircraft capable of limited diving attacks, operating from primitive forward airstrips. The result was the Mitsubishi Ki-30. It was a highly reliable, if not outstanding, aircraft and was used in China and the Philippines. The Royal Thai Air Force also took delivery of a number of these aircraft and used them in combat against the French in January, 1941. (Robert and Misake Piper)

◀
Another good shot of a Mitsubishi Ki-30 over Malaya early in the war. (Author's collection)

German technicians assisted with its production and development. The following description applies to the best-known version with fixed undercarriage, details of a reported development, having a more powerful engine and retractable undercarriage, not being available. T99s have been manufactured by the Aichi and Mitsubishi concerns.'

It is obvious that confusion existed between the Aichi, later to be codenamed by the Allies as 'Val', and the newer, but not to be operational for several years, Yokosuku D4Y1 Suisei (or Comet), which was later to be codenamed 'Judy'. They were totally different concepts of course. German participation was minimal, although the pre-war purchase of a Heinkel He 118-V4 prototype, which was then shipped to Japan for evaluation, may possibly have had some influence on the Judy's designers.

A similar mix of fact and fiction followed in the 1941 report. Thus under the heading 'Employment' this exclusively dive-bombing aircraft has listed 'Dive Bombing/Fighting/Probably reconnaissance. Designed for operations from aircraft carriers.' It was correctly described as a low-wing, single-engined, cantilever monoplane having fixed cantilever undercarriage with streamlined wheel fairings, a radial engine and 'transparent cockpit enclosure'.

'Photographs show that the construction is of all-metal stressed-skin type. Apparently the wing differs in design from that of the T97 bomber but details are not known. The tips are rounded and trailing-edge flaps are fitted inboard of the ailerons. It is probable that diving brakes similar to those of the Ju 87 are fitted beneath the wing behind the trailing edge. The fuselage is of clean design and it appears that the cockpit enclosure is shorter than that of the T97 which is probably explained by the fact that a crew of only two is carried. This feature, in conjunction with a fin of increased area, has caused the machine to be described as being similar to the Saversky 2-seater fighter.

Photographs show that the undercarriage is of very clean single-leg cantilever design, the wheels being faired by large spats. The 14-cylinder two-row air-cooled radial of Kinsei or Kaishin type is enclosed in a long-chord gilled cowling and drives a three-bladed VP airscrew of Hamilton type. The comparatively small diameter of the engine and the forward position of the pilot permit a good view over the nose for dive-bombing.

Two fixed forward-firing 7.7mm guns are fitted in the top cowling and are synchronized to fire through the airscrew arc. In addition there is a free gun of the same calibre on a manually operated mounting in the rear cockpit. For short-range operation a single 250kg bomb and two 60kg bombs can be carried, but for long-distance work the smaller bombs are omitted. Details of ejector gear are not known.

Deck arrester gear is fitted and radio is known to be installed. Maximum speed 256mph at 10,000 feet, cruising speed 204mph at 10,000 feet, cruising range

450 miles and Service ceiling of 26,000 feet.'[7]

'Closer study' was duly afforded when the Val dive-bomber squadrons embarked in the aircraft carriers of the Nagumo Force followed up their achievements at Pearl Harbor by devastating Darwin and Colombo harbours, while at sea they easily sank the British aircraft carrier *Hermes* and the heavy cruisers *Cornwall* and *Dorsetshire*, in addition to a whole host of lesser warships during their April 1942 sortie into the Indian Ocean. Thereupon British interest ended; the Royal Navy withdrew from the area in double quick time and the Aichis' turned eastward toward Rabaul, the Solomons and their duels with the US carriers in the Coral Sea and at Midway.

Despite increasing losses, its short range, and steadily falling standard of aircrew, the Val was destined to fight on for most of the war against increasingly heavy odds, inflicting many severe defeats on the US Navy before being finally shot out of the sky.

The replacement for the Aichi, the Judy, was a splendid design, lean, fast and powerful. It is thought by some to have been the most aerodynamically perfect bomber of the Pacific War. Like the American Helldiver, it was subjected to numerous production and design problems and its entry into service, as a dive-bomber, was long delayed. By the time it did appear in any numbers the Japanese were on the retreat and it failed to make any impression during the disastrous Battle of the Philippine Sea in June 1944. Nevertheless, although in penny-packet numbers, the Suisei did carry out some of the most spectacular and devasting conventional dive-bombing attacks of the Pacific War.

The Yokosuka D4Y1 Suisei's development problems caused long delays in preparing this superb dive-bomber for combat and although two were embarked as early as the Battle of Midway in 1942, it was only as high-speed reconnaissance aircraft because they were

▲
A trio of Japanese Navy Yokosuka 'Comet' dive-bombers etched against the magnificent backdrop of Mount Fuji. (Author's collection)

▶
These photographs show the outward difference between the Yokusuka Suisei (Comet) as originally designed, with the in-line engine, and as re-designed, with the radial. Both reveal the grace and clean lines of a classic aircraft. (Author's collection)

▶
The radial engined version of the Yokosuka D4Y 'Comet' produced a very powerful machine of high performance, but it arrived far too late to influence events in the Pacific War. (Author's collection)

▶

Two Aichi Type 99 carrier-borne dive-bombers in a classic pose. Aircraft were boldly marked during the early stages of the Pacific War reflecting the superiority enjoyed by the Japanese Navy for the first year of the conflict. Black or red noses and tail and coloured 'spats' were later replaced by drab olive green as the dive-bombers started operating from jungle airstrips. (Sadao Seno)

1. The most famous Japanese dive-bomber pilot of them all, the legendary Egusa, who led the dive-bombers in their early days and later died attacking the US Fleet on 14 June 1944. (Mrs Kiyoko Egusa)

2. A D3A2 Val on a jungle airstrip in the South Pacific. (Tadashi Nozawa)

3. The clean and pleasing profile of the Yokosuka D4Y 'Judy' dive-bomber. The in-line engine proved too temperamental and not powerful enough for the rugged combat missions of the Pacific Zone and had to be replaced. (Author's collection)

4. Japanese Vals warming up at a Rabaul airstrip in readiness for another mission, *circa* August/September 1942. (Bob and Misake Piper)

restricted from diving. This was due to persistent 'wing-flutter' experienced in the flying prototypes. It would be many valuable months before this defect was ironed out. Even when the Aichi company began turning out the aircraft in numbers, the performance of the original Atsuta in-line engine, although it had resulted in an aesthetically pleasing line, proved inadequate for the demands of dive-bombing and the more powerful 1,560hp Mitsubishi MK80 Kinsei 62 radial engine had to be used in its place on later models. This gave the 'Judy' a top speed of 357mph, a marked improvement on the Aichi 'Val' which was still carrying the bulk of the dive-bomber burden as the tide of war flowed against Japan. In truth, the Suisei, although a superb fighting machine, arrived too late, and in too small numbers, to influence the outcome of the naval war. By the time enough were available for battle, most of the best dive-bomber aircrew had been killed and almost all the aircraft carriers had been sunk.

1.

2.

3.

4.

▶

The Brewster XSBA-1 prototype flight testing on 2 June 1936. From this design, advanced when it first appeared, much was expected, but in fact little or nothing resulted, either with the US Navy's SBN-1 or the USAAC Buccaneer or RAF Bermuda follow-ups.

▶▶

By contrast, the big experimental Vultee single-seater combined dive- and torpedo-bomber concepts. The XA-41-VU, which appeared late in 1944, although a potent and powerful machine in every respect, arrived too late to be adopted as by then existing types of heavy fighter were able to carry the same bomb loads with almost equal accuracy and the concept was abandoned. Only the single prototype shown here ever flew. It was a single-seater weighing some 23,359lb all-up and had a span of 54ft, length of 48ft 8in and was powered by a single Pratt and Whitney XR-4360-9 3000hp engine giving a top speed of 353mph. It had the designation Vultee 90 and was similar to the single-seater Navy torpedo aircraft of the VBT Classification which were discarded under the new A (for Attack) classification. (US National Archives)

6. The US dive-bomber types

BY far the largest selection of dive-bombers, featuring the most modern concepts of the art, came from the USA. There not only did the war in Europe cause a huge expansion in the numbers of carrier-borne dive-bombers ordered by the US Navy, but it awakened the interest of the US Army Air Corps in this type of aircraft. Further home demand was almost swamped by foreign orders during the years 1939–41, particularly from Great Britain, France and The Netherlands.

A number of well-established designers and companies, such as Vought, Curtiss and Douglas, brought out new designs, but such was the impetus of foreign demand that new companies sprang up to produce dive-bombers of varying capability, performance and usefulness: Vultee, the regenerated Northrop, Brewster and North American. We have space here to devote but a cursory glance at this huge outpouring of talent, skill and expertise. That not all parts of this great mushrooming of ideas and talent managed to mesh correctly, in the pressure and frenzy of war production, can be seen from the story of the USAAC's dive-bombing.

'A flock of airplanes we don't want'

If the Fleet Air Arm had trouble getting the aircraft it wanted out of the Admiralty, this was as nothing compared to the trauma which shook the US Army Air Corps. The sensational results of the Stukas in Europe in the summer of 1940 made an enormous impact across the Atlantic. At this time the US Air Corps was undergoing a rapid and huge expansion programme under the dynamic leadership of General of the Army, Henry 'Hap' Arnold. At that time the Air Corps had no dive-bombers and no interest in them. They were committed to the 'attack' type of twin-engined light bomber and these were growing progressively larger and larger. The current model then in production was the Douglas DB-7, which became the A-20 (known variously as the Boston, Havoc or Invader) and export orders included large numbers for France and the United Kingdom. Douglas knew how to build dive-bombers, but did the A-20A have dive-bomber potential? It did not! However, like the RAF with the Vickers Wellington and the Luftwaffe with the Heinkel He 177, some people in high places were persuaded that the A-20 might be made into one.

On 1 June 1940 the Chief of the Air Corps requested information from General Brett on the possibility of 'converting the A-20 type for dive-bombing'. The response next day from the Material Division recommended 'procurement of

either late model Navy dive-bombers, or from a design competition and *not* to re-design the A-20'. At a Staff Conference held on 19 June, General Arnold laid it on the line. 'The Corps would have to furnish two groups of dive-bombers to operate with armoured divisions.'[8] The German combination of such forces had just swept across northern France from Sedan to Dunkirk and in four weeks had knocked out the bulk of the Allied armies. No nation could afford to ignore such potential.

Thus the '2181' Programme originally contained an urgent order for 200 SBD-2 Dauntless dive-bombers, and Wright Field was told to negotiate with Douglas for them, but this was later changed to 78 A-20s to agree with the already approved programme. Another conference was held which was attended by General Arnold, Colonel Echols and Dr Meads on 2 July. France had surrendered and Germany held Europe in captivity. The American Air Chiefs decided to procure only 78 A-24s (as the Army classified the SBD) initially and substitute the other 122 of the original order back to A-20 bombers. However, General Arnold specified that, 'All light bombers of the A-20 type procured on the 18,000 Programme should be capable of dive, glide or horizontal bombing.'

The 78 Navy dive-bombers were to be procured from Douglas as options on Navy contracts, while the dive-bombing requirements of the Army were to be met by procuring light bombers with dive-bombing as one of their capabilities. But it was not that easy. To cover all bases it was further specified that: 'The Research and Development Program provide for four dive-bombers of the light bomber class, procured from two different manufacturers under Project B-71 for a total estimated cost of US Dollars 1,832,000.'

Material Division was instructed to set up:

'(1) Immediate study to see what steps are necessary to permit Navy type dive-bombers to use Air Corps bombs and other equipment.

(2) Immediate engineering studies to modify the A-20 type airplane so that it is capable of dive, glide and horizontal bombing.'[9]

The latter proved impracticable and was dropped. As for the former, the Army eventually ended up ordering no less than four different types of dive-bomber, two as adaptations of Navy types and two brand-new designs straight off the drawing-board. All were failures as far as US Army operations were concerned. Only one, the SBD-Dauntless-based A-24, being the most far advanced, ever saw combat; its

combat missions are described later. In total the Army placed orders for 168 SBD-3s (which they called the A-24 Banshee) of which the only difference from the US Navy Dauntless was that they had provision for a pneumatic tail-wheel instead of a solid rubber one and featured no tail-hook for carrier landings. Procurement of the A-24 was maintained in 1942 with 170 SBD-4s being completed as A-24A and 615 SBD-5s as A-24Bs.

The other ex-Navy type selected was the Curtiss SB2C-1 Helldiver (designated the A-25 and named Shrike). An initial order for 100 was placed on the last day of 1940. More orders followed from the Army, 900 in April 1941 alone, until no less than 3,000 had been procured. The entire output of the St. Louis plant of Curtiss had to be allocated exclusively to the Army version, while the Navy Hell-divers had to be turned out in a brand-new plant at Columbus, Ohio. In the event the SB2C hit so many production problems that its entry into US Navy service was considerably delayed. Earlier ideas of standardization of the two lines soon were dropped. The Army needed the A-25 to be fitted with larger mainwheels, a soft tailwheel, an Army-type radio and extra armour protection, but strangely the Army initially accepted folding wings, although it was later

standardized with fixed wings. Thus it was not until 29 September 1942 that the first prototype Shrike flew, and the first of ten pre-production models did not leave St. Louis until March the following year.

The third type to be ordered was the A-34; some 750 of these Brewster SB2A-1 Buccaneers were asked for. The Royal Navy ordered 140 as the Bermuda, and the Netherlands Government placed orders for 162 (the Dutch aircraft of course were never delivered but went to the US Navy as the SB2A-4). Developed from the SBA/SBN design, the Brewster SB2A, like the Helldiver, was plagued with production problems. In short the rapidly expanding companies took on more than they could initially cope with and chaos resulted. Although eventually large numbers (771) of this dive-bomber appeared, it was two years too late and the need for them had gone. Many were relegated to the target-tug role on both sides of the Atlantic while others came straight off the production line into store and then were scrapped, earning the Brewster the unenviable (if unearned) epitaph of 'the worst American production aircraft of World War Two'.[10]

Not everyone agreed with this savage epitaph however. One former US Navy officer, Burton S. Block, told me:

'It is my opinion that this airplane, condemned by many as a notorious failure, was in fact well thought of by many in later years. I make this statement after combat duty flying the SBD Dauntless, the Curtiss Helldiver and the TBM Avenger with the Navy.

I was stationed at the Naval Air Station, Vero Beach, Florida, in July 1943. Here, unknown to many, radiomen/gunners training at Vero Beach served double duty, flying approximately 60 per cent of the time with US Navy pilots and 30 per cent of the time with British Navy pilots who were also undergoing operational training in the same SB2A-2, -3 and -4 aircraft. The main purpose of the crewman was to call out altitudes and pull-outs. From my logbook I can verify 26 flights during the month of August 1943 with a total of 32.3 hours. Of the 26 flights, 19 were practise dive-bombing with a general average dive of from 10–12,000 feet down to 3,000 feet.

As there were other groups of British and US Navy personnel using the same aircraft at the same time it is possible that the aircraft were averaging better than 60 hours and 200 dives with green, new pilots, per month, which certainly exceeded the requirements of combat duty.

It is therefore my opinion that properly utilized, and with all inter-service politics cleared out of the matter, an unbiased record would show the SBA Buccaneer performed better than various historians down the years have credited it.'[11]

The final dive-bomber of the quartet was the A-31 Vultee Vengeance. Originally built to the specification of the French Purchasing Commission of 1939 and adopted and modified by the British after the fall of France in June 1940, the Americans took over large numbers of these even before Pearl Harbor. On 1 July 1941 the Assistant Chief, Material Division at Wright Field sent to the War Department, Air Corps, Materials Division in Washington, DC the following Memorandum:

'Returned herewith as approved June 28 1941 by the Under Secretary of War, are three numbers of Contract DA-W-553 AC-119 with Vultee Aircraft Inc Downey, Cal covering procurement of 400 aircraft Model A-31 Dive Bomber Airplanes, Spare parts and Data at a total cost of US Dollars 31,619,280.00.'[9]

The A-31 was a big aircraft and contained many innovative and advanced features – perhaps too many because the design and production was again plagued with problems involving management/worker difficulties. Once more, despite early progress on air testing and prototype, final production was delayed. Eventually so many differences appeared between the British specification and the American one that,

◄◄
The US Army Air Force had adopted the Vultee A-31 dive-bomber, but insisted on numerous alterations to bring it up to their specifications. So many alterations were demanded that a whole new Mark, the A-35, was developed and two production lines were maintained. As with the Shrike/Helldiver concept, this resulted in delay, manufacturing difficulties, frustration and, ultimately, abandonment of the whole idea. Here an early A-31 is flight tested over California. (US National Archives)

◄
After many experiments and failures with conventional dive-bombers, the US Army finally found a perfect machine by default when, to keep the Mustang programme alive, 500 were converted for dive-bombing with dive brakes and bomb racks. Known as the A-24 Apache or Invader, they proved splendid dive-bombers in every way and saw much combat in the Mediterranean and Far East from 1943 to 1944. (Hugh V. Morgan)

as with Curtiss and the US Navy, two production lines were rolling, one at Downey, California and one several thousand miles away at Nashville, Tennessee, plus sub-contracting from Northrop at Hawthorne. In the end, Vultee was turning out virtually two different aircraft: A-31s for the RAF, A-35s for the USAAF. The fate of the Vultee was to be a slightly happier one than that of the Brewster. Eventually it did achieve extensive combat service and great success as we shall see, but this was with the RAF, RAAF and Indian Air Forces. The US Army found only problems with it until it threw in the towel.

With so many problems causing such headaches and long delays, coupled with the poor results and high losses of the few A-24s, the A-35 *had* managed to get into service, it is little wonder that the US Army began to detest the dive-bomber and everything to do with it. In frantic efforts to get some aircraft off the static production lines attempts were made to swap types with the Navy, but this only caused more friction.

Colonel Sassons and General Wolfe met in 1942 to discuss the chaotic situation. Wolfe told Sassons that Nashville were in a very precarious position with respect to materials and components for the A-35s. There was 'talk about pulling the A-25 from priority and substituting 200 A-31s'. It was confirmed that the contract was being re-worked and that the Navy had agreed that the Army had the paramount interest in the St. Louis plant and could do as it pleased with their share of the aircraft. 'What the hell business is it of the Navy or anybody else if we want to kick the A-25s out of the place that the A-35 occupied,' demanded the General. Colonel Sassons agreed that they then discussed the many modifications required on the Curtiss and how Burdie Wright at that company was shying away from introducing them as it would delay the aircraft even more. This would mean Curtiss laying off workers. They felt that because of this they were being pressurized. Wolfe stated that all favoured the A-35 in preference to the present A-25 and Sassons agreed this was so. General Wolfe exploded, 'God dammit, Burdie is just manoeuvring around us to make us take a flock of airplanes we don't want.'

Vultee were also producing the AT-6 training aircraft. The Vengeance was supposed to have a higher priority, but AT-6s were coming off the line in a flood while very few A-35s were appearing. Sassons suggested this was because the trainer had been in production a long time and components were available. Also he thought it was unfortunate that the components were not interchange-able and so could not be redirected to the A-35. So trainers kept coming but dive-bombers did not. The General was not convinced. He listed some of the shortages that were holding up the Vengeance line: 'Weatherhead actuating cylinders, Stewart Warner cheaters, Chromoly tubing, cable terminals, Klatic stop nuts, Bendix valves, Parker fittings, ball and roller bearings, oxygen manifolds. Now every darn one of those things are on the AT-6 and the AT-6 gets every one they need, apparently, 'cause they delivered 500 airplanes last month!'

They decided to allocate all available items to the priority aircraft despite any objections from Curtiss. They also decided that the best answer was still to insist on the A-25 being re-jigged to Army needs leaving out 'stuff not essential to us', like folding wings and the like. They agreed the A-25 was 'in a hell of mess' so it was wrong that it should be in a higher priority than the A-35. The only danger they felt was that Curtiss would 'go to the Navy and say, "Well the Army doesn't like the airplane, you people do. Why don't you make a deal with the Army to take the first three or four or five?"' Wolfe summed up this possibility: 'Well, lets find out who's dumb an' who's smart, the Navy, Curtiss or us!'[12]

In the event all the wheeling and dealing was to no avail. The final termi-

Famous aircraft, classic viewpoint. A Douglas SBD Dauntless lowers her distinctive 'cheese-grater' dive brakes to land aboard a carrier. The mainstay of the US Navy in the Pacific theatre, the faithful 'Slow But Deadly' sank more enemy shipping than any other weapon. It turned the tide of the war at Coral Sea, Midway, Guadalcanal and a hundred other air/sea battles and was still in front-line service with the US Marines in the Philippines and with the French Navy and Air Force in Britanny in 1945. (ECP des Armées, Fort d'Ivry)

▶

The unmistakable shape of the Vultee A35 Vengeance dive-bomber. Developed from scratch to a French order, the RAF took it over and modified it and the USAAF also placed orders for large numbers. Yet again, many teething problems caused many delays before it entered service and it was abandoned by the Americans. None the less it performed notably in combat with the RAF, RAAF, Indian and French air forces from 1942 to 1945, mainly in the Far East. (Smithsonian Institution)

nation of US Army Air Force interest in conventional dive-bombers came about with the convening of a Board of Officers for the purpose of evaluating all the dive-bombers then in production. They met at Wright Field, Dayton, Ohio on Friday, 19 March 1943. The officers present at these historic meetings were:
Colonel Ralph F. Stearley, AF HQ, Washington, DC
Colonel Ernest K. Warburton, Flight Section, Wright Field
Colonel William B. Karns, AF HQ, Wright Field
Colonel John D. H. Davies, Orlando School of Applied Tactics
Lieutenant-Colonel Frank R. Cook, Production Engineering Section, Wright Field
Lieutenant-Colonel Lee B. Coats, Production Engineering Section, Wright Field
Lieutenant-Colonel Melvin B. Zipp, 405 Bombardment Group, Drew Field
Major Whitmell T. Rison, Production Engineering Section, Wright Field
Major Guilford R. Montgomery, AAF Proving Ground, Eglin Field
Major Daniel G. Hawes, AAF Proving Ground, Eglin Field
Captain R. L. Hodges, AAF Proving Ground, Eglin Field
Lieutenant Charles A. Appel, 485 Bomb Squadron, 339 Bombardment Group, Drew Field

Certain members of the Board had flown the A-35 in flight tests at Eglin Field and in Third Air Force. The A-25 had been flown by certain members of the Board 'in active theatres', and other officers stationed at Wright Field, who had experience with the A-24, were consulted. The A-25, A-35 and A-24s at Wright Field were flown by various members of the Board. In comparing the three craft the following points were considered:
1. Provision for forward gun fire.
2. Ability to place a bomb on the target from a dive.
3. Ease of maintenance.
4. High speed at low altitudes.
The report also recorded that: 'In considering the recommendations as to further production of these types of aircraft for active theatres and recommendations as to types of aircraft to be used by dive-bomber groups contemplated in the present program the following points were considered:
1. Vulnerability to hostile fighters.
2. Ability to take evasive action, including high speed.
3. Accuracy at the target compared to the fighter-bomber types (A-36, P-51 and P-39) equipped with the N-3A modified gunsight, etc.'
The conclusions of the Board were fairly predictable.

'(A) Considering the suitability of the three types in regard to flying characteristics, maintenance and high speed, the types are listed in the following order of worth: A-25, A-35, A-24.
(B) (1) The three types are not tactically suitable in an active theatre. They are extremely vulnerable to hostile fighter's action and need close fighter support at all times, especially at the time of the individual dive, pull-out and reforming.
(2) The high speed at low altitude is not sufficient to evade hostile fighters or limit the number of attacks by hostile fighters.
(3) The accuracy of these types at the target will not be equal to that of the fighter-bomber types (A-36, P-51, P-39). Also, the fighter-bomber can better protect itself against hostile fighter action; this by its speed and other fighter characteristics. If these types are used with the N-3A modified gunsight in low-level attacks to gain accuracy, the inherent lack of speed is costly.'
Finally, to pre-empt the obvious question of why the US Army could not use dive-bombers when the US Navy was practically winning the Pacific War with them the Board commented:
'The Navy's need for a dive-bomber does not indicate an Army need for a dive-bomber. Hostile navies or task forces clash and the issue is quickly decided. The dive-bomber, primarily

An experimental Vengeance. This 3-bladed special conversion, with air scoops under the wings, was used as a flying test bed for new engine designs. (Author's collection)

Vultee Vengeance over the mountains of Burma en route to another dive-bombing mission against the besieging Japanese troops at Kohima and Imphal in 1944. Six squadrons of these aircraft were used to mount continuous sorties during these crucial battles. (Kenneth J. Gray)

Northrop-built V-72 Vengeance for the RAF, showing how the aircraft was prepared for crating prior to shipment overseas from the manufacturers. (Northrop)

The Vengeance was sub-contracted to Northrop while Vultee themselves built a modified version for the USAAF. Here ground crew at Northrop's Hawthorne plant in California load live rounds into the ammunition boxes and wing guns of a V-72. (Northrop)

designed to operate from a carrier, can in a naval action account for itself well.

Losses, even though large, may be accepted, since the action is vital and often final. The Army Air Force, in a normal theatre will operate daily. Large daily losses will cause a particular type to be classed as other than operational. The fighter-bomber type will suffer far less combat losses than the dive-bomber types.'[13]

All of which of course begged the very large question of the dominance of the German Ju 87 and the Soviet Pe2 in the world's most extensive and combat-intensive war zone, the Eastern Front. It also ignored the fact that daily operations by the heavy bombers of Eighth Air Force over Europe were resulting in huge losses, far greater than any dive-bomber casualties, but that this did not negate the B-17 one iota in the Army's eyes! However, their report terminated officially any question of the Army having to accept the dive-bomber as a specialized type. What of course it did *not* do was eliminate the requirement for a dive-bomber type, which, as soon as they became embroiled in real land battles, made itself very evident, despite their lofty academic disdain for it. So, having rid themselves of dive-bombers, the USAAF (as it had by then become) was to utilise dive-bombing to a high degree in

Sicily, Italy, Burma, China and France from 1943 to 1945. Luckily, mainly by chance and default, it had an outstanding dive-bomber with which to accompany its dive-bombing needs. This was the North American A-36.

Apache or Invader?

The story of the North American P51 Mustang has been told and retold. Everyone agrees it was one of the most outstanding fighter aircraft of the Second World War. What is less known is that versions of it became the best dive-bombers of that period. One early adaptation, the A-36 Apache, was built for the job, while the P-51D was almost as efficient with slight modifications. But the strangest twist to the story is that the conversion of the P51A to the A-36, came about more as a 'political' ploy by 'Dutch' Kindleberger to keep North American's production lines working rather than any firm commitment to dive-bombing on behalf of her designer, Edgar Schmued. Out of such machinations appeared a brilliant long-range fighter aircraft and an outstanding dive-bomber. Stanley Worth had a long period with North American at this time and he gave me his 'behind the scenes' version of these momentous events at North American as they unfolded.

'The 150 P51As built under Lend Lease

were to be the last of the Mustangs since the US Army Air Corps had been so convinced that it was a poor airplane that they did not want it and would not authorize any more under Lend Lease for the UK. However Dutch Kindleberger was determined to keep the airplane alive and the production line going and since dive-bombers were the "in" airplane he convinced Hap Arnold that the P51A with four 50cal in lieu of the four 20mm together with dive brakes was just what the US needed. I don't believe anybody really believed that dive brakes would be effective on a laminar flow wing. I know Dutch didn't, but desperate measures were needed even if it meant distorting the truth.

A contractor's word meant a lot, more then than it does now and if there had been no A-36 there would have been no P51D – which was an absolute winner. When the A-36 went into the USAAF in North Africa they soon recognized it as a far better fighter airplane than the P40 or P38. There had been some wing beef-up in the dive-bomber role, but it was minor and initially there were many flight restrictions placed upon the A-36. Some A-36s did carry long-range external drop fuel tanks but I think they were more for ferry purposes than anything else.'[14]

The A-36 differed in having a modified engine to give a better low-altitude per-

formance to help offset the drag of the bombs. Wind tunnel tests were conducted and these resulted in modifications to the radiator scoop to improve airflow. Bomb shackles for carrying two 500lb bombs were fitted under each wing, being located under the wing machine-gun trays outboard of the undercarriage. The most obvious feature was the fitting of hydraulic dive brakes of the lattice type which opened both above and below the main plane thus giving a more stabilized control in the attack dive. However on early models the hydraulics proved not up to their job. Imbalances often caused one brake or the other not to extend. In such an awkward configuration the aircraft could not be held on target, and in extreme cases all control was lost resulting in some spectacular crashes.

The first A-36 of an order for 500 rolled off the production line at North American's Inglewood plant in September 1942, joining their fighting units the following month. Originally it had been planned to name the P51A the Apache, but the British name Mustang was chosen and the name Apache was passed to the A-36. It failed to stick however. Following its initial operating usage at Pantelleria and Sicily one of the pilots of 27 Bombing Group (Dive) suggested calling the A-36 Invader,

'because we keep on invading places'. And so it became the unofficial name for the A-36 in the Mediterranean theatre. It was never officially adopted, having already been assigned to the A-20, and the A-36 squadrons with the CBI in Burma still used the old name Apache, but more generally A-36 and this also applied to the Italian theatre later.

What was the A-36 like to fly? One person who can answer that is Roland W. Tapp, ThD. He had wide experience in dive-bombing having flown 115 hours on the A-24A Banshee, soloed on the A-31 Vengeance and had 121 hours (including combat) on the A-36A Apache. He gave me this fascinating account of his early experience and the dive-bombing methods as taught by the US Army at that time.

'Wings growing out of your shoulders'

'I was in 55 Squadron of 48 Bomb Group (Dive) at Key Field, Meridian, Mississippi. I think that when the decision was made to use the A-36 instead of the A-31 they transferred us from 57 Squadron to 55, but am not really sure why. We went from Key Field to Harding Field in Baton Rouge, Louisiana, to 305 Squadron of 85 Bomb Group (Dive).

The first training was in the A-24. My memory says that it carried ten smoke-

bombs under each wing. We climbed to about 8,000–10,000 feet, opened the dive brakes, did a push-over dive straight ahead, and frantically looked around for the target, dropping the bomb at about 3,000–4,000 feet. Much to the disgust of the range officer who was supposed to score our hits (he was in greater danger than the bull's-eye, as I recall).

So this meant about twenty dives a day. Far more than any of us ever did in combat (so most of us had eye, ear or nose trouble by the time we got to Italy). But our Colonel was insistent that all of his airplanes stay in the air from dawn till midnight EVERY day. I think he thought it made him look good. The result, of course, was that we lost more airplanes to mechanical failure than the Germans ever shot down.

Since there was extra flight pay for aircrew, we had no trouble getting would-be gunners to ride in the back seat. Once a pilot decided to do a loop on the way home from the range. He looped it all right, but the gunner did not have his seat belt on and so tumbled right out. Fortunately, he was able to open his parachute before he hit the ground. But this caused quite a flap for a few days.

The A-24 was a good, stable airplane. But it was too slow for the kind of flying

48

◄◄
The new generation of US dive-bombers being developed when war broke out included the Curtiss SB2C Helldiver, known to the USAAC as the Shrike. Unfortunately the shared interest and enormous orders placed, coupled with teething problems, caused endless delays and the aircraft did not enter service until late in the Pacific War. (Imperial War Museum)

◄
The Curtiss SB2C-1 undergoing flight testing at Port Columbus, Ohio in 1942. After a series of demonstration flights this aircraft was destroyed in a crash and the programme was put back. (US National Archives)

we were expecting in Italy against the Luftwaffe's Me 109s and FW 190s. I think the decision to go to the A-36 was because that airplane could act in both capacities: it really was the ideal fighter-bomber. When we dropped our bombs, we became fighter aircraft. Up to about 14,000 feet that is! The Allison engine was not supercharged and so was pretty much out of it at higher altitudes.

The A-36 gave its pilot the feeling that the wings were growing right out of his shoulders and the A-24 never did that! Also, the A-36 was a very good low-altitude machine for strafing. In Italy, when we completed a dive we were often down between two hills, so the only way out was a low-level run up the valley, shooting whatever was in your gunsights. I doubt that the A-24 or the A-31 could do that. I mean at altitudes like 20 feet! (I can remember an Italian farm woman flapping her apron at me as I went by!)

Advanced cadet training was in the AT-6, so the A-24 was a big change. But the speed was not all that different, either take-off or landing. The A-36 was really different! It landed at about 90–100mph. Cruising was about 265 or so. And the cockpit was so small that even a little guy like me (5ft 6½in) was crowded. I remember once I got lost on a cross-country flight in a rainstorm. When I broke out of it, I couldn't determine

where I was, and I was sitting on my map (under my parachute). I could NOT raise myself high enough to get my hand under the seat to extract the maps! (Finally found a railroad track and followed it.)

Training in the A-24 and the A-36 was like this: Fly from dawn till noon (two or three landings, but mostly diving and formation exercises . . . like: "You're too far away! I want you six inches from my wingtip!". Ground school from 2 p.m. till 4 p.m., engines, meteorology, map-reading, etc. Then back in the air right after dinner until midnight. Night formation flying, night cross-country, night landings (in formation yet!!!).

The dive-bombing training was mostly trying to put smoke-bombs inside a 300ft circle from various altitudes (none of them high). Gunnery practice in the A-36 was using the six 50cal guns to hit ground targets, and then the towed target. I think that the guns were calibrated to give you a 100ft cone-of-fire at about 300yd, but memory gets foggy after forty years!

I do not remember that we *ever* had any instruction from either Navy or Marine dive-bomber pilots. Maybe our higher officers did, but it never filtered down, as far as I know. Nor did we have any films of tactics of the Stukas or anybody else. Which meant we knew nothing whatsoever about dive-bombing until we actually joined a combat unit in

Italy. We also had a gunnery range off the coast at Mobile, Alabama when we were flying A-36s from Harding Field at Baton Rouge and an A-31 towed the target for us.

Towards the end of our A-36 tactical training in Baton Rouge, it was discovered that sometimes one of the dive brakes would begin to open a bit ahead of the other. This caused the airplane to become uncontrollable. (In fact, one of our men crashed into Lake Ponchatrain, near New Orleans, and the assumption was that this had happened to him.)

So, for about the last couple of months of training, the dive brakes were wired shut and not used. When we reported this to the Colonel of 27 Bomb Group in Italy, he sniffed and said, "Not over here, you don't wire 'em shut . . . you use them!" So we did. So, if your research turns up anyone (in fact almost *every* air historian so far) who says that the A-36 dive brakes were never used in combat, tell him that he is wrong. We used them consistently in every dive, and never had any trouble. At least, I never did!

I have also read that the A-36 had only four 50cal guns, two in each wing. Not so. There were two in each wing and two mounted in the engine fairing, firing through the propeller arc. These guns had to be cocked in the cockpit, but were fired from the same trigger as the others.

◀

A Brewster Buccaneer dive-bomber and team of aviators at the US Naval Air Station, Vero Beach, Florida in August 1943. Mixed teams of American and British naval pilots practised their art here with a high degree of accuracy and a very low accident rate, but the Brewster never saw operational service. (Burton S. Block)

▶

After the fall of France the Royal Navy purchased batches of the Vought, which it named the Chesapeake. During extensive squadron testing it was found to be a very good aircraft, apart from its long take-off run, and ideal for dive-bombing from large carriers or shore bases. The Admiralty, however, chose to evaluate it as an anti-submarine aircraft operating from small escort carriers, and abandoned it in favour of the Swordfish. (RAF Museum)

True. There were also stories that once in awhile someone shot a hole in his prop, but this was *not* standard operating procedure!

North American made only 500 A-36s. Two groups were sent to Italy, two groups went to CBI in India, and two stayed home for training. When these aircraft were shot down or otherwise used up, the combat units first went to old P-40s, then to P-47s. There were no more A-36s and no more true dive-bombers. (All of us genuine dive-bomber pilots don't consider a 45–60-degree dive to be a real dive!)'[15]

The Beast!

The Army Board had decided that the Curtiss A-25 was the best of the conventional dive-bombers in production, even if it then went on to decide it still didn't want it. Yet the US Navy, firmly committed to the dive-bomber and daily proving its merits, had to wait a long, long time to get their hands on the SB2C-1 Helldiver. The many modifications required on this temperamental and rugged dive-bomber alone could fill a book the size of this one, and all this was coupled with plant difficulties and endless delays due to the fruitless inter-Service feuds trying to 'harmonize' what had become two very different aircraft. The first prototype Helldiver flew on 30

June 1942 soon after the Battle of Midway. This did not indicate early introduction to battle because the SB2C-1 production line at the Columbus, Ohio plant had to incorporate yet more changes. This was after structural weaknesses were exposed in diving tests, which had led to fatal accidents at NACA Langley, causing the -1 Helldiver to be restricted in its prime role, and clean high-speed dives were ruled out. Not a good start for an aircraft whose entire *raison d'être* was high-speed diving attack!

The first fleet carrier squadrons to be equipped were VS-9 and VB-9 embarked aboard *Essex* in December 1942. It soon became apparent that she could not take them to war, faults and accidents escalating alarmingly. She sailed to meet the Japs with the old reliable SBDs instead. Next VB-17 took over the Helldivers and put them through their paces aboard the trials carrier *Santee* for sea tests in April 1943. At first they appeared to hold up, but then the catalogue of tailwheel failures, hook malfunctions and spin-ins began to mount again. Yet more modifications resulted and VB-4 and VB-6 aboard *Yorktown II* were equipped with the resulting aircraft. They lasted only a few weeks; during the carrier's initial shakedown cruise enough accidents and further faults took place to lead her

skipper, Captain J. J. Clark, to request the Navy to scrap the whole Curtiss programme. He also took the old 'Slow But Deadly' to war and yet a third major modification programme was begun. Non-retractable tailwheels were fitted to end the string of collapses; much greater structural strength was built in; the longitudinal control had a bobweight added to give higher forces in the recovery of the dive; self-sealing fuel tanks were fitted in the fuselage and so on. In July 1943 VB-17 took three dozen of these heavily changed SB2C-1s aboard *Bunker Hill* to try their luck![16]

7. The British experience

IN the Fleet Air Arm Great Britain had a champion of the dive-bomber and eventually they managed to get one built in time for the outbreak of war. This was the Blackburn Skua. Only a few were built, but they served well if briefly before events overtook them. Then the stark reality of the threat of invasion in June 1940 forced the British to follow the French example and turn for succour to the USA.

A formidable sea bird

The Blackburn Skua was the solitary representative of the true dive-bombing type to see combat service with British forces during the first year of the war. She was hardly an elegant aircraft nor was she speedy by any stretch of the imagination, but she *could* perform her main function to perfection. What is more the Skua was one of the first to show just how superior dive-bombing was against military targets, and in particular, against medium and small warships. Unfortunately nobody in Britain took the hint but our German opponents did. As Britain had most of the warships and Germany had all the dive-bombers the unpleasant consequences, handed out in increasingly liberal doses off Norway, Dunkirk, Greece, Crete and Malta in the years which followed, were rather predictable if bitter reminders of this truth.

Captain T. W. Harrington, DSC, RN, had a wide experience of flying all types of single-engined aircraft with the Fleet Air Arm during the war. He started off flying Skuas, however, and his all-round expertise gives him a rather more credible viewpoint from which to judge this much-maligned aircraft than its many armchair critics post-war.

'From the UK point of view, I think that the Admiralty was the first British Service to achieve a specific aircraft with designed (and achieved) dive-bombing characteristics. This was the Blackburn Skua (named after a formidable sea bird, which dives bodily into the sea for its food) and was intended to fill both the role of dive-bomber or fighter. We had three or four such squadrons of up to twelve aircraft apiece based in aircraft carriers like *Ark Royal* at the beginning of the war and so they were spread in both home waters as well as the Med! They first made their mark as makeshift fighters but achieved their full measure in the Norwegian campaign. It was here that, despite the skill and vigour of people like Bill Lucy and a host of other determined operators, the Skua was shown up as a non-starter in the fighter role against the most modern German land-based aircraft.

The Skua then became mainly used in her correct role as a dive-bomber rather

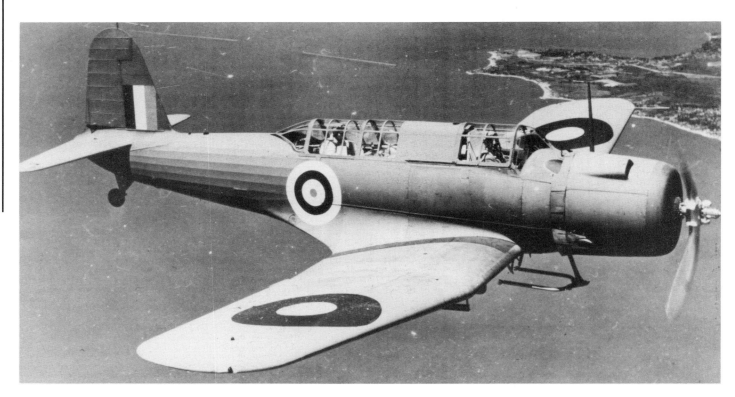

than as a "fighter". Indeed, one of the earliest attacks made in this strike-role was on the first or second day of the war, when one of our stalwart flying Royal Marines, dive-bombed a U-boat, causing a bit of damage. However, the real lesson learned (shades of Sutton Bridge range and peacetime training) was that he went so low in his enthusiastic attack, that the bomb (not an anti-submarine one) also blew him up and he finished up in the sea. In those early days (of gentlemen) the German Navy were gallant to their brothers-in-arms and the damaged U-boat collected our "Royal" and took him back to the Fatherland for the rest of the war.

Probably the most striking example of the Skua in its dive-bombing role was at the end of the Norwegian campaign, when the remnants of several squadrons flew from the Orkneys (Hatston) and sank the German cruiser *Königsberg* in classical style while she was alongside in Bergen harbour. After this the main role of the Skua was fixed, but by that time there were not too many Skuas left around, just enough to keep Nos. 800 and 801 Squadrons going, and finally just No. 800 Squadron.

The Royal Air Force had also put out a staff requirement for a dive-bomber and Hawker's famous Sidney Camm produced a typical Camm solution, the

Hawker Henley with his classic lines, as remembered and seen in the Hurricane, Tempest and Sea Fury. It flew beautifully, had excellent dive brakes and no doubt would have been a formidable strike aircraft. However, the fates and conflicts of priority in this defensive period had the effect of turning the excellent Henley into a target-towing workhorse – a great waste and a great pity in the event.

One notable characteristic the Skua had in a long steep dive was that, as the speed built up, the aircraft tended to rotate round its axis. This was easily controlled and was caused by the setting of the ailerons being adjusted for normal flight conditions. One countered this by the controls plus laying one's sighting to let a natural creep take place. The old girl also had a bomb-throwing crutch which took the main bomb on the belly clear of the propeller, an essential for a steep dive.

After Norway, No. 801 Squadron were flown into RAF Detling in the second half of May just in time to start helping to cover the collapse in France and during the German thrust through Belgium. We left in the last days of June and flew back to Hatston (Naval Air Station) in order to continue the strike role off the Norwegian coast. The squadron was embarked from time to time for either strikes off northern Norway or to provide

strike/fighter or research role for special convoys taking RAF fighter aircraft to West Africa for onward reinforcement of Wavell's desert war efforts. It was during this period we were sent to RAF St. Eval for the "Salmon" and "Gluck" (planned, but never carried out) dive-bombing attacks on the German battle cruisers *Scharnhorst* and *Gneisenau* holed up in Brest harbour effort, which in turn was ended when the German Air Force counter-attacked St. Eval and severely mauled our poor old Skuas while parked near the control tower.

From mid-1941 I was never in anything other than pure fighter types of which the best of the bunch was the Grumman Hellcat. The Hellcat was a rugged, formidable and flexible fighter from which the then new rockets could be fired and napalm plonked into an enemy nest. It was a great fighter but of course had no form of dive brakes or speed-spoilers. This meant you had to have a lot of airspace to be offensive with a dive-bomb attack; even this was at the expense of accuracy and effectiveness.

It was not really until well after the war was over that the development of special weaponry took place and the attack role was capable of being married into designed attack aircraft and being really cost effective in terms of accuracy, surprise and results.'[17]

◄
The Chesapeake was evaluated by the aircrew of 811 Squadron, Fleet Air Arm at Lee-on-Solent. Note the prominent bomb fork and the composite construction of the fuselage fore and aft. (RAF Museum)

►
Again, with the fall of France Britain took over outstanding orders to prevent them going elsewhere. The CW77Fs were named Cleveland in British service, but only a handful were assembled and test flown. Obviously obsolete, they were used for secondary purposes and at engineering schools. (Imperial War Museum – RAF Museum)

►
A small batch of Helldivers were evaluated by the Fleet Air Arm, but never used operationally, nor were orders placed via Lease-Lend. Instead the Royal Navy used torpedo-bombers such as the Fairey Barracuda and Grumman Avenger in the shallow dive-bombing role. (RAF Museum)

▲

Conceived as a dive-bomber that could also act as a fighter far out at sea in naval battles, the Blackburn Skua had to be dragged from a reluctant RAF by the Royal Navy. When war came it was used as a fighter against first-class enemy opposition and only rarely in its correct role. However, when it *was* allowed to dive-bomb it was a success, sinking the cruiser *Königsberg* at Bergen in April 1940, the first large warship to be sunk by aircraft. (RAF Museum)

▶▲

The USAAF used the A-36 dive-bomber and later found that the standard P-51 could be adapted, with hard pads for bomb-carrying, to perform almost as well in this role. The RAF evaluated the A-36, but as usual, rejected the dive-bomber concept, and the only unit it equipped with this aircraft was used for reconnaissance purposes in the central Mediterranean theatre. (RAF Museum)

◀
◀

The initial production orders placed by the RAF for the A-31 were fulfilled by sub-contracting to Northrop which had wide pre-war experience of the dive-bomber. They produced on time to the original specification. These two photographs show early production models on the concrete at Hawthorne prior to flight testing, crating and shipping to Britain or India. (Stanley Worth)

And so, that was the end of true dive-bombers in British service until 1943 when the much delayed Vultee Vengeance began to join squadron service with the RAF, the RAAF and the Indian Air Force. In the two-year gap there was a great deal of controversy in Press and Parliament, but the only other serious contender was an American import, the Vought 'Vindicator'.

Paradise lost

When the Navy Skua was phased out of service the Navy was left with no dive-bombers at all, and was forced to use torpedo-bombers in the dive-bomber role instead. Although they evaluated batches of Douglas Dauntless and Curtiss Helldivers they never utilized them. The same fate befell a small batch of Vought–Sikorsky Vindicators (given the British name of Chesapeake) that came their way in the summer of 1940. Perversely, having a dive-bomber totally suitable for use on fleet carriers, the Admiralty tested it exclusively with anti-submarine operations from a small escort carrier in mind! Like the Skua this dive-bomber refused to perform in a totally alien role and again the aircraft was blamed not the testers!

An interesting and highly entertaining personal account of this charade was given by one young FAA pilot (now Lord

Kilbracken) who was involved. After a period of flying Fairey Swordfish bi-planes he was posted to No. 811 Squadron, then working-up at Lee-on-Solent airfield. He arrived on 15 July 1941 expecting more of the same and was: 'envious to see, dispersed at intervals round the airfield perimeter, nine gleaming gull-winged monoplanes among the Stringbags and Albacores. We were supposed to be able to recognize every aircraft that flew. But these I had never seen before.'

Next day he discovered that he was to fly these newcomers.

'Vought–Sikorsky Chesapeakes, Pratt & Whitney Twin Wasp Junior engines, newly-arrived from the States. Closed-cockpit dive-bombers, all mod cons, Jesus what a line! Having imagined myself almost certainly Stringbag bound, grown to love the old lady *faute de mieux*, the mieux suddenly materialized. As though a sex-starved male, newly married off to a comfortable if pie-faced lady of very uncertain age, had been suddenly thrown into bed with a captivating and extremely willing bobbysoxer.'

The question we had to answer was whether our glamorous Cheesecakes (as they soon became known) were suitable for the rough-and-tumble of hunting U-boats from a small carrier in mid-Atlantic, the work for which *Archer* was

intended. Our CO was Lieutenant 'Pig' Lucas, an extremely experienced, very old pilot. He must have been getting on for thirty! Senior pilot Alan McTurk also had two stripes and long experience. Four rookies: the author, Lieutenant Commander (A) John Godley, RNVR; Eric Cooper and Robin Shirley-Smith. Peter Bentley (*nom de guerre* of a French flyer) another two-striper, Murray Willcocks, plus Jock Sayer and Denis Fuller.

Like the girls of the same period she doesn't look much today when I examine her faded photograph, but in 1941 the Cheesecake seemed a wonder and a joy. Unlike the Stringbag she looked like a warplane and felt like one – more than twice as fast, fully aerobatic, flaps and VP prop, glasshouse, the lot. An unusual feature was that the undercarriage (retractable of course) was designed to be used as an airbrake; you lowered it before going into a dive and this kept your speed below 250 no matter what.

The Cheesecake was well suited for low-level attacks on U-boats, presumably the most usual employment foreseen for us, or for general reconnaissance, but was designed as a dive-bomber. As such it was remarkable. The technique was quite unusual: position yourself ten thousand feet or so immediately above your target and then des-

◀
Vengeance production line rolling at Northrop's Hawthorne plant in 1943. (Gerald Balzer)

▶
An early production model Vengeance in RAF markings ready for delivery. The enormous nose of this aircraft ruled it out for anything but vertical dive-bombing. The bombs were stowed in a large internal bomb-bay. (Author's collection)

◀▼
Night-work on the Northrop assembly lines. The size of the Vultee's engine is very apparent. (Gerald Balzer)

cend vertically – and I do mean vertically – upon it. There wasn't any bomb-sight, you aimed the whole plane. Hold her thus to as low a height as you dared, press the tit and pull out. Well you could hardly miss. In a less steep dive you had to judge how far past your target to aim. As a bonus it is very hard, sometimes impossible, for a ground gunner to bring his weapon to bear on a target immediately overhead or for a fighter to keep after you.

Funnily enough it isn't too easy to dive vertically, not absolutely vertically, until you get the hang of it. If you just shove the stick forward and hold it there, you feel you're vertical before you reach sixty degrees. By the time you reach ninety degrees, which takes quite a steady nerve, you may well be past your target. And it feels like past the vertical. The trick was to do a half-roll so that you were momentarily upside-down, then simply pull back on the stick till your target was sitting on top of your engine cowling. You couldn't help being vertical, it's a geometric certainty. Hold her till you press the tit, then pull out, no problem.'

Actually there were problems. Far from being designed to use the under-carriage as a dive brake, the Vought used this method because the real dive brakes did not work properly! But

nobody had told them that, certainly not the Americans who had also sold this aircraft to the French as we have seen. Nor was it as simple as all that to control the Chesapeake; Godley wrote off AL 936 in a bumpy landing at Starvell Farm, Kiddington near Oxford. Nevertheless, compared to what had gone before and was to come after, the Vought dive-bomber was very welcome. Alas, it did not last.

'We had been given no inkling of it, about our *coup de foudre* with the sexy American teenager was coming to an end. The ample bosom of the Stringbag, once deserted wife-mother, compla-cently awaited us. We'd been putting in thirty hours a month subjecting the Cheesecake to every trial and indignity. But Their Lordships from Pig's reports didn't like what they had heard. A few days after my birthday Pig broke the news. We'd be leaving next week for Arbroath to re-equip with Swordfish. Our Chesapeakes would be demoted to non-operational duties.

Jesus what a come-down. It seemed a totally incredible decision. The verdict had been that our sweethearts were under-powered, would too often be unable to carry an adequate load from a small carrier. But the power of the Twin Wasp Junior, and all the performance data had been well known before we

started. Our exhaustive three-month trials had shown no defects, drawbacks, shortcomings. It seemed totally inexplic-able, a perverse step backwards to what we'd thought *temps perdu*, as though My Lords were determined at all costs that Navy pilots should never have a halfway modern kite to fly.

Like trying to drive a truck. That's how it seemed to us to be once more driving a Stringbag after the Chesapeake's de-lights. Can the controls always have been so ponderous, needing a ham-handed thrust on the stick, an almighty boot on the rudder-bar, to get any real response, when our silvery Cheesecake had soared and gyrated to the smallest touch of a finger? No more the easy rolls and effortless loops, with perhaps a stylish half-roll off the top among the clouds, then the breathtaking vertical dive with the needle beyond 300. And no more the comfort and class of a closed cockpit . . .'[18]

Diving the Vultee

The main mount with which most RAF, RAAF and Indian Air Force wartime dive-bomber operations were conducted, in Burma, New Guinea and the Eastern theatre generally, was the big, powerful but slow Vultee A-31 Vengeance. Alto-gether a much larger and heavier dive-bomber than almost all its single-

▶

At work on the unpredictable Cyclone. Supplies of the early Vengeance to all units were marred by the unreliability of their power plants. Heavy oil consumption, the tendency to sieze up or catch fire while aloft and many other problems, delayed the entry into service of this aircraft by a year. However the squadrons solved their own problems thanks to the dedication of the armourers and mechanics, the unrecognised 'Erks'. (RAF Museum)

▶▶

A North American A-26 dive-bomber with British markings in March 1943. This aircraft was undergoing flight tests at Martlesham Heath. (RAF Museum)

engined contemporaries, the Vengeance has, since the war, received a largely unjustified 'bad Press' by misinformed historians. 'The Vultee', as it was generally known in Allied service, was in fact rated as 'probably the most accurate dive-bomber in service other than the Stuka'[19] by people who really count, such as senior test pilots who flew all types. It was also highly rated by the majority of its aircrew of whom the author has contacted a very large number. One such is Flying Officer L. F. Foster, who gave me this account of the VV's qualities.

'I converted to this aircraft at No. 152 OTU at Peshawar from July to September 1943. I was a WOP/AIR/ASU/AG ex-Costal Command and crewed up with an ex-Spitfire pilot after he had done a six-week familarization course on the VV and I had done a Navigator's course in order to make a "fully self-contained" crew of two. We both then did a further six weeks as a crew, doing practise dive-bombing, air-to-ground gunnery and cross-country navigation.

In September, we both joined No. 82 Squadron in East Bengal as they had just commenced operations in VV aircraft, having been a former Blenheim squadron in the UK. All told, I did about 130 trips in the Vengeance, 69 as ops on our Tour.

We mostly operated in the Arakan area in South Burma, being used as "Immediate Call" bombers to support the Army, although on many occasions we bombed strategic targets such as the airfield at Akyab. When Kohima was besieged, we moved to North Burma in March 1944 to bomb forward Japanese troops and positions from Kumbhirgram airfield, returning to the Arakan area late in April.

The Vengeance was uncannily accurate and we did 90-degree dives from 10,000 feet (pulling-out at 1,000 feet) almost all the time and our accuracy was invariably maximum error of 25 yards. Usually we carried two 500lb bombs in the interior bomb-bay and a 250lb bomb under each wing.

Controlled dive speed with dive brakes opening above and below the wings, was 286mph, although my log-book records, on 4 March 1944, during an attack on Japs at Letwedt, my pilot forgot to put out the dive brakes and we reached 450 knots plus IAS (we had duplicate controls and instruments in the rear seat which is how I knew!)

For defensive armament we had twin .303in Brownings in the rear and two .300in Brownings in the wings. One of the last VVs I flew in was No. 82 Squadron's 'D' serial, EZ986. We started with the AN series and finished up with

FBs (i.e., Marks I, II, IIa and III)'.[20]

In total four RAF squadrons, two Indian Air Force squadrons and five RAAF squadrons employed this aircraft most successfully on dive-bomber operations from 1942 until mid-1944. It was also used extensively on subsidiary duties by the RAF, Royal Navy, RAAF, USAAF, Brazilian and Free French Air Forces, the latter in North Africa, being employed mainly as coastal anti-submarine aircraft and target-tugs. Unfortunately the later Mark IV models, which were much improved, never saw action, arriving too late. The main faults with the Vengeance, which prevented its more widespread use earlier in the war, was the initial unreliability of its Wright Cyclone engines which were rendered inefficient and uneconomical by shoddy parts and workmanship. Once these difficulties had been resolved at squadron level the Vultee became a highly dependable aircraft. During the intensive operations at the siege of Imphal and Kohima, Vultee squadrons maintained enviable sortie rates for long periods in difficult conditions.

Alas, such real achievements have been either belittled or ignored in the various official and unofficial histories, but its war record was both a remarkable and a positive testimony to the dive-bombing of jungle targets.

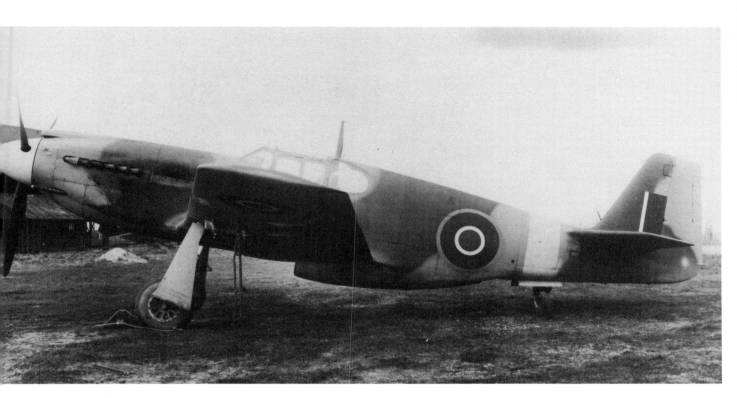

Commonwealth types

Compromise dive-bombers were hardly ever successful. Many such were tried, from the Soviet conversion of their standard SB medium bomber through the French Breguet 698 concept to the Messerschmitt Me 210-AO dive-bomber variants. Conversely, on occasion even some of the least likely contenders performed more than adequately. One such duckling that turned into a part-time dive-bombing swan, was the Commonwealth A-20 Wirraway.

The original aim of the Wirraway concept in Australia dated back to before the war when the Australians' need to build-up their own aircraft industry to help in the expansion of the RAAF had led to the choice of the North American NA-33. What was required was a simple rugged all-round aircraft on which the fledgling industry could cut its teeth while providing a useful aircraft for the Air Force's inventory at the same time. This they did. The wartime demands placed on this little aircraft (which was really a modified version of the standard training aircraft known as the T-6 Texan in the USA and the Havard in the UK) were many and varied. It had to act as trainer, combat front-line fighter, reconnaissance aircraft and artillery spotter. Perhaps it didn't perform all these duties as well as specialized types, and it was

very optimistic to expect it to act as a fighter (which is why the single-seater derivative, the CAC A-46 Boomerang, was developed), but it filled gaps left by the absence of anything better at a crucial time.

Its combat dive-bomber origins can be traced back to the desperate days of the Japanese invasion of Malaya from December 1941 onward. A detachment of five of No. 12 Squadron's CAC Wirraways, with mixed Australian and New Zealand aircrew, had been stationed at Kahang as an advanced flying training flight. This was hastily made an operational unit when the Japanese stormed ashore. They were fitted for carrying light bombs and a further 'unofficial' refinement in their new role as dive-bombers was the installation of sirens made from soup plates which turned in the slipstream to produce Stuke-type screams in their attacks. It was hoped this would scare the Japanese as the Allied forces had little else with which to do so!

Their big moment in this role came on 19 January 1942 when all five made a concerted dive-bombing attack on Japanese invasion barges and landing craft crossing the strategic River Maur. The attack was successful but they lost one of their number to defending fighters, and were too few to affect the issue. The long-awaited dive-bombers

(Bermuda and Vengeance) ordered from the USA had not materialized as promised and something had to be done to give the Army close and accurate air support. No. 12 Squadron was therefore reorganized as the RAAF's first dive-bomber unit and equipped with the Wirraway for this work pending the arrival of the Vultee, which did not happen until April 1943.

Early modification of the standard Wirraway had already taken place with this employment in view, and involved the strengthening and redesign of the wing and tail units to take the added stresses, as well as fitting light bomb-carriers below the wings. In addition of course, the standard split flaps were supplemented by proper dive brakes. This development produced the CA-10A dive-bomber variant, and they saw considerable action in this role.

▶

A group of smiling Russian women pilots of a Pe-2 dive-bomber Regiment. These women's regiments flew with great gallantry and suffered heavy losses. (Author's collection)

▶▶

The Soviet Petlyakov Pe-2 twin-engined dive-bomber was an inspired design. Changed from a high-speed high-altitude interceptor into a dive-bomber, the result was far ahead of its time. From hesitant beginnings in 1941, a vast fleet was built up and these dive-bombers spearheaded the Red Armies' drive to Berlin from 1943 to 1945. (Novosti Press Agency, Moscow)

8. Soviet Developments

HAVING compared the dive-bombers of the United States and Great Britain *vis-à-vis* those of the two principle Axis partners, attention must be given to the designs maturing at this period in the Soviet Union, a nation not hitherto much concerned with the art.

'Astounded our boys considerably'

That the Western combatants knew little about their potential enemies' aircraft may seem strange, but they knew even less about the capabilities, or even the very existence, of some of the main combat aircraft of what was to be their major Ally. Thus the fact that the Soviet Union widely employed one of the most advanced and successful dive-bombers seen anywhere in the world has remained a generally ignored fact ever since. Everyone has heard of the ground-attacking Shturmovik, but apart from certain dedicated enthusiasts, few know much about the outstanding Petlyakov Pe-2 dive-bomber, which was so advanced that it was still equipping front-line Eastern Bloc air regiments in 1947.

The former main wing designer for the Soviet aircraft manufacturer Tupolev was Vladimir Petlyakov. He, together with his mentor and 450 other irreplaceable aircraft designers and aeronautical specialists, were arrested by Marshal Stalin and thrown into labour and special NKVD internment camps during one of that paranoid leader's brainstorms. Typically, Stalin later recalled these men whom his meglomania had so abused and ordered them to create new types of aircraft with which to face his enemies. It is indicative of the Russian mentality that they unhesitatingly did so. Thus, when Stalin demanded a dive-bomber, Petlyakov took his much-cherished high-altitude fighter design, the twin-engined VI-100, and swiftly transformed it into an aerodynamically clean dive-bomber of outstanding performance. It was a remarkable achievement considering the circumstances under which he was working, and even more so when it is remembered that the then prevalent theory in the West was that modern high-speed aircraft would be unable to carry out dive-bombing at all! For this achievement the brilliant young designer obtained his 'freedom' once more.

In April 1941, just prior to Germany's

invasion of Russia, State Aircraft Factory No. 22, where the new aircraft was being built, was visited by representatives from the Luftwaffe's Technical Office. The Germans do not seem to have realized any more than anyone else, just what sort of aircraft they were looking at. It was later to prove their bane. A Soviet deputation had visited the leading aircraft firms in the Reich as early as March 1940, when the two powers were still close allies and friends. Among the aircraft viewed was the Junkers Ju 87, but the delegation turned down the opportunity to purchase examples of the Stuka, despite Stalin's interest in dive-bombing, because they considered it was obsolete and slow. With hindsight we can see why they were able to turn up their noses at the then leading exponent of the art.

However, the formation of the first Soviet *Pikiruyushchi bombardirovochny* (dive-bomber) Regiments were a long time coming. By the end of 1940 only two Pe-2s had been built. By the outbreak of war in June 1941, the VVS-VMF had 460 of the new Peshkas (so nicknamed by its pilots after the pawn of the chess-board) in service. This included one special 'Test Pilot's Regiment' formed to evaluate air-

craft in combat conditions. Vast reorganization in the production plants, newly transported beyond the Urals, soon produced a flood of these very versatile aircraft for front-line service. Technique lagged behind production, but the Pe-2 proved to be the outstanding dive-bomber of the Eastern Front.

From July to October 1942, two British Hurricane squadrons were sent to northern Russia to provide fighter protection. They were used, in part, to escort attacks by one of the few active Regiments of Pe-2 dive-bombers then operational in ground-attack missions against Finnish ground forces. It was from these RAF fighter pilots that the first true inkling was received in the West of this brand-new, and hitherto unsuspected, dive-bomber. In view of the fact that the then current official British line was to denigrate all dive-bombers and dive-bombing at every opportunity, it is not surprising that the reports were received with some incredulity and were not subsequently given very wide circulation. Indeed four years later high officials in the RAF were denying any knowledge of the Soviet use of dive-bombers!

One comment above all may have

made them purse their lips. Flight Lieutenant H. Griffiths stated that the British fighter pilots found, that, 'in an operation which lasted as long as an hour they had to go all-out to keep station' with the Soviet dive-bombers, and that these aircraft, 'climbed and flew at a rate that astounded our boys considerably.'[21]

As early as 11 September 1941, a full report was in British hands on the Pe-2 which the British test pilot described as 'one of the most notable aircraft produced in Russia' and one which was 'a type with no counterpart in the RAF'.

'The Pe-2 is a twin-engined low-wing monoplane of metal construction. Details of the airframe construction are not available although photographs suggest that this is of fairly conventional stressed-skin type. The tail has twin fins and rudders and is remarkable for the pronounced dihedral on the tailplane.

All control surfaces are fabric-covered and aerodynamically balanced, the elevators by set-back hinges and the rudder by a section of the surface which encroaches into the fin. Two M-105 (Hispano-Suiza type) 12-cylinder liquid-cooled engines, giving about 1,000hp at 12,000 feet, are fitted. The radiators are

under the nacelles and the temperature of each engine is regulated by a flap at the rear of each radiator housing. Oil coolers are fitted in the wings immediately inboard of the nacelles. These coolers are of circular formation and air is admitted to them through ducts in the leading edge. Muffs, similar to those on Merlin installations on Beaufighter aircraft, are fitted over the exhaust pipes.

All three wheels of the undercarriage are retractable. Two fixed 7.62mm machine-guns are installed in the nose and are fired by the pilot. The navigator has charge of a third, 7.62mm, gun on a "rocking pillar", somewhat similar to the Fairey "high-speed" mounting. Firing through the floor is a 12.7mm gun which is fired by the radio operator.

Four 100kg bombs are stowed internally in the same fashion as on the Wellington. All heavy bombs are carried externally, alternative combinations being two bombs of 500kg; four bombs of 250kg; or four bombs of 100kg. Additional stowage is provided in the tails of the engine nacelles for two bombs of 100kg.'

The report on the speed of the Peshka gave the following figures:

Height	Indicated airspeed	RPM	Boost
1250m (4,100ft)	400kph (248mph)	2500	91
1800m (5,900ft)	390–kph (242–245mph)	2500	91

The report concluded:

'Accurate data are not yet to hand, but an approximate estimate based on a span of 57 feet shows that the maximum speed of the aircraft without external bombs, would be of the order of 300mph at 14,500 to 15,000 feet.'[22]

However you looked at it, the Soviets had pulled off a master-stroke. That their technical prowess in producing the Pe-2 had not yet been matched by the equivalent operational skill in using it in the role for which it was designed was something that was also soon to be overcome, mainly through the dedicated efforts of some outstanding Soviet pilots.

Soviet 'piggy-back' dive-bombers

Although best remembered for the superlative Peshka dive-bomber, the Soviet Union did experiment with other types less successfully. Colonel N. Denisov noted in his book *Boyevaia*

Slava Sovetskoi Aviatsii that during the period 1933–38 the dive-bombing types VIT-1 and VIT-2 had been produced. Better known was the belated attempt to turn the Tupolev SB-2bis twin-engine light bomber into a dive-bomber. This, the Arkhangel'ski SB-RK (RK means Reduced Wing), was designed in 1938 and first flew a year later. It was ordered into production late in 1939 at Stalin's insistence but was not a great success. Only 210 were actually completed in 1940–41 and production and maintenance difficulties called an early halt to it. However some survived to take part in the early fighting on the Eastern Front, becoming re-designated Ar-2 in 1941. Stalin made impossible demands of Andrei Tupolev to pressurise him into making the Tu-2 capable of dive-bombing, but the designer bravely stuck to his guns and refused.

Far more interesting in the experimental dive-bombing role was the unique concept of 'piggy-back' dive-bombers. The idea originated with a young *Nauchno-ispytatel'ny institut* (Scientific Test Institute) engineer, Vladimir S. Vakhmistrov, who in 1932 had envisaged long-range bombers

One of the most bizarre dive-bomber concepts was the adaptation of the little Rata I16 fighter plane to a bomb-carrying dive-bomber variant. Two of these machines were carried below the wings of the giant Tupolev TB-3 bomber and released when adjacent to the target. They carried out their attacks in steep dives then flew back to base. It was not just a concept; actual combat missions were conducted against targets in Roumania in the early months of the war, with relative successes and no losses. (Novosti Press Agency, Moscow)

▶

A mixed group of men and women pilots and aircrew pose with their camouflaged Peshka somewhere on the Eastern Front. (Author's collection)

taking their own defending fighters into battle slung from underwing cradles. Nothing came of this, but the idea was modified to provide the *Voenno-vozdushnye sili* (VVS or Air Forces) with a long-range dive-bomber. Basically the concept called for two of the stubby little Polikarpov I-16 Ishak ('Donkey') fighters, each adapted to carry a pair of 250kg (551lb) underwing bombs, re-designated as the I-16SPB (*Skorostnyi Pikiruyushchii Bombrdirovshcik* or Fast Dive-Bomber). Their original fighter armament was reduced, the cannon taken out and only two machine-guns retained. They were to be carried to the vicinity of the target slung below one of the giant Tupolev TB-3 bombers. Once there they would be released, drop free and then carry out their dive-bombing attacks under their own power before using their full fuel tanks to make their exit.

This idea was put into effect. Late in 1940, 92 Fighter Regiment had pilots trained in dive-bombing techniques in readiness. Six of the converted TB-3s and twelve of the little I-16SPBs were assembled at Yevpatoria airbase in the Crimea, and further trials were conducted. Obviously the lumbering TB-3s

and their charges were highly vulnerable, but all dive-bombers and dive-bombing depended on the element of surprise and certainly the enemy would not expect dive-bombers to operate so far behind the front line as was envisaged for the SPBs. A range of 730 miles was estimated.

On the outbreak of war in June 1941, this unit was placed on full alert and Vakhmistrov flew down to supervise the actual war preparations of his brain-child. The targets selected were across the Black Sea in Roumania. By 1 August all was ready and the first attack was directed at Constanza. This sortie was followed up on 10 August when two TB-3s each with a pair of SPBs under the overall command of Captain A. Shubikov made a night attack against the strategic Danube bridge at Chernovoda. Another attack was made on 13 August. Subsequently it was claimed that the dive-bombers had destroyed a 150yd span of the bridge together with its accompanying kerosene pipeline. Other targets were equally important and the SPBs were sent against the Ploesti oil refineries, and Axis ships berthed in Constanza harbour. A cargo ship was

claimed as destroyed in this attack. They also hit the vital Dnieper rail bridges over which Axis supplies and reinforcements were hastening to the southern front in the aftermath of their victory at the Uman Pocket in September. None of the Soviet dive-bombers was lost in these attacks.

The German land advance finally reached the Perekop isthmus and to defend this crucial area the piggy-back dive-bombers were thrown in regardless of losses, which were heavy. Of the few surviving aircraft from this carnage, the long-range bombers were pulled back to the Caucasus and the remaining SPBs were used up as makeshift fighters until Sebastopol fell. Even if their accomplishments were far less than claimed at the time, the operations of this unique dive-bomber force gave the enemy much pause for thought and gave the Soviet defenders a much-needed boost to morale after the earlier débâcles of their air forces.

1.

9. Other European systems

FINALLY, a brief look at some of the dive-bomber ideas that were current among other European nations' air forces at the outbreak of war reveals that only a few got beyond the planning stage and saw combat.

Although Poland did not develop a dive-bomber until far too late, the Wilk never becoming operational, she did operate the PZL P-23 Kara light ground-attack bomber. It is claimed that the Bulgarian designer Lazarov was influenced by the Polish aircraft when he modified the DAR 10 fighter-bomber into a dive-bomber in 1941. Certainly the resulting DAR-10F, a two-seater dive-bomber, had common features with the Kara, including the fixed, spatted undercarriage like their more famous counterpart, the German Junkers Ju 87 Stuka. Thus do designs and ideas percolate across continents.

In neutral Sweden the air force was still equipped with obsolete license-built Hawker Hart biplanes which formed the main dive-bomber squadrons until well into 1940. Aware of her exposed position, sandwiched between Soviet-dominated Finland and German-occupied Norway, the Swedes were anxious to modernize their dive-bomber arm. They imported the American Northrop 8A-1 Attack bomber, which they utilized as a makeshift dive-bomber under the designation SAAB B5. They speeded introduction into service of their home-built SAAB L10, which, like the Northrop, was a single-engined monoplane. It formed two dive-bomber Wings in 1943. Finally, it developed the SAAB B17, a twin-engined monoplane of great potential. In addition to aircraft, Sweden alone

64

1. During the war Sweden's purchasing of foreign types of aircraft was restricted, but licensed-built variants continued to feature. Here three SAAB L 10 (B 17) light bombers, adapted for the dive-bombing role, are seen over northern Sweden in 1943. Special dive-bombing sights were fitted to these aircraft to increase their potential. (Flygvapnet) **2.** The ultimate Swedish dive-bomber type to see service was the twin-engined SAAB B18A. This one belongs to F 1 Squadron which has a strong dive-bomber tradition. Known as light bombers to the outside world, the Swedes developed them specifically for dive-bombing, although later ground attack and torpedo-bomber variants were also produced and continued to serve post-war for a time. Note the folded dive brakes outboard of engine on the left-hand side of the photograph. (Flygvapnet) **3.** A nice in-flight view of the Swedish SAAB L 18 B (B18 B) dive-bomber on patrol in 1944/45. At this time the threat of the Soviet advance was causing considerable concern to neutral Sweden and constant war footing patrols were maintained. (Flygvapnet) **4.** A close-up of a SAAB L 18 on a snow-bound airstrip in the winter of 1944/45. (Flygvap net) **5.** Behind the headlines of the front-line applications were the dedicated men working away to perfect the dive-bomber technique. Sweden had been early in the field in embracing this method of precision attack, but to make the best use of her limited resources and manpower she strove to perfect an automatic dive-bomber sight. While other powers went down this road to a greater (Germany) or lesser (USA) extent, none produced a really satisfactory answer, but Erik Wilkenson, working with SAAB, stuck to it and produced a fully automatic dive-bombing sight later in the war, which was embraced post-war by many of the leading air-minded nations. (Eric Wilkenson)

among the smaller nations, devoted a great deal of research into perfecting a workable dive-bomber sight.

Improvised dive-bombers which proved quite successful in service were the Roumanian IARB1 and UARB1A. These were single-engined monoplane fighters of the IAR80 and 80A types adapted for dive-bombing. The changes were minimal, involving the fitting of underwing dive brakes which in turn meant lengthening and strengthening the aircraft's wings. Bomb racks were fitted for light bombs and a single 551lb weapon was carried below the fuselage. Being a fighter modification it was a fast aircraft, 317mph, and although less than 300 were finally built, they did see service on the Russian Front.

The Hungarian air force set up its own dive-bomber units equipped with

Junkers Ju 87s, but later in the war were unique in being the only air force which employed the German twin-engined Me 210C in its original dive-bombing configuration with *102 Onallo Zuhanobombazo Osztaly*, also against the Soviets.

The flying banana

From the sublime to the ridiculous. Another dictator had been duly impressed by the work and results of the Luftwaffe's Stukas in the Spanish Civil War, as well as his own air force's experiments there. Benito Mussolini had towering ambitions, but these were not backed up by the industrial base to give his military muscle a credible status. Thus all his grandiose schemes were superficial. It was thus with Italy's home-grown dive-bomber, the Savoia-Marchetti SM85.

The one thing that Mussolini resented above all else was the fact that Italy's self-proclaimed dominance of the Mediterranean (Mare Nostrum), was made a mockery of by the very presence of the British Mediterranean Fleet which sailed the length and breadth of that waterway with arrogance. What he wanted was a machine which would hurt the one enemy and render it ineffective. He thought the answer lay in the dive-bomber. He was right, as the Luftwaffe was soon to prove time and time again, but unfortunately Italy's own efforts at producing such a weapon came to a rapid and humiliating termination.

The SM 85 was a twin-engined, high-winged monoplane, produced rapidly to satisfy Mussolini's ego, but it was of wooden construction, grossly under-powered and lacked both the structural

The IAR-81, together with the IAR-81A, was a further refinement. With bomb racks (and the provision of four 7.92mm cannon in the 81A), some 260 of these dive-bomber variants were built. (Passingham collection)

Another rare bird! The Bulgarian DAF-10F was that nation's only home-built dive-bomber and was an adaptation of the DAF-10 light bomber. Given structural strengthening, they first flew in 1941. They were used against Yugoslav partisan forces before being replaced by Junkers Ju 87s. (Passingham collection)

A passing glance! Just about all this dive-bomber was ever worth. High-ranking Luftwaffe dignataries are shown Mussolini's answer to the Stuka, the Savoia-Marchetti SM85. This twin-engined machine was rushed to completion to meet the need for a precision weapon for use against the Royal Navy in the Mediterranean, but proved a hopeless failure in service. (Author's collection)

Hazy, but very rare and valuable photograph, the only one to show a massed formation of SM85s airborne. Their one mission, in July 1940, was a failure and their last. (Author's collection)

strength and technical expertise to dive-bomb in peacetime, let alone combat. Its fuselage had a marked upward sheer both fore and aft resulting in the immediate derisory nickname of 'The Flying Banana' from its aircrew who were only too well aware of its limitations. Only a handful had been produced by the time Italy entered the war in June 1940. These were concentrated on the island of Pantelleria ready to strike the decisive blow should the Royal Navy venture near. They were soon given their chance; at the Battle of Calabria on 9 July 1940, Admiral Sir Andrew Cunningham's fleet chased an Italian fleet to within a few miles of its own main naval base of Augusta.

The SM85s of 96 *Gruppo Bomardamento a Tuffo*, two squadrons totalling eighteen aircraft, were thereupon dispatched to do their worst. They returned to base within a few hours having failed to even find the British ships, let alone attack them! Subsequent exposure to the heat of the central Mediterranean warped their wooden structures which, coupled with damp nights parked in the open, deteriorated rapidly. Within a few months they were declared inoperational. As in so many other things Mussolini was forced to turn to his Axis partner for help, and all subsequent dive-bomber missions by the Regia Aeronautica were flown in German-built, Italian-crewed Stukas!

The French take urgent steps

In 1939, France only had one aircraft carrier, her aircraft industry had been run-down and the ancient aircraft provided from the 1920s onward were obsolete and slow.

Towards the end of the 1930s, spurred on by the growing menace of the Fascist dictatorships in Italy, Germany and Spain, all on her borders, France began to re-arm. She hastily sought dive-bombers from America after witnessing their power in the Spanish conflict, but this was meant to be a stop-gap measure and plans were also put in hand to build her own home-grown version. Thus the Loire-Nieuport Aircraft Company was commissioned to design and produce for the Navy their own carrier-based dive-bomber for use against enemy fleets. It was also expected that the precision and accuracy of such methods would prove invaluable for combating the submarine menace at sea.

The result was the LN 40 concept. This was a single-seater, low-wing mono-

◄
An A-36 'Invader' or 'Apache' dive-bomber which was evaluated by the RAF but only used by one Flight in the Mediterranean zone for a short period. (RAF Museum)

▶
Side view of a Loire-Nieuport LN 420 which was developed from the LN 401/LN 411 design of 1939–40. It incorporated a 1,100hp HS 12Y-51 engine and its basic fuselage remained the same as the earlier versions. Hidden away during the German occupation, development continued on this aircraft after the Liberation in 1945. However by then it was obvious that it was too obsolescent to proceed with any further and, after a test flight on 24 August 1945, was disposed of. (Musée de l'Air, Paris)

▶
The French Navy's Fleet Air Arm, the Aéronavale, had to order Vought dive-bombers from the USA, French manufacturers being unable to supply them quickly enough. They were forced to use them from land bases. Here ground crew help a French Navy pilot check out his immaculate V156F in the spring of 1940. (ECP des Armées, Fort d'Ivry)

◄
The Roumanian Air Force adapted its IAR-80 fighter, seen here, to carry one 551lb bomb under the fuselage and four 110lb bombs under the wings thus giving it limited dive-bombing capability. (Passingham collection)

plane, designed by M. Pillon for the *Aéronautique Navale*. This little dive-bomber made its maiden flight in June 1938. Visually, especially from dead ahead, it resembled very much the Junkers Ju 87 which was its main inspiration. It had the same inverted gull-wing layout with a single tail-fin equipped with the same small endplates. The French machine had a retractable rather than a fixed undercarriage and was powered by a single Hispano-Suiza 12-cylinder engine. To help it perform as a dive-bomber the central rudder was split vertically so that it could open right and left and act as a dive brake.

Six further prototypes followed and a production order was placed in February 1939 as the LN-401. This was the Navy version, but belatedly the French Armeé de l'Air decided it also required a dive-bomber and placed further orders. This type became the land-based LN-411. Forty machines were originally ordered but most were later delivered to the Navy instead, as the sands of time ran out.

For the rest it was the Curtiss CW77 biplane and the Vought V156F monoplane on which the immediate dive-bomber potential of France was to be placed. Of the former none got farther than embarkation (via Canada to comply with American neutrality laws) and they were dumped ashore at Martinique in the French West Indies where they rotted or were destroyed by sabotage. A few of the latter reached France in time, but were overwhelmed in the débâcle of May and June 1940.

1,2,3. Another American dive-bomber which the French purchased in their desperation was the Curtiss SBC4, classified in its export version as the CW77F. To get round the American 'neutrality' embargo these aircraft, already re-painted in French dazzle scheme and roundels, were flown to the Canadian border and pushed over. The French 'matelots' in full uniform negating the pretence. Once over the border they were loaded aboard barges and shipped out to the waiting aircraft carrier *Béarn* for shipment to France. But France was overrun before she could sail and she was diverted to the French West Indies where the CW77Fs were dumped ashore and rotted away in the semi-tropical heat. (Jean Cuny – Imperial War Museum – Jean Cuny)

1▲

2▲   3▼

4. Strangely, Curtiss Helldivers did eventually join the French Navy in the post-war years when they were flown against the Viet-Minh in Indo-China. Here a Navy Helldiver is seen over the dense jungle of what is now Vietnam, en route to Dien Bien Phu. (ECP des Armées, Fortd'Ivry)

5. French Navy pilots examine their bomb loads aboard the carrier *Arromanches* prior to another dive-bombing mission over Dien Bein Phu. (ECP des Armées, Fortd'Ivry)

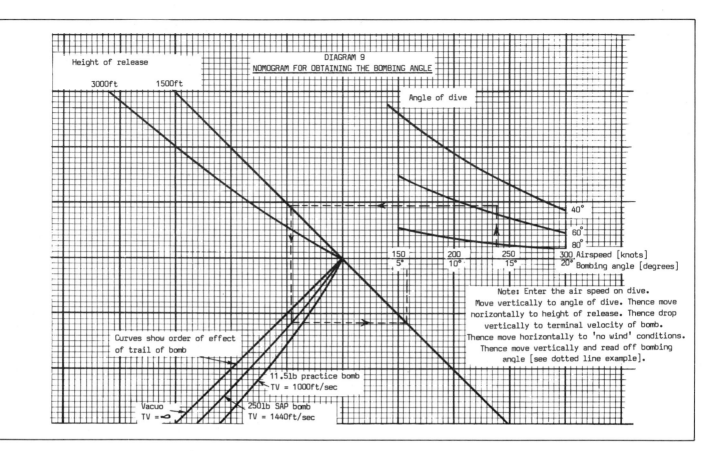

Height of release

3000ft   1500ft

DIAGRAM 9
NOMOGRAM FOR OBTAINING THE BOMBING ANGLE

Angle of dive

40°
60°
80°

150   200   250   300 Airspeed [knots]
5°   10°   15°   20° Bombing angle [degrees]

Note: Enter the air speed on dive.
Move vertically to angle of dive. Thence move
horizontally to height of release. Thence drop
vertically to terminal velocity of bomb.
Thence move horizontally to 'no wind' conditions.
Thence move vertically and read off bombing
angle [see dotted line example].

Curves show order of effect
of trail of bomb

11.5lb practice bomb
TV = 1000ft/sec

Vacuo
TV = ∞

250lb SAP bomb
TV = 1440ft/sec

10. The dive-bombing sight

THE basics of dive-bomber aircraft design had become well established by 1939. Strengthened construction, good all-round visibility, automatic pull-out equipment, bomb-crutches to carry the missile clear of the propeller arc in a dive. Aiming at the target had not developed in the same way as the aircraft themselves. This remained much as it had been back in 1918, by the pilot's judgement alone. Much thought had been devoted to the development of a computer which would carry out this function, but the variants and calculations necessary, wind-speeds, cross winds, angle of approach, evasive action by the target, etc., were of such complexity that only compromise solutions had been reached by the outbreak of the war. Germany was farthest advanced in producing and using an automated system, but this was not completely automatic and even in its existing form, far ahead of any rival, it was a complicated and time-consuming instrument, easily misused, and most German pilots still relied more on their own judgement.

Three other nations also devoted a great deal of time and effort in seeking machine solutions to the same problem during the war years, and were ultimately to come up with the same truth. Great Britain and the United States persevered with varying degrees of enthusiasm, but no really satisfactory solution was reached. As there were few dive-bombers in Britain pre-war, the spur was more from the desire of the Navy to have such an instrument than any fear by the RAF of German developments. It was not until during the early war years that they discovered how far advanced the Germans had been in this field, but by then it was too late. The third nation, Sweden, thanks to the persistence and dedication of one man, Erik Wilkenson, kept on and finally developed the sight required. By that time, however, the war was over.

Other areas of dive-bomber experimentation during the war principally concerned trials with aircraft not specifically designed as dive-bombers in the hope that somehow they could be made to do the job despite their limitations. This often resulted in some quite novel, or even bizarre trials, like the RAF attempting to dive-bomb with Wellington bombers! A few of these tests, some surprisingly successful, others not, are

Anatomy of a dive-bomber. Showing in detail the pilot's, navigator's and armourer's views of a Northrop-built A-31 Vultee Vengeance. (Gerald Balzer) see also following pages

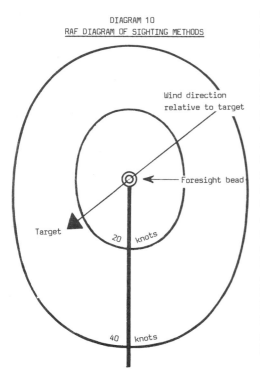

DIAGRAM 10
RAF DIAGRAM OF SIGHTING METHODS

Wind direction relative to target

Foresight bead

Target

20 knots

40 knots

included here for completeness.

The earliest experiments in dive-bombing techniques had been conducted by the fledgling RAF at Orfordness in 1918. They used the Sopwith Camel fighter and a mixture of experienced and novice pilots to get a fair spread of expertise. The standard Aldis gun-sight, a telescopic tube mounted forward of the cockpit, was the aiming sight utilized for a special series of these tests. The conclusions reached were that if a pilot concentrated on his target through such a device he tended to forget his rapidly dwindling altitude during the dive. Moreover they found that the percentage of direct hits by 'eye-sighting' only, as against using the Aldis, favoured the former. This official verdict was backed-up by the pilots themselves and eye-shooting became the accepted norm for dive-bomber pilots the world over. The rapid strides in aviation between the wars and the development of increasingly more sophisticated bombing sights for level altitude bombers, culminating in the American Norden sight, led to a renewal of demands for a fully automatic dive-bombing sight as well.

The British Experience

In Great Britain the response was split in two diametrically opposite camps: the Royal Navy, who were strongly in favour of dive-bombing, constantly called for a special sight, while the RAF were at best lukewarm and thus afforded it very low priority status, when they considered it at all.

Typical of many pre-war conferences of the Bombing Committees and Sub-Committees was one held in London in 1937 and attended by representatives of both viewpoints. Mr Meredith from the RAE discussed the problems associated with dive attacks on ships and said that it might be worth considering the use of a repeater from the DR compass to fix the wind direction, and that a special repeater for this job could be set at the appropriate angle in front of the pilot. The magnitude of the speed could then be judged on the repeater. For the Navy, Captain Langley pointed out that possible alteration of the target vessels course would remain unaccounted for. What was needed was a vector sight in which the enemy course could be adjusted for avoiding action.

This gave Meredith a chance to bring

73

up an earlier proposal he had made for an automatic dive sight, and he strongly advocated concentration on the development of such a line of research. He considered this would provide the only really satisfactory tactical solution. Mr. Bowen of Research Development/ Armament 2b Section then intervened. 'Were we justified in developing at considerable trouble, a complicated sight for a type of bombing which might be obsolete in the very near future? Such a sight, the development of which would take at least two years before it reached the Service, might be useless by that time if the type of aircraft which could dive at angles of about 40 degrees had then disappeared.'

He was backed up in this view by Wing Commander Davis, RAF, of RD/ Arm.1. 'It was wrong to develop a special sight for dive-bombing only.' Captain Langley replied that the Navy did not look upon level bombing as the primary form of bombing and that dive-bombing was considered as of first importance. He agreed with Meredith that 'The possibilities of an automatic sight were well worth investigating.'

Because of lack of resources available

to the RAE Bowen advocated that the multi-directional sight, 'without any further additions or complications', should be tried on a modern aircraft which could dive steeply. This was agreed to, 'as soon as the gyroscopic release was ready'. The tests were to be conducted using a Fairey Swordfish aircraft or, failing that, with a Hawker Hart. The angle of dive was to be less than 50 degrees, 'to simulate future conditions'. The question of the use of bomb-distributor gear when diving with such a sight was then raised. The distributor could be set on a time interval based on the angle of dive, but of course, if the pilot varied his rate of pull-out this would result in varied spacing.

The Navy still held out for the fully automatic dive-bombing sight which they felt 'would cut out a tremendous amount of elaboration and would be much simpler for the operator'. Captain Langley stated that what the Navy needed 'was a far more accurate method of sighting'. Theoretically, he considered that the automatic principle was undoubtedly the best one, and he recommended that it should be examined without further delay.

But the other members of the Committee again closed ranks against these. The AOC, Armament Group queried whether they could 'allow research on these items to proceed without holding up something which might be of greater national concern than a dive-bomb sight which, although it was considered of importance, had only a limited use'.[23]

And there things stuck. By the end of 1939, with the example of the Luftwaffe's combat use of dive-bombing in Poland and in attacks on the fleet before them, a few British experts were having belated second thoughts. Christopher Deanesly told me of one such awakening.

'In the autumn of 1939 I was a pilot with the newly formed No. 152 Squadron at Acklington. We were all taken to Blyth harbour where the Navy had salvaged a Junkers Ju 88 which had been shot down. The AOC No. 13 Group, Air Vice Marshal Saul, was there together with a high-level 'boffin' from Farnborough and it was evident that the latter was amazed at the design and features of the aircraft.'[24]

An RAF report issued on 1 February 1940 still claimed confidently that 'it would seem that there is little to choose

between the probability of hitting when making high-level or dive-bombing attacks'. The report continued, 'The German standard of dive-bombing accuracy in which pilots have been intensively trained is disappointing.' Of course Norway and Dunkirk were soon to remove that naïve attitude. The report did grudgingly conceed however that: 'If an accurate automatic dive-bomb sight is produced, the whole aspect of dive-bombing may then be changed.'[25]

So, although Smith's Instruments were working on a dive-bombing sight prompted by wartime glimpses of German work and spurred by a growing list of wartime losses due to dive-bombing, it all proved far too late. By the end of the war, with Allied fighter-bombers ranging across northern France in search of targets, dive-bombing had been generally re-adopted by the RAF and was proving invaluable, but it still relied on eye-sighting or relatively primitive sights to achieve the desired results.

Wing Commander W. F. Blackburn, Commanding AFDU, commented on trials that were carried out in June and July 1944 to determine the advisability of using direct sighting or the two-spot

method for dive-bombing with the North American Mustang III. The actual aircraft utilized in these trials was FZ107 which expended thirty 10lb practice bombs and twenty-nine 500lb MC Mk 7 sand-filled, short-tail bombs in the process. The 500lb bombs were carried on standard American bomb shackles, the 10lb on a British Light Series Rack fitted to the Mustang's port wing.

The actual sighting device utilized was a normal GM2 Sight and the sighting view over nose of the aircraft was 5 degrees. A modified GM2 sight could be used, but this made the method of calculating wind allowance unfeasible due to the impracticality of estimating ring radii from the top of the range bar which was at no time at the centre of the ring.

Blackburn observed that: 'The Mustang III is considered to be one of the best aircraft used for dive-bombing by this Unit, on account of its superior handling qualities in the dive. The change of trim required at the recommended speed of release of 370mph was found to be comparatively small. This reduced the tendency to skid, which is common to all types of fighter aircraft.'[26]

During the trial, sighting in both 45-

degree and 60-degree dive attacks was studied. The 5-degree view over the nose enabled direct sight to be used in the 60-degree dive, but for a 45-degree dive the height of release using direct sighting was found to be too low to allow a sufficient safety margin for pull-out. The latter angle, which accordingly required the use of the two-spot method of sighting, was therefore abandoned in favour of the 60-degree dive 'where the simpler form of sighting produced very satisfactory results'. It should be noted that this was in direct variance with the RAF's pre-war advice (and repeated claims since). Sixty-degree dives were made from a cruising height of 8,000 feet, with a release at 4,700 feet and a pull-out height of 2,600 feet, a very high level compared to other nations' dive-bombing. This probably reflected the superior AA weaponry of the German Flak units in France at the time. Bombs were dropped in pairs and the average distance between the bombs on impact was 46 yards.

The main factors affecting accuracy were *height of release*, which could be controlled by an audible contracting altimeter which gave a correct height

Later standard Mustang fighters were equipped with special bomb racks and used most successfully as dive-bombers from Normandy onward. This close-up shows the specialized racks used by those aircraft.
(Public Record Office)

report within plus or minus 200 feet; *angle of dive* and *speed of release*, which could only be attained accurately if the pilot could position himself correctly for the entry into the dive; *skid*, which, to avoid as much as possible and to ease stick forces, meant trimming the aircraft before the dive for 'hands and feet off' at the moment of release; and finally, *wind allowance*, in which the recommended method was to take the Met forecast of wind over target and use the gunsight to measure the necessary allowance by offsetting the sight from the target a certain angular allowance. As a rough guide, offsetting one ring radius allowed for 20mph wind. In other words, in live 1944 combat conditions the RAF was using the same methods as advocated in 1937 and the automatic sight was nowhere in evidence.[27]

But did this matter? Apparently not, for desired accuracy and results were being achieved by this method, as analysis of two dive-bombing attacks by Bomphoons on ground targets in northern France on 23 and 24 December, showed clearly. The Bomphoons used 500lb bombs, and one of the aircraft carried a cine-camera to enable results to be

analyzed fully.

The dives were made at angles varying from 33 to 47 degrees, with height at pull-out 4,300–6,600 feet. Slant range varied between 2,400–3,000 yards. The duration of dive before the pull-out was between 3 and 7 seconds at .7 to .9g rate.

In view of the use of such high-performance fighters as the Mustang III and the Hawker Typhoon ('Bombphoon') for wartime combat dive-bombing, the viewpoint expressed by RAF experts in 1937 that 'new aircraft would be unable to carry out dive-bombing . . . owing to the diving limitation of new high speed aircraft'[28] seems all the more bizarre. One cannot help feeling that it was inter-service politics which led to British backwardness in dive-bombing rather than any practical problems.

American Methods
When asked to define dive-bombing during the Second World War, an American 'Helldiver' pilot is reputed to have given this description: 'When we speak of dive-bombing, we mean *straight down* . . . right on the smoke-stack. If your airplane doesn't stand on its nose and lay eggs in their lap, then

you are not dive-bombing.'[29] Not all Navy pilots shared that extreme view, but it indicated the precision of such a method.

Although it had been the British who had first used dive-bombing in combat on the Western Front in 1917, the Americans were not far behind and the basic tactics claimed to have been 'perfected' at the Quantico test center shortly after the end of the First World War. Certainly it was US Marine Corps flyers who revitalized the concept in Nicaragua and brought it back to the forefront of military aviation, and by 1928 the Corps were using aircraft designed and built specially for the purpose. As in Britain, however, this enthusiasm did not extend to the US Army Air Corps in general. Although the USAAC had used the technique, with much success, on Mexican border patrols in the early 1920s, it had fallen into disfavour after the shrill and vocal clamour of the heavy bomber school of thought, with General Billy Mitchell at their head, had captured the media attention.

The German Blitzkreigs of 1939–40 made the US pause and reconsider, and, as we have seen, some tentative moves

Rear view of the capacious internal bomb-bay of a Northrop-built A-31 Vengeance dive-bomber. Clearly visible are the twin bomb forks which swung the weapons out and clear of the prop arc in a dive. (Northrop)

back were made, but with little enthusiasm and therefore correspondingly little success. Not until the arrival in squadron service of the A-36 Invader of 1943 did the US Army Air Force (as it had become), get a dive-bomber worthy of their fuller attentions. So the problems of perfecting automatic dive-bombing sights, and of developing new skills in that field, remained very much a Navy problem and it was the US Navy Bureau of Ordnance which was chiefly concerned with USA progress in those fields during the war. It was recorded later:

'Long before the outbreak of hostilities, the Navy was aware that dive-bombing held more promise than horizontal bombing. Year after year in the last decade before the war, fleet practices demonstrated the superiority of dive-bombing. Even when horizontal bombers were equipped with precision bomb-sights, dive-bombers, employing simple gunsights to establish a line of sight to the target, ran up the more impressive scores. Against a manouvering target they held a practical monopoly of effective attacks.'

Even so, the Bureau of Ordnance was as anxious as the Royal Navy in Britain to

increase efficiency by the development of a better bomb-sight 'that would increase the lethal probability of each dive'. They enlisted the help of the Norden company, whose altitude bomb-sight was probably the most advanced of all such high-level devices at that period. By 1942 Norden, despite massive commitments to the heavy strategic bomber sphere and USAAF requirements, had been able to come up with a new instrument, initially known as the Norden Aiming Angle Sight, later simplified to the Mark 16.

The Mark 16 was constructed specifically to allow aircraft to release bombs above 5,000 feet while retaining the dive-bomber's accuracy and the inherent advantages of shorter time of flight and high-velocity strike power. A simplified version of this device appeared soon afterwards, known as the Mark 17. Both were subjected to extensive testing by the Bureau during 1943 and 1944 and once more the claims of the inventors were found to have exceeded the actual performance of their product. In the Bureau's words: 'Though the computations of the instruments were highly accurate, satisfaction was confined to the

theorists. Both sights had to be used with flight techniques not normally expected of even highly trained pilots. Neither bomb sight was placed in full scale production.'[30]

This just about ended the American hunt for a specialized dive-bombing sight, but some improvements and additions to existing equipment was found to be possible and it was hoped that pilots would at least find these more helpful than just plain gun sighting. The basic Aircraft Telescope Mark 3 used for aiming had a dive angle indicator incorporated. However the basic obsolescence of such sights 'antiquated the new with the old' and proved of little or no value. Nor did the attempt to introduce a visual indicator for slip and skid – two vital factors in dive-bombing accuracy – meet with any greater success. It still required too much pilot concentration in addition to actually controlling the diving aircraft and aiming it at the target. The pilot had no spare time to pay attention to a whole range of further instruments.

Therefore it had to be admitted that, although the gunsight was not a scientific answer to the problem, it gave the pilot a line of sight and was both simple and

available. The need of the pilot to keep the flight path of his aircraft above the target by a sufficient amount to compensate for the gravity drop of the bomb after release prevailed. The simple gunsight gave an obvious datum reference point to attain the desire line of sight. It did not provide an indication of the inflight line to be followed to ensure a hit, and the deviation between this and the correct flight path still depended on many variable factors, speed and altitude, dive angle, wind speed as well as evasive turns by the target vessel. Although the deviations in mils as measured on the gunsight's recticule pattern could be worked out for any given situation, no pilot could possibly carry all the aiming allowances in his head and no useful purpose was to be gained by the attempt.

Like most other nations then, eyesighting of the target remained the vogue for dive-bomber pilots of the three US services that used them, Navy, Marines and Air Force. In the first two services, however, one final attempt to help was the adoption of squadron doctrines, 'Grouping the factors into fixed combinations, and specifying a point of aim

and release for each. The tactical rigidity imposed by the procedure was the price paid for bombing with gunsights, but the tactics were realistic. They provided naval aviators with a method of attack that remained far more effective than the highly mechanized horizontal bombing.'

It remained for one small nation, not even involved in combat operations in the Second World War, but on the fringes of it, to show just how the problem could be resolved with dedication and patience.

Wilkenson and the Swedish Dive-Bombing Sight

The small and neutral state of Sweden was both early in the field of development and followed through to perfect a dive-bombing sight. If this be thought strange, it should be remembered that Sweden shared with many states a particularly pertinent appreciation of the value of dive-bombing. Her leading scientist in this field, Doctor of Technology, Erik A. Wilkenson, spelled this out succinctly.

'There is a general desire in air bombing to achieve the greatest possible precision in bombing without exposing

the bombers to too great risks from the active air defence, fighters and anti-aircraft artillery. In regard to the military conditions, however, the problem varies, in accordance with the size of the country, its military position and national policy.'[31]

For a small country like Sweden the needs of its small bomber force, as stated by the Commander-in-Chief, General Jung, as late as March 1947, were: 'attacks against an invading enemy and his advanced bases'. The theory was simple, and again detailed by Wilkenson (who was commissioned by the Saab Corporation in the spring of 1940 to devote his whole time to first developing a trial dive-bombing computer), so that:

'By using smaller aircraft it will be also possible to maintain a greater number on the limited appropriations allotted for this purpose. Regard must also be paid to certain special factors; the potential invader will probably have mastery of the skies, and the direct military objects ... will be small (and mobile) and therefore difficult to hit.

The points of view set forth above indicate that in Sweden there have been

1.

2.

special reasons to study precision bombing from aircraft operated on mobile tactical lines. In point of fact the Swedes have been pioneers in dive-bombing since 1932.

As aircraft became more rapid and heavier, dive-bombing was rendered more difficult. The nearest approach to solving the problem was found to lie in the reduction of the diving speed by dive brakes. But these did not eliminate other disadvantages and thus the idea originated to try an entirely different bombing method, thereby facilitating the task of the pilot and making bombing more effective from the military point of view.

A detailed discussion of the proposed method showed that it would be worth making great efforts to realize the proposal. The task was therefore to study carefully the possibilities of constructing the instrument necessary for automatic precision bombing during pull-out. First the ballistic problems were studied so that a calculation of errors could be made. This implies that the required accuracy of instruments and mechanism, could be estimated so that the target misses should not be too frequent. It was found that demands on the measuring

instruments would have to be much greater than could be met by existing instruments. For instance, the dive angle must be measured by a gyroscope with only a fraction of the marginal error of existing instruments. The altimeter and the speedometer should give correct data with much greater exactitude than standard instruments, even in the dive, where altitude and speed vary rapidly. In studying the detail problems, therefore, it was deemed difficult, but not absolutely impossible, to overcome the obstacles in some way or other.'[31]

To help him develop this new instrument Saab gave him full cooperation backed with money. Wilkenson, himself, born in 1914, was a pilot, but, as he told me recently, 'My flying experience dates back to 1936–38 when I was trained as a fighter pilot in the Air Force on the Swedish Jaktfalken, the Bristol Bulldog and the (then) very modern Gloster Gladiator. No dive-bombing!' However he was joined in his work by another pilot, Torsten Faxen. The two became close friends and Faxen himself 'became a "Helldiver"'. Thus the latter 'for several years was directly responsible for a great part of the work in which his

training as both a dive-bomber and a graduated engineer was invaluable'.[32]

As Wilkenson told me, dive-bombing became his, 'greatest interest from 1940 onwards. As a matter of fact we had a flying test model of our equipment as soon as nine months after the original idea, i.e., we flew and made test bombing in August 1940. From late 1942 all aircraft from Saab were equipped. It is true that we were very isolated from foreign developments in dive-bombing, not only during the hostilities but for a long period after 1945.'

'A period of experimenting began in summer 1940, with the definite object of building a trial model of the bombing instrument. In a small laboratory which had been equipped for the purpose, we studied the possibilities of carrying out the various suggestions for the solution of the technical detail problems, and under Mr Faxen, the designing of the trial instruments began.

Many difficulties were encountered. The rapid change of altitude and speed in the dive made great demands on the immediate reaction of the instrument. Various causes for time delays were therefore carefully studied, but only after

The back-room boys. Behind the hell and sudden death of dive-bomber operations and combat missions in whatever war zone, it was the dedicated work of the unsung heroes, the groundcrew and armourers, that kept the machines in the air and flying round the clock. Here are illustrations showing the same dedication, whatever the nationality and whatever the dive-bomber. 1: At a forward Stuka air base of Beloretschenskaja in the Caucasus in October 1942, an SC 1,000lb bomb attracts a lot of attention from aircrew and armourers alike. In this photograph are Heinz Bucker, the Squadron commander, Burkhart Oelschalger and Alois Menrad. The weapon was designed to be dropped in the water close alongside the target ship and to cause massive internal damage through the 'water-hammer' effect, like the British 'B' Bombs. (Oelschlager). 2. Groundcrew (both men and women) undertaking maintenance in the field at a forward Peshka air strip on the Eastern Front in 1943. (Author's collection). 3. French Navy men work on the Douglas SBD Dauntless dive-bomber in readiness for another sortie in 1945. (ECP des Armées, For d'Ivry)

3.

producing a few interesting inventions of details did we obtain the basic conditions for achieving accuracy in spite of temperature changes, vibrations and external acceleration.

From the outset the air tests proved that the fundamental idea was correct, namely, that the pilot could accurately and easily direct his aircraft towards the target in a medium steep dive and that the pull-out from the dive could be made in the calculated manner. Until these preliminary tests had been made, it was of course impossible to determine whether this bombing method would be practicable. The functioning of the trial instrument was first checked by electric measuring devices and lamps which registered the bomb release during pull-out. When the results appeared favourable, the first releases of practice bombs were begun. The results showed well-concentrated hits, which promised well for the future.

The first trial instrument was not entirely automatic. It carried out measurements and calculations, but it had to be served by a man between releases. It remained to devote considerable efforts to the further development of the instru-

ment until completely automatic function was obtained and to design it in detail so that maximum reliability could be achieved. We drafted a design for such an instrument and suggested to the Air Force that it should be ordered for the Swedish light bombers. The suggestion was carefully studied and adopted.

The little group of engineers who had hitherto taken part in the work were now set a more difficult task. First, the number in the group had to be increased, that is, many beginners had to be taught, and secondly, we had to design reliable instruments for serial production. At that time Sweden's instrument industry was deluged with orders from the armed forces for the production of such precision parts as had earlier been procured abroad. At Saab practically no experience had been gained in instrument design and manufacture; we therefore had to start by establishing a standard for designs, tools and machines. In six months the designing group was increased sixfold and the work was in full swing. An instrument workshop was started, production began, orders were placed with other industries and as early as the summer of 1941 the first instrument

of a series production type could be tested in the air.

In conclusion one might perhaps venture to say that the new dive-bomb sight made possible a highly advanced bombing technique for Swedish aero-strategic conditions and that Saab contributed in this respect to heighten Swedish military strength during the latter half of the war.'[33]

These words were written in 1947, but the Swedish work on the dive-bombing sight had other material rewards, including exports to the United States itself. Wilkenson recently listed deliveries of the various marks of the Saab Dive Bombing system as:

	Customer	Aircraft	Year	Number
BT2	Swedish AF	B17	42–44	Many
BT3	Swedish AF	B18	44–46	Many
BT9	Swedish AF	A21	47–49	Many
BT9B	USAF	F84–86	52–53	250*
BT9C	Swedish AF	A32	55–58	256
BT9F	French Navy	4M(AMD)	62–63	70
BT9H	Swiss AF	Hunter	64–65	70
BT9J	Danish AF	F100D/F	66–68	50
BT9H	Swiss AF	Hunter	74–77	90

*Plus licence to manufacture in the USA.

A novel and rare view of an old friend in a rare guise. This is a Soviet Pe-2 Peshka dive-bomber proudly displaying the Swastika markings of its most hated enemy. The reason is that it is one of those supplied to the Finnish Air Force who also used the symbol as their National Insignia. (Passingham collection)

11. Other experiments

ALL the combatants conducted strange experiments once the true power of the dive-bomber had been demonstrated with the fall of France. The RAF held what they euphemistically termed 'high dive-bombing' trials in which a Wellington was dived to see if it could perform like a Stuka. After extensive tests the bewildered crew (and no doubt indignant Wellington) came to the unsurprising conclusion that it could not! Strangely the one aircraft which *could* have been converted to a very good dive-bomber instead of the much mooted Blenheims, Battles and others, was ignored and soldiered on overlooked or deliberately spurned, as a target-tug. This of course was the Hawker Henley, originally designed as a dive-bomber and with clean lines and a great heart. Many people have scratched their heads over this strange omission down the years.

But the RAF were not the only ones to make strange decisions. Udet and other Luftwaffe chiefs became obsessed with dive-bombing and even insisted that their new four-engined heavy bomber, the Heinkel He 177 *Greif*, be fitted with dive brakes! Although designer, Siegfried Guenther, did his best to comply with the Technical Office's demands, the necessary beefing-up of the big bomber's airframe to take the stresses of diving attacks was one more

factor which delayed this aircraft's introduction into service until too late to be of use. That some aircraft were just not suited to this type of operation was emphasized when the second prototype crashed during diving trials (killing test pilot Rickert), as also did the fourth prototype.

A special technique had to be worked out by the test pilots before such a big aircraft could be dived effectively. Speed had to be reduced immediately prior to the dive itself, but once in the dive angle the sheer bulk of the Griffon built that speed up to critical levels very quickly and pull-out had to be initiated equally fast, leading to overstressing. So this needless requirement was dropped from the specification prior to production.

Of the makeshift types hastily pressed into service, these ranged the whole spectrum from brilliance (North American A36 Invader), adequate (Commonwealth Wirraway and Boomerang, Fairey Albacore), through mediocre (Messerschmitt Me 210) to bizarre (Gloster Gauntlet, Hawker Hector, Vickers Wellington!), and we shall attempt to mention most of them. However this is *not* a technical history and so we shall examine them mainly through the eyes of their combat aircrews or test pilots. Some of the more outrageous experiments are covered in the appropriate chapter.

PART THREE
COMBAT AND CREWS

HAVING set the scene and described the history and developments of the dive-bomber and dive-bombing, given details of both the aircraft and the methods of the main users of this weapon on the outbreak of war, and itemized some of the most pertinent experiments and advances in hardware apertaining to its use, the rest of this book covers descriptions of the battles and actions in which it featured. As befits the title of the book I have tried to make these descriptions valid historical documents by interviewing the crews who flew the dive-bombing missions. Many have given me their own unique memoirs of these actions while for others I have quoted from official documents, battle reports and pilots' log-books.

There was no more personal form of bombing attack than that of the dive-bomber. One threw one's machine, and therefore oneself, straight at the enemy, unflinchingly facing all he had to give in return. A cavalry charge against a square of enemy infantry, or full-tilt at a prepared artillery position, would no doubt be the closest equation in land fighting terms, and a torpedo attack by a destroyer against an enemy battleship its naval equivalent. Courage was therefore commonplace among such aircrew, it could not be any other way. Much like fighter pilots, dive-bomber aircrew could regard themselves as an élite. Not for them the objective and almost casual involvement of altitude bombing from great height using telescopic sights or radar; theirs was a very personal war where one could see one's enemy and it was destroy or be destroyed.

Although the dive-bomber pilots were the heroes one should never forget their gunners and navigators. The pilots had something to do, the target to hit, wind-drift and height calculations to be constantly made and the actual bomb-release computed, which all occupied their time and kept their brains actively working. There was little time for anything else. They could see what was happening and their blood was up. The rear-seat man could only watch the sky behind for fighters, try to ignore the angry Flak bursts coming from (for him) the unseen enemy and trust his pilot's judgement. On top of all this he was going into the stresses of the high-speed dive *backwards!* Only at the final pull-up and evasion did the man in the back seat come into his own. Now *he* could see the results of the attack and his pilot could not. On him therefore mainly depended the accurate reporting, not only of hits and near-misses, but of enemy counter-attacks. He was the sole defence against eight-gun fighter aircraft able to outrun and outshoot his vulnerable aircraft. Now he fought or died.

And it should not be forgotten that, on the Eastern Front anyway, this bravery was not the sole perogative of men. A whole regiment of women pilots served with the Soviet airforce's dive-bombers in this bloody conflict. The exploits of the women night-fighter pilots has been given wide coverage in the West; the equally outstanding performances of the female dive-bomber pilots deserves the

► Stuka Pilot Major Frank Neubert on the occasion of his award of the Ritterkreuz of the Iron Cross on 22 June 1941. (Frank Neubert)

▼ ► Another outstanding Stuka pilot who gave the author much detailed information on operations and missions was Hauptmann Hans-Joachim Lehmann, here also seen on the awarding of the Ritterkreuz on 23 November 1941. Born 18 August 1912, Hans-Joachim served right through the war in Stukas. He flew with 3./St.G.2 Immelmann in Poland and later served as this unit's Technical Officer in the French, Balkan, Crete and early Russian campaigns. One of his outstanding achievements was the destruction of a Soviet Armoured Train east of Mga on 14 September 1941. He later served in Tunisia, then in southern Russia with St.G.77 in 1943, and finally with I.St.G.2 again before ending the war as an instructor with the Fliegerausbildung. Hans-Joachim flew some 339 missions in the Stuka. He died on 17 April 1982. (Gisela Lehmann)

same respect. Nor were these special qualities confined to one nation, any more than was dive-bombing itself. The same attributes could be found if the crew were German, French, Italian, British, Russian, Australian or Canadian, New Zealander or Japanese. Wherever dive-bombers flew into battle, courage and dedication prevailed.

The very first bombing attack of the Second World War was carried out by a dive-bomber, a Stuka which attacked a Polish railway bridge some time *before* the official declaration of war by Germany on Poland. Thereafter the dive-bomber played a prominent part in all the great land and sea battles, and dive-bombers conducted almost the last combat battle actions of the air war, in Burma and off Japan itself against the Allied Task Forces in July 1945. The dive-bomber became the first aircraft to be shot down in the war, the first British aircraft to shoot down an enemy aircraft, the first to attack a submarine, the first to sink a major warship, the first aircraft to actually sink a battleship by bombs alone, in that conflict, the only aircraft to take on a whole fleet at sea and defeat it and many other remarkable achievements, many of which are preserved here. The dive-bomber therefore holds a unique place in the history of air warfare.

► Stuka target. The blitzed remnants of a Polish mobile column caught in the open by St.G.77 in the first days of the war. The Poles were the first army to experience the power and accuracy of dive-bombing and it proved a harrowing lesson. (Peter Schwarzkopf)

12. The European Theatre, 1939–42

MAJOR Frank Neubert, known to his contemporaries simply as 'Frankie', typified the German Stuka pilots of the Second World War. He was in action from the first day of the war, including the first ever combat victory by any German pilot, and he was still fighting at the end of the war in the ground-attack role. Nor was he unique in this achievement. The fact that, like Hans-Ulrich Rudel, Walter Enneccerus, Paul-Werner Hozzel, Bruno Dilley, Hubertus Hitschold, Oskar Dinort and others, Neubert flew Stukas for most of that period and survived both the war and a long post-war career, and is still alive at the ripe old age of 72, belies the myths of the vulnerability of the Junkers Ju 87. The breathtaking deeds which these famous pilots achieved with the most famous dive-bomber of all need books of their own to do full justice to them. We must content ourselves with just the one to serve as an example of the other's work.

Frank Neubert was born at Herrenalb/Schwarzwald on 28 September 1915. He joined the Luftwaffe as a *Fahnenjunker* at the age of eighteen, undergoing the normal military introduction to life in the *Sturzkampffliegerverbande*. This long training period completed, 'Frankie' joined the famed St.G.2 'Immelmann'

Stuka Group in 1936, and was later promoted to Leutnant. He flew his first combat mission on 1 September 1939 against Poland when he was Kettenführer in the 1. Staffel. 1/St.G.2 at that time was commanded by Oskar Dinort and the Junkers Ju 87s made their initial attack against hangars and runways at Crakow airfield at 0600 that morning. The Poles had dispersed their aircraft to secret airfields, however, and little positive result was achieved. On the return the Polish fighters came up to intercept the dive-bombers and in the very first air combats of the war, Neubert's Kette were attacked by Polish PZL 11c fighters from a nearby airstrip. Frankie Neubert succeeded in shooting down one of the Polish attackers – probably the first aerial victory of the war. It was certainly one of the swiftest kills and it early on belied the later endless propaganda that Stukas were helpless against fighter opposition![34]

That same afternoon I/St.G.2 found a straggling column of Polish cavalry and horse-drawn vehicles near Wielun and their precision bombing, followed by strafing attacks, reduced masses of men and animals to disorganized and demoralized chaos. On the second day of operations, I/St.G.2 caught a train full of Polish troops at Piotrkow and pulverized

Flak damage over Warsaw and other heavily defended targets was common. Often the Stukas returned to their front-line bases with gaping wounds, so that Kesselring was later to record his wonder that they still flew. The rugged sturdiness of the Stuka was a factor which made it so successful in combat for so long. Critics have always concentrated on its lack of speed, as if this were all that mattered in a precision weapon. Too often they ignore or forget this little aircraft's many merits which more than compensated for its deficiencies. (Peter Schwarzkopf)

A Loire-Nieuport LN411 dive-bomber of the French Aéronavale at their base near Cherbourg in June 1940. These aircraft were built for land operations with the Armée de L'Air, but were handed over to the French Navy just before the Blitzkreig struck. Francis Laine commanded Escadrille AB4 which was still equipping with this aircraft when thrown straight into the desperate battle. (Admiral Francis Laine)

Stuka victims. This burn-out Polish railway station is just one example of how the accurate attacks of the Junkers Ju 87 paralyzed enemy troop movements during the Blitzkreig campaigns. An entire Polish regiment was caught detraining here by St.G.77 and wiped out from the air before it could deploy or scatter. (Peter Schwartzkopf)

The main loco sheds of a railway terminal on the outskirts of Warsaw after the Stukas of St.G.77 had paid a brief visit. Such clinical demolition of key targets led to confusion and slow reactions by the defending armies enabling their encirclement, trapping and piecemeal destruction in campaigns that lasted weeks instead of years. (Peter Schwartzkopff)

it. Whole enemy armies were trapped in a huge pocket between the Rivers Vistula and Pilica at Ilza. Another army threatened to take the German advance in the rear, but was encircled on the Bzura. From 8 to 13 September both enemy army concentrations were subjected to non-stop dive-bombing until the dazed and frightened remnants laid down their arms *en masse*. The Stukas then pounded the city of Warsaw itself which the Poles had turned into a fortress. The final dive-bombing attacks reduced the fortress of Modlin on 26 and 27 September 1939.

The rapid defeat of Poland was followed by a period of reorganization during the winter, but in the spring the Blitzkreig tactics of Stuka and Panzer in close combination was again unleashed, this time against the forewarned, but arrogantly unready, Allied armies of the West. From 10 May until July 1940, Frank Neubert was *Staffelkapitän* of the 2.Staffel and from the latter date until September 1941, was that unit's *Staffelführer* and as such he fought in all their major combats. In Belgium and France the Stukas again led the way. The initial audacious seizure of Fort Eban Emael was supported by St.G.2 and on 12 May the unit attacked Allied armoured formations west of the fortress town of Liège.

Keeping pace with the swift advance to the sea by the German tanks, the Stukas moved base almost daily to maintain their combat sorties. Soon missions were being flown against the French ports and Dunkirk was an early target. On 24 May St.G.2 moved into Guise airfield, near St-Quentin, from where they could just about reach the sea. That day and the next their targets were British and French destroyer flotillas operating off the French coast in bombardment and evacuation roles, and they soon began to cause damage and casualties to these warships.

On 26 May the target was the citadel at Calais where the British were making a last stand. A concentrated attack by Stukas brought about its surrender that afternoon. From 27 May until 1 June the most frequent targets were the mass of shipping off Dunkirk, and scores of vessels were sunk and disabled in repeated attacks.

In the space of six short weeks the dive-bomber had transformed military thinking the world over.

Laine's Loires fight back

It is a little-known fact that there was also a 'Frank' flying dive-bomber missions for France against the Stukas during the brief Blitzkreig battles in France. Born

into a family with a long tradition of service in the Mercantile Marine of France, Francis Laine first saw the light of day on 16 October 1909. On 1 October 1926, at the age of just under seventeen, Francis entered the Navy Officer's College, *l'Ecole Navale*, the French equivalent of the British Britannia Naval College, as a cadet. 'That began a 43-year career in the Navy which I look back on with pride and great affection,' Francis, now a retired Admiral, told me recently. Later, when the Aéronavale called for volunteers for their Fleet Air Arm, young Francis was one of the first to step forward.

Ever since September 1939, Francis had been working at a desk job as Liaison Officer to the *Direction Technique et Industrielle du Ministère de l'Air*. Laine told me that he was glad when eventually a reserve officer arrived in November 1939, to take over from him.

'I now determined to gain for myself the job of Commanding Officer of a Fighter squadron,' Francis told me, 'and I approached the Navy's Director of Personnel accordingly. However during my time supervising aircraft supply, these plum jobs had been taken. Two other openings arose at this time, one was as commander of a Seaplane squadron then forming for service with the fleet, the

An ex-Army, Navy-flown land-based Loire-Nieuport LN 411 from AB-4 (Nbr 12) which was shot down by Flak near Villereau, France on 19 May 1940. The unique tail assembly can be clearly seen. (Musée de l'Air, Paris)

Another LN 411 victim, unit unknown, being examined by German soldiers after being shot down over northern France in May 1940. (Musée de l'Air, Paris)

The French Navy dive-bombers were thrown into the inferno of the German Blitzkreig and were sacrificed in a few brief sorties. Here is a Loire-Nieuport LN 401, (Nbr 10) from AB-2 unit, which was shot down by Flak near Berlaimont on 19 May 1940. (Musée de l'Air, Paris)

other was forming a new land-based dive-bomber squadron for the Navy, with the LN-411s made over from the Army. I had no wish to return to biplanes and quickly made my preference known at the Ministry. Thanks to some good comrades there I was named as commander of the dive-bomber squadron in the last days of 1939. My new command was AB-4, which was to be formed from scratch and eventually equipped with twelve LN-411s as soon as they came from the manufacturers' plants. At the time only three aircraft had been delivered from the factory of the SNCAU (*Société Nieuport-Astra*) at Issy-les-Moulineaux.'

Laine took over his squadron at Orly airfield on 4 February 1940. He was told to prepare his squadron for service by the beginning of July, but unfortunately Adolf Hitler's timetable was rather in advance of that of the Navy Ministry and Francis was to be allowed only two months to receive his aircraft, train his aircrew, assemble his ground staff, learn his trade and fight. The first aircraft actually arrived at the squadron at the end of February 1940, and Francis took it aloft to see what it could do. Others followed in a steady trickle as did the officers and men to form the squadron.

'During March and April,' Laine told

me, 'small parties arrived and were given their tasks, receiving and making the aircraft ready for service, training, arming and modifications of the planes and so on. On 17 May, at 1500 hours, and still a month-and-a-half in advance of the predictions given me, the squadron, which was still three short of its assigned twelve aircraft, was ordered urgently to pack up and entrain from the airfield at Querqueville for its assigned operational base at Berck. Here it was to go into combat right away.'

The urgency was plain. On 10 May the German Army had launched its great attacks on the Western Front and now, a week later, the dam had burst and the Panzers were in full flood across northern France, preceded by the dive-bombing Stukas which broke all resistance. Now AB-4, with its half-trained pilots and untested aircraft, was supposed to dam this floodtide! They did their best but it was a hopeless sacrifice.

The squadron flew to Berck near Cherbourg in two sections of three aircraft each, led by Lieutenants de Vaisseau Laine and Habert respectively, arriving at 1800 that evening. Here they were immediately armed with two small bombs apiece. AB-2 was ordered north into battle in Holland, but AB-4 was held in reserve. This did not suit Laine at all

and he made contact with the base commandant and got permission to conduct offensive patrols over the Dunkirk area. By 18 May nine aircraft were readied and, at 1815, they flew north led by Francis. Their target was enemy armour concentrations at Berlaimont and they attacked at 1930 through heavy Flak in 60-degree dives, from 1,200m down to 600m, delivering their twelve bombs on a German motorized column dispersed in the woods and fields there. On their return they were heavily engaged with equal intensity by the AA gunners of the German, French and British armies! As a result only Laine and three others returned to Berck at 2030, the other five becoming scattered among various airfields in the area or being shot down and their crews made prisoner.

The few survivors combined with other French dive-bomber units, AB-4, AB-1 and AB-2 equipped with Voughts, and made further desperate attacks during the days which followed, notably two contributed to the gallant attack on the bridge at d'Origny. On 21 May Laine himself led another attack of a mixed Loire force from AB 2 and AB 4, surviving attacks by Heinkel He 111s, British Hurricanes and Dornier 217s all in the space of a few hours, to find and attack a German column approaching Berck.

◀
June 1940. The beaches at Dunkirk immediately after the evacuation taken in a low-level pass by Tom Harrington's Skua dive-bomber. (Tom Harrington)

▶
June 1940. Tom Harrington's Blackburn Skua returning from an attack on Bergen, Norway, with a Flak cannon hole through the cockpit. (Tom Harrington)

They even managed to shoot down one of the Dorniers as a bonus!

With the enemy closing in on the Channel ports, the surviving dive-bombers had to keep shifting their airfields between missions, but in the process lost most of their ground staff and had to write-off damaged aircraft before they could be repaired. Admiral Laine gave me this description of the LN-411 from his viewpoint:

'The first requirement for any dive-bombing attack is to get up-sun of your target. This hides your approach from enemy AA fire and gives you a clear view of your target during the dive. The Loire-Nieuport was certainly an "exceptional" aircraft! But it was not very fast (250kph in horizontal flight, 320 in the attack dive). It was also indifferently armed for defence having only one 20mm cannon and two machine-guns. Its bomb load, being designed for use against submarines, was also light, only 150kg bombs being carried. It had little protection against fighter attack and had to be protected during daylight missions. There was, for example, no armour protection for the pilot. The engine was heavy on oil and tended to catch fire easily when pushed hard. The fuel tanks were small and not self-sealing and the radio equipment, as in all French planes

of this period, was poor. They were in fact specialized aircraft, even for dive-bombers, being produced to attack submarines from aircraft carriers out at sea, not to attack German tanks protected by fighters and Flak on land.'[35]

By 4 June it was virtually all over in the north. Only a few of the LNs had survived the carnage and Laine led these south from the Calais area to Hyères on the Côte d'Azure. There were only fourteen LNs of both types left in flying condition. The new enemy was the Italians, who had tried to take advantage of the German victories in the north by attacking across the border. They were soundly thrashed for their pains. Among AB-4's contributions to this humiliation was an attack by thirteen Loires against Imperia and Novi-Ligure on 18/19 June. They had to cross the Alps to reach their targets and lost two aircraft in bad weather doing so. Their attacks were conducted with their usual gallantry, but two more Loires were destroyed by Flak over the target and one was so badly damaged that it crashed on landing.

Eight Loires now remained and at 1600 on 24 June Laine was ordered to fly these to a French base in North Africa while there was still a chance of saving them. At 1815 he took off from Palyvestre with these eight dive-bombers accompanied

by a Loire 451 bomber with some of their crews aboard. They landed at Ajaccio-Campo and then flew on to Bone, but only six made it, two crashing en route over Sardinia. On 24 June they were ordered to move again, this time to Sidi Ahmed, near Casablanca. Here the remaining six dive-bombers were joined by twelve new Loires handed over by the Army, but in September all of these were ordered to be placed in store as the unit was to be converted to American-supplied Glenn Martin 167F medium bombers for future operations as Escadrille 7B. Historically, the end of AB-4 came on 18 December 1940, at Oran-Tafaraolli airfield, when it was wound-up as an operational squadron. The final epitaph for the gallant little Loire-Nieuport dive-bombers of France was written during the Allied North Africa landings in November 1942, when they were all destroyed in their hangars by the covering bombardments.

Skua Missions – 1940

The best-known exploit of the Royal Navy's Blackburn Skua dive-bomber was the sinking of the German cruiser *Königsberg* at Bergen, Norway in April 1940. This was the first major warship to be sunk by dive-bombing, but this great achievement was given little publicity at

the time (save by the BBC who declared, 'The RAF has done it again!') and has been largely ignored by historians since. Given more publicity was the later attack on the battle-cruiser *Scharnhorst*, when half the attackers were shot down by defending fighters who were in the air waiting for them. The one bomb which hit failed to explode.

Aside from these two attacks the Skuas had an extremely active war during this traumatic period, none more so than No. 801 Squadron. In a recent interview Captain Tom Harrington, DSC, RN, kindly gave me a very detailed account of their work at this time, which is supplemented by his Flying Log Book. He starts by describing events soon after the fall of Norway, the Low Countries and France. It was a time of high tension and great uncertainty, but rightly or wrongly, the feeling was that a German invasion of Britain was imminent. From 11 June onward No. 801 Squadron was based at RAF Detling and their Skuas and Rocs were flying a variety of missions, convoy escorts in the Channel, dive-bombing attacks on the German-held Channel ports, dive-bombing German heavy gun sites on the French coast near Cap Gris Nez and photo-reconnaissance missions up and down the Channel. Between times they would be sent north to Scotland for

the odd mission off Norway. They also were embarked aboard aircraft carriers from time to time for longer-range jobs from north Norway to Dakar in West Africa. It was a hectic period and nobody had much spare time on their hands in No. 801 Squadron. The actual dive-bombing of German E-boats in Boulogne harbour was carried out, not by the Skuas but by their fighter equivalent, the Blackburn Roc acting as dive-bombers. Harrington conducted the first such attack on 12 June and repeated the process the following day.

'When we went to Detling we were working under RAF Coastal Command, not Fighter Command. And our main function was to do reconnaissance from Boulogne right the way up to beyond Zeebrugge, Dieppe and Dunkirk, because the threat at that time was that Uncle Adolf was going to get his troops barged up and start coming across. It was most interesting because the Blenheims of the RAF and ourselves used to do the thing completely differently. The Blenheims used to do their recce at about 6,000 feet, obviously to take advantage of the cloud and that sort of thing. Our experience taught us that if you did your recce 1–1/2 in above the ground contour, nobody then troubled you, you troubled them.

If you were going to do Calais and Boulogne you were going one way round the hills. You came down through the valley and went through the harbour and you would take photographs because that's what you were there to do. It was most interesting. We learnt one or two little tricks, for instance Boulogne harbour. If you came down the valley you had the hills on either side and you could pop unexpected into the harbour below the level of the cranes. There was a very good reason for doing it this way. The dear old squarehead would have his 37mm light Flak waiting for visitors. He was a dedicated chap, he would aim at you and of course he'd forget about his chums on the other side of the harbour. So you'd go through there low and fast and out of the corner of your eye you'd see cranes being cut-down and falling on either side of you and the like. Indeed on one occasion, in order to try and get the 109s on to us, they had some of these fairly heavy calibre coastal defence guns. They were firing at us out at sea with these great water geysers laying down a splash barrage. Just single shots so obviously they were not trying to hit us, but point out where we were. You could see these 109s hunting us by the splashes. Of course they had great difficulty as we had sea camouflage which

◄

Tom Harrington and the other Blackburn Skua pilots of Number 801 Fleet Air Arm Squadron busy about essential duties aboard *Furious* in 1940. (Tom Harrington)

▼◄

An undignified arrival. A Skua from 801 Squadron having lost one wheel while returning to *Furious* off the West African coast in the autumn of 1940. (Tom Harrington)

►

Emergency repairs on a pranged Skua aboard *Furious* in the autumn of 1940. Note the size of the Pegasus engine, three-bladed prop, two-tone pattern of Skua painting at this stage of the war, still 'North Sea' grey in the tropics, and crew's mixture of tropical outfitting which one could describe as 'practical but hardly flattering'. (Tom Harrington)

▼

Two Skuas wait on the lift in *Ark Royal* in the light of the midnight sun off northern Norway. Their forlorn attack on the battle-cruiser *Scharnhorst* in June 1940 was both costly and abortive. (Author's collection)

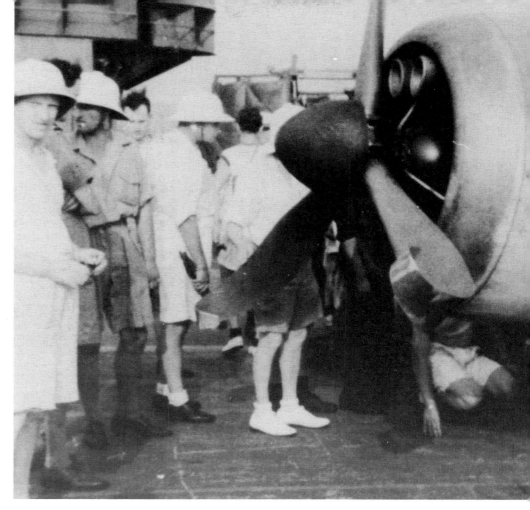

The Italian Stukas were taken straight from German production lines, and, despite wartime rumours, none were ever built in Italy. They equipped many squadrons and saw hard service in Sicily, Greece, the Balkans and the Western Desert, as well as disputing control of the Mediterranean with the Royal Navy from 1941 to 1942 in many a hard-fought Malta convoy battle. (Nicola Pattella)

▶

Italian Stukas, Junkers Ju 87Rs (Richards) with long-range tanks under their wings, huddle on a Sicilian airfield after delivery from German factories in 1941. (Nicola Malizia)

had great advantage to us. But as with all points this had two sides, the great disadvantage was that we used to get attacked by the RAF as well! The fighter boys hadn't much of a clue regarding aircraft ID. They wondered who were these extraordinary, foreign-looking aircraft and, looking for scalps, were not too particular whose they got!

We couldn't talk to them about the error of their ways, as we had different frequencies on the primitive R/T that was in existence in those days. So we did the only thing we could do. We just went flat out. It was like going flat out in an Austin 7. You just waited for them to come and then took counter-measures. You turned and played with your flaps, made them overshoot. If you happened to be driving a Roc you'd fire a warning burst over them, which again, with a cloud of red-hot golf balls coming out of the back, would make the odd Blenheim or fighter think twice and pause for thought. Then we'd just disappear as best we could again at sea level.

They would have been told we were going out, but I don't think the cross-communications were frightfully good. I mean this was early on in the war and co-ordination between one control unit and another control unit of the same command was very much interogative,

let alone between Fighter Command and anyone else. I think everyone was really very much on the defensive in an aggressive way at this period and anything they couldn't see and understand was to be wiped out.

It could be most amusing in that, even when you were doing convoy protection duty off Dover or somewhere like that, you would go and be relieved by a Blenheim and the first thing you knew of your relief would be the Blenheim coming in to attack you. Their attitude was, there's a funny-looking aircraft over our convoy, it can't be on our side, and we will hack it down! You'd think that as you were stooging around in a level plod rather than screaming down with your flaps out onto the ships or being fired at, that they would get the clue you were friendly and not hostile. But no. Perhaps because one of the aspects of convoy spotting with a single machine is not to destroy the convoy yourself, but to bring the intelligence to bear so that you could organize a proper co-ordinated attack. So that you would try and stay there so that they would know the position, so that anyone 'shadowing' a convoy wasn't necessarily being aggressive in a direct way to the convoy. But would have hostile intent.

The formation we adopted for these

runs across the Channel depended on what we were going to do. A convoy would probably be a single aircraft. If you were doing a reconnaissance we'd sometimes go as a pair. For instance we did the first attack on the Cap Gris Nez guns. We spotted the chaps digging. How it all came about was because we were doing this 'barge-spotting' intelligence-gathering. The whole thing started with our intelligence-gathering from these ports, and we would be flying to and from Boulogne and Calais. Cap Gris Nez was in between so we spotted them building the gun positions and took pictures. As a result we had to go back again, this time to bash them.'

The first such attack took place on 21 June. Harrington's log-book tersely recalls the results. 'Too many fighters. Day shot down.' One of the swift transfers north to Hatston in the Orkney Islands followed this and on 5 July the mission report shows 'Blitz after a phantom cruiser.' On the 7th, during a dive-bombing attack on Bergen harbour, Tom Harrington nearly lost his head. Literally! He was later to describe it this way.

'We operated from Hatston airfield (mainly a small straight road with telegraph poles removed). Here, we could either fly direct to the coast of Norway (just) or, by embarking on one of the few

remaining aircraft carriers and thereby having a great choice of naval targets on the vast west coast of Norway, with its mass of offshore islands and deep fjords running inland.

On 7 July 1940, seven of us took off from Hatston in the dark (not too much of that during July) and flew low across the north part of the North Sea (to avoid detection by German radar, etc.). Our target was the shipping in the port of Bergen and our plan was to climb to our most effective dive-bombing height (*circa* 15,000 feet depending on the thickness of the target's building materials and the type of bomb we were carrying, i.e., semi-armour piercing, etc.). On this particular party, we climbed up to about 'ten grand' (10,000 feet), because we started to run into thicker and lowering cloud as we crossed the outer islands. This not only forced us to fly lower, but also meant that we were having difficulty to avoid 'bunching' together, which in turn meant an easier target for enemy gunners and from our point of view, we had less 'room' to roll into our dive-bombing run, when we had selected a worthwhile target.

I found myself behind a friend of mine as he pushed his aircraft over into its dive and put out his dive brakes (this allows you dive "steadily" at some 70–80 degrees towards your target). The effect of these dive brakes is to make your aircraft steady, but also causes the aircraft to track forward during the dive. This means that when an anti-aircraft gun fires at you when he has you in his sights and fires, he will often miss you because of this forward moving and the shell often goes below you instead of hitting you! (Good News!).

Because of this cloud and the fact that I was stuck behind my chum, I was in fact getting all the Flak aimed at him and this was whizzing over the top of my diving aircraft. Not a very comfortable situation. It also did not help too much in my "tracking" of my target (a ship alongside a jetty).

As you know, when things start going wrong, you often start experiencing the effects of "sod's law" – when lots of not likely other things also start going wrong! In this case, I noticed that my fuel gauges were reading zero, and my flap position indicators were showing the wrong reading (I smelt an electrical problem). When I selected my bomb release (another electrically operated button) the bombs did not release.

I did not have too much spare time left in my 75-degree dive, with clouds of red hot "golf balls" flying over the top of my canopy, so I had to screw my head round to my emergency bomb-release levers on the righthand side (starboard) of my cockpit, in order to grab them and when steady, release the bombs – all of this came to pass, but while my head was bent down to the emergency panel, one of the 40mm enemy shells hit the top right part of my canopy, passed over where my head would normally be and left my aircraft through the port-side of the canopy – making a nasty smashing noise!

Anyway, after letting my bomb release go, on its target, I found myself no longer chewing gum but munching some nasty tasting "sawdust". So I lifted off my oxygen mask and blew out this newly created (non-chewing) material which I blew all over the place, giving a rather new type of non-skid and high-traction" finish to many parts of the cockpit.

The trip home was not too comfortable – not so much because of the draught caused by the German shell – but because of the electric failure, which in turn meant that I had no physical indication of my fuel situation. We had three tanks and it was bad news to let any one of these tanks drain dry because the engine took a long time to come on-stream again. The flight out and back took four hours and thirty minutes, which

in weak mixture meant that we were very, very close to nearly not making it! I made for Sumburgh airfield in the Shetland Islands, it being the nearest base.

When I filled up with petrol, I found that I had used all the capacity of the three tanks except for 7½ gallons (i.e., about two gallons in each tank left) – about ten minutes' flying in weak mixture.'[36]

Although there were only a handful of Navy dive-bombers for Britain to hit back with, they did their best. At least they managed to hit their targets, and in attacks from April to December 1940, naval aircraft sank six ships and damaged thirteen more. By comparison the RAF failed to do any damage at all. Captain S. W. Roskill was to record why.

'. . . at the outbreak of war the belief had prevailed that a good percentage of hits would be obtained on ship targets in medium- or even high-level bombing attacks. Disillusion came quickly, but the mistake resulted in neglect of the dive-bomber and in our fighting the first two years of the war with no aircraft of this type except for a handful of naval Skuas. The change from medium- to low-level attacks was slow and, even when accepted, did not produce results comparable to those regularly obtained by German dive- and low-level bombers.'[37]

Fighter Bait

After the fall of France, only the twenty-two miles of water known as the English Channel stopped the German onrush completely. So once again the sea proved Britain's 'Sure Shield'. To get over it required that the Royal Navy be removed. The Stukas proved themselves quite capable of doing that, by driving the destroyer flotillas from Dover in short order with heavy casualties, but to keep them away for long enough to enable Admiral Raeder to get his makeshift armada ready for the invasion would clearly take a lot longer. That, in turn, would depend on the elimination of the RAF's fighter defences. Thus the Battle of Britain – and the end of the dive-bomber as a viable weapon of war, or so we have been constantly informed.

What were the Stuka methods employed against British Channel ports at this period? We have a detailed account contained in a 'Most Secret' report to the War Cabinet on the use of the ridiculous UP weapon (Unrotated Projectile, or rocket, which fired parachuted projectiles with trailing wires that had explosive devices attached – an aerial minefield and one of Lord Cherwell's more scatter-brained concepts). The report was based on observations at Dover of a Stuka attack which took place there at the

beginning of the campaign.

'The second raid took place at 7.36 a.m. on 29 July, and took the form of a massed dive-bombing attack in two waves of 16 and 22 Junkers 87 bombers. The attack was carried out from NE to SW and the aircraft started to dive from a height of approximately 4,000 feet to heights of between 500 and 1,000 feet.

It was not possible to get the barrage up quickly enough to catch the first six of the raiders in the first wave, but the remainder had to face it and take what avoiding action they could. By swerving hard to port several aircraft managed to pass through the gap in the barrage, but the rest were unable to manage this manoeuvre successfully and were forced to pass through either of the two curtains. One of the four bombers passing through was seen to become entangled and was brought down. It appears probable that the crash of this bomber was caused by the UP barrage, but this cannot be stated definitely as no explosion was observed. Another bomber was entangled in the curtain and an explosion took place in the machine when flying approximately at the height of the cliffs behind the harbour. The description given by the observer (Captain Jarman, RA) in my opinion leaves no room for doubt that in this case the aircraft was

2.

3.

4.

5.

1. During the war Sweden's purchasing of foreign types of aircraft was restricted, but licensed-built variants continued to feature. Here three SAAB L 10 (B 17) light bombers, adapted for the dive-bombing role, are seen over northern Sweden in 1943. Special dive-bombing sights were fitted to these aircraft to increase their potential. (Flygvapnet) **2.** The ultimate Swedish dive-bomber type to see service was the twin-engined SAAB B18A. This one belongs to F 1 Squadron which has a strong dive-bomber tradition. Known as light bombers to the outside world, the Swedes developed them specifically for dive-bombing, although later ground attack and torpedo-bomber variants were also produced and continued to serve post-war for a time. Note the folded dive brakes outboard of engine on the left-hand side of the photograph. (Flygvapnet) **3.** A nice in-flight view of the Swedish SAAB L 18 B (B18 B) dive-bomber on patrol in 1944/45. At this time the threat of the Soviet advance was causing considerable concern to neutral Sweden and constant war footing patrols were maintained. (Flygvapnet) **4.** A close-up of a SAAB L 18 on a snow-bound airstrip in the winter of 1944/45. (Flygvapnet) **5.** Behind the headlines of the front-line applications were the dedicated men working away to perfect the dive-bomber technique. Sweden had been early in the field in embracing this method of precision attack, but to make the best use of her limited resources and manpower she strove to perfect an automatic dive-bomber sight. While other powers went down this road to a greater (Germany) or lesser (USA) extent, none produced a really satisfactory answer, but Erik Wilkenson, working with SAAB, stuck to it and produced a fully automatic dive-bombing sight later in the war, which was embraced post-war by many of the leading air-minded nations. (Eric Wilkenson)

among the smaller nations, devoted a great deal of research into perfecting a workable dive-bomber sight.

Improvised dive-bombers which proved quite successful in service were the Roumanian IARB1 and UARB1A. These were single-engined monoplane fighters of the IAR80 and 80A types adapted for dive-bombing. The changes were minimal, involving the fitting of underwing dive brakes which in turn meant lengthening and strengthening the aircraft's wings. Bomb racks were fitted for light bombs and a single 551lb weapon was carried below the fuselage. Being a fighter modification it was a fast aircraft, 317mph, and although less than 300 were finally built, they did see service on the Russian Front.

The Hungarian air force set up its own dive-bomber units equipped with Junkers Ju 87s, but later in the war were unique in being the only air force which employed the German twin-engined Me 210C in its original dive-bombing configuration with *102 Onallo Zuhanobombazo Osztaly*, also against the Soviets.

The flying banana

From the sublime to the ridiculous. Another dictator had been duly impressed by the work and results of the Luftwaffe's Stukas in the Spanish Civil War, as well as his own air force's experiments there. Benito Mussolini had towering ambitions, but these were not backed up by the industrial base to give his military muscle a credible status. Thus all his grandiose schemes were superficial. It was thus with Italy's home-grown dive-bomber, the Savoia-Marchetti SM85.

The one thing that Mussolini resented above all else was the fact that Italy's self-proclaimed dominance of the Mediterranean (Mare Nostrum), was made a mockery of by the very presence of the British Mediterranean Fleet which sailed the length and breadth of that waterway with arrogance. What he wanted was a machine which would hurt the one enemy and render it ineffective. He thought the answer lay in the dive-bomber. He was right, as the Luftwaffe was soon to prove time and time again, but unfortunately Italy's own efforts at producing such a weapon came to a rapid and humiliating termination.

The SM 85 was a twin-engined, high-winged monoplane, produced rapidly to satisfy Mussolini's ego, but it was of wooden construction, grossly underpowered and lacked both the structural

◀

A mission with 209 Squadriaglia. Sergeant-Major Tarantola Ennio and his wireless-operator/rear-gunner, Ricci. (Ennio Tarantola)

▶

Two Italian Stuka pilots of 209 Squadriaglia, Sergeants-Major Tarantola and Cappelli. (Ennio Tarantola)

definitely destroyed by the UP.'[38]

If it was, then it was the only occasion ever when this device worked successfully. This attack set the seal on the Stukas' victory over the anti-invasion flotilla, for it sank the destroyer depot ship *Sandhurst*, damaged in previous attacks. Not that it mattered, because the destroyer flotilla she had served had already been decimated by dive-bombers, and the last undamaged destroyer had sailed the day before. Destroyers were forbidden to sail through the Straits of Dover in daylight. When one was sent out contrary to these orders, as was HMS *Dainty*, which sailed from Portland, she was quickly sent to the bottom.

The dive-bombers now turned their attentions to the RAF airfields along the south coast. The Stukageschwader were distributed on airfields adjacent to the Channel. As part of VII Fliegerkorps Stukageschwader 1 had its Stab (Major Walter Hagen) and I (Hauptmann Paul-Werner Hozzel) and III (Hauptmann Helmut Mahlke) Gruppen at Angers; Stukageschwader 2 had its Stab (Major Oscar Dinort) and I Gruppe (Hauptmann Hubertus Hitschold) at St-Malô and its II Gruppe (Major Walter Enneccerus) at Lannion; Stukageschwader 77 its Stab (Major Clemens Graf von Schonborn-

Wiesentheid), I (Hauptmann Friedrich-Karl Freiherr von Dalwigk zu Lichtenfels), II (Hauptmann Waldemar Pleweg) and III (Hauptmann Helmut Bode) Gruppen at Caen. Under II Fliegerkorps were II./St.G.1 (Hauptmann Anton Keil) in the Pas-de-Cais and IV (Stuka)/ Lehrgeschwader 1 (Hauptmann Bernd von Brauchitsch) were based at Tramecourt. In all they could muster 336 Stukas, of which 280 were operational.

After preliminary skirmishing for several weeks over the convoys, the battle started in earnest in mid-August. On 12 August the airfield at Lympne reported dive-bombing attacks from 1740 to 1800 hours, which caused damage to hangars and offices.

It was on 13 August that *Adlerangriff* was scheduled to begin, but bad weather postponed it until the afternoon. Prominent among the Stuka attacks this day was that made by IV (Stuka)/LG.1, commanded by Hauptmann von Brauchitsch, son of the German Army's Commander-in-Chief. Their target was Detling airfield, a Coastal Command base near Maidstone, which they hit at 1716 hours that afternoon. The dive-bombers planted their bombs with clinical care on this target. They hit and destroyed the Operations Block, among the casualties being the station CO, and also hit

hangars and the mess halls as the airmen were going to tea, killing sixty-seven of them. Twenty-two aircraft, eight Blenheims of No. 53 Squadron and four Ansons of No. 500 Squadron, caught sitting on the ground, were destroyed and the runways heavily cratered. All the Junkers Ju 87s returned safely to base.

Patrol 'A' of No. 56 Squadron, scrambled five Hurricanes at 1530, but one aborted. The remaining four, Pilot Officer Page, Flight Sergeant Smythe, Sergeant Hillwood and Sergeant Whitfield, caught II./St.G.1 led by Hauptmann Kiel (which had originally been sent against Rochester airfield, but was later switched to attack Lympne) over Canterbury this day. Gleefully they put their noses down for a feast of easy kills as the Stukas jettisoned their bombs. However, return fire from the dive-bombers caused heavy damage to the attackers and they were forced to break off the attack without result. Sergeant Whitfield, flying P2922, failed to return. 'We were taught a sharp lesson,' was the comment by one of the fighter pilots after this encounter.[39]

On 15 August there was another major effort. This time von Brauchitsch dispatched two Staffeln to RAF Hawkinge near Dover, while II./St.G.1 was to strike at nearby Lympne airfield. Both targets

◄ ▲
An Italian Stuka swoops low over a sinking British supply ship, caught, dive-bombed and sunk while trying to keep the isolated garrison at Tobruk supplied. (Ennio Tarantola)

◄
Further near-misses finish off the already sinking supply ship off Tobruk while the Stukas circle their prey. (Ennio Tarantola)

▲
Mission accomplished. A trio of Italian Stukas of 209 Squadriaglia returning along the Libyan coastline after yet another successful attack. (Ennio Tarantola)

were heavily hit. Two Staffeln of IV (Stuka)/LG.1 together with II.St.G.1 were sent against Hawkinge and Lympne. They were intercepted by fighters from Nos. 54 and 501 Squadrons. At the first target LG.1 caused considerable damage to the airfield and its buildings but the Staffel commander, Hauptmann Munchenhagen, was shot down. However, return fire from the Stuka caused severe damage to the Spitfires. The Operational Records Book of Hawkinge records the attack lasted ten minutes from 1135 and that there were two hangars hit, and one other building damaged, but no casualties. The latter target was put out of action for 48 hours. Again the ORP describes the raid:

'Cloudy-Fair. 1040. Aerodrome subjected to dive-bombing. Heavy bombs were dropped in repeated dive-bombing attacks. Hangars damaged. Two wooden buildings used as paint stores and an Armadillo was burnt out. All power and water services cut. Direct hit on Station sick-quarters. Orderly Room, Accounts Section and Sick-quarters evacuated to empty houses near aerodrome in the evening.'[40]

Eight machines from II./St.G.1 and IV(Stuka)/LG.1 attacked Dover harbour once more, sinking some small ships. Four aircraft from Staffel 10/Lehrge-schwader 1 were shot down by fighters while circling to attack a convoy.

On 16 August Tangmere was hit at 1300 by St.G.2. It was another classic Stuka bombing attack which struck the base dead centre, devastating it and destroying seven Hurricanes and six Blenheims on the ground. The station ORP stated that 17 Stukas hit between 1300 and 1320.

'Following casualties were sustained: – 10 Service personnel, 3 Civilians and 20 personnel injured. The following buildings were destroyed· All Hangars, Workshops, Stores, Sick-Quarters, Pumping Station, "Y" Hut Officer's Mess and Salvation Army hut. Many buildings damaged but promptly made fit for habitation. The following services were temporarily put out of action: Tannoy Broadcasting System, all lighting, power, water and sanitation. The following aircraft were destroyed or damaged: 3 Blenheims (Written Off), 3 Blenheims, 7 Hurricanes and 1 Magister. 6 Merlin Engines damaged but repairable. 7 MT and 30 private cars damaged beyond repair. A large amount of equipment was buried under débris and salvage work was put in hand immediately.'[41]

However, the dive-bombers subsequently lost seven of their number when jumped by Nos. 601 and 609 Squadrons

while reforming afterwards. Ventnor radar station, already damaged on the 12th, was hit by seven Stukas again just as it was coming back into action. They inflicted so much damage in this attack that it was off the air for a week.

On 18 August four Ju 87 Gruppen hit the airfields of Gosport, Thorney Island and Ford as well as the radar station at Polling, attacked at 1430 by 25 Stukas from I./St.G.77. They inflicted heavy damage but no casualties, and a makeshift set was installed which carried on the plot. Ford and Thorney Island were also punished heavily. These Stukas were caught without fighter escort, again by the Spitfires of No. 152 Squadron and the Hurricanes of No. 43 Squadron, before they could concentrate for the return flight. They took heavy punishment, losing thirty aircraft, including twelve of the twenty-eight machines belonging to I/St.G.77, among them its CO, Hauptmann Herbert Meisel, shot down over Selsey Bill. He had only recently taken command when Hauptmann Freiherr von Dalwigk zu Lichtenfels had been shot down on 13 July. Meisel had fitted extra armoured plate which he salvaged from smashed-up French Moraine fighters, but this extra protection only slowed his aircraft down and did not save the lives of the crew.

99

The other two leading machines were piloted by Kurt Scheffel (who was the unit Technical Officer) and the Mechanics Adjutant, Oberleutnant Karl Henze. Thirty-eight years later, Scheffel's eye-witness account of this much-publicized 'Stuka Massacre' was recounted by Heinz Sellhorn.[42]

'18 August. 1430 hours. Three Stuka-gruppen, totalling 90 Ju 87 dive-bombers set out from France across the Channel "Gegen England." In the lead of I.Gruppe of the Sturzkampfgeshwader 77, at the head of the three planes of the Stabskette, Hauptmann Herbert Meisel, the new Kommandeur, who today would be making his first and last flight with this unit. Just behind him the Ju 87s of Kurt Scheffel, the Technical Officer, and the Adjutant and that of Oberleutnant Karl Henze crouched. Behind them were 25 Ju 87s in Reichsspreitentagsformation.

At a height of 3,500m they sighted the British airfield ahead, close to Portsmouth and started to get into their attack formation. A slight left-hand curve changed the formation. All was proceeding as routine – and then began the Vengeance from Hell!

Scheffel himself was watching the approach of the target point below, not the sky of death. "Fighters coming in from the right and above," the leading aircraft began violent avoiding action. Thirty seconds later his radio operator, Otto Binner, began shifting violently and going crazy, firing with his rearward-facing machine-guns. And now it was that Scheffel remembers: Bright tracer paths then hammer blows against the fuselage. An instant of fear! Blows against his front *Reflexvisier*, and his instruments flying asunder under a rain of hits, their transparent covering spiking back into the pilot's eyes with countless Plexiglass daggers.

Scheffel was not then aware that he also had, in addition, 40 or 50 splinters sticking into his back, or that he had been hit in the lungs. However he was well aware that he could not move his left arm at all and that aluminium shreds projected from his right hand which clasped the control column. And he also instinctively knew that his Radioman behind him had made his last operational flight: Binner had shouted once more and then had stopped and had collapsed over his machine-gun.

All Kurt Scheffel remembers next is a mêlée of hurtling aircraft with Stukas, English and German fighters all dimly discernible, no longer as formations but firing and diving everywhere: "You must not remain in this mess – if you do somebody will quickly or accidentally shoot you down," he thought to himself.

The blood rushed to his head as he threw his aircraft at the target airfield, going quickly into an 80-degree dive, releasing his bomb and then clawing his way out to sea.

"I felt strangely tired and weary. I had a mist before my eyes and as a result I attempted to pull out some of the glass splinters which were obscuring my sight," he recalled. "I remember seeing an English Defiant fighter position itself directly in front of my nose and turning its turret, with its quadruple machine-guns, directly at me. As soon as I was aware of him I instinctively threw my agile aircraft into a sharp turn and he was gone. A Flak tower on the Isle of Wight, shooting hard from every gun, loomed up in front of me, filling my vision with mushrooms of bursts. I glimpsed a Stuka down in the water. As I sped away I was not more than ten metres above the wave-tops . . ."

Scheffel achieved the impossible: somehow he nursed his shattered little bomber back to his home base of Caen-Maltot airfield, despite the pain and the damage, and got her down in one piece. Many rushed to help and he was lifted from aircraft, and so, tragically, was his dead Radio-operator borne gently away. Those on the ground later counted no less than 120 machine-gun holes in his

◄
Futile zig-zagging of the Australian destroyer *Waterhen* under attack by Italian Stukas off Tobruk. Near-misses which crippled her can be seen close alongside. Although taken in tow she later had to be sunk. (Ennio Tarantola)

►
Moment of impact as a Junkers Ju 87 Stuka crashes in the Western Desert, a victim of AA fire on 23 July 1942. (*Illustrated London News* Picture Library)

►
The pilot and radio-operator of a crashed Stuka being taken prisoner behind Allied lines in North Africa, summer 1942. (*Illustrated London News* Picture Library)

►
The Forgotten Men! In the eastern desert during 1942 the Fairey Albacore biplanes of the Fleet Air Arm – dumped ashore when their carriers had been Stukad out of the sea – were considered obsolete relics. However their young crews were highly skilled and conducted a series of classic dive-bombing attacks on Axis installations during this time, even if they were ignored by the Press and completely forgotten by the Admiralty. (Fleet Air Arm Museum)

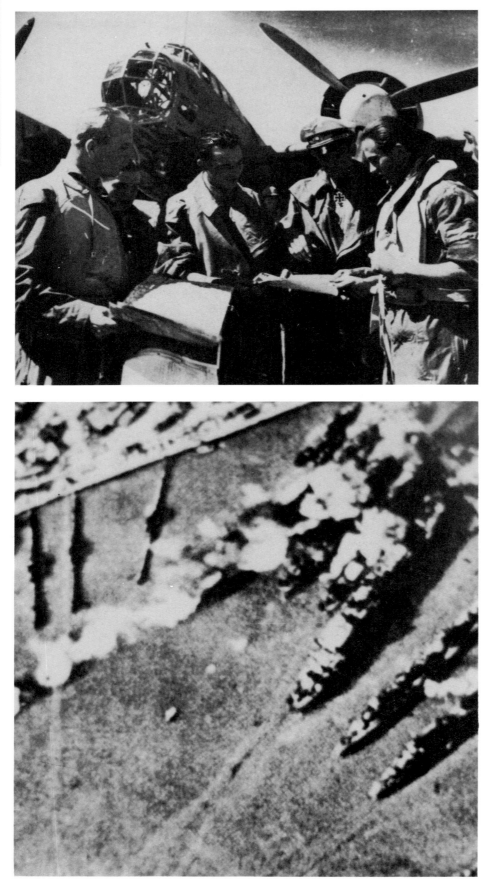

The most outstanding of the Junkers Ju 88 aircrews was that led by Joachim Helbig who specialized in anti-shipping operations with great success. His famous 'Helig-Flyers' even earned the grudging respect of the British for their exploits. Born in Berlin on 10 September 1915, Helbig joined the Luftwaffe in 1936 and quickly went on to make his mark. But it was as leader of 4./LG 1 that he first made a big impact during the Battle of Britain, smashing Worthy Down airfield. When his unit moved to the Mediterranean, Helbig's operations crippled the Royal Navy's movements. On one occasion in mid-1942 he sank three out of four destroyers from a British flotilla in a single afternoon. (Author's collection)

Another outstanding Junkers Ju 88 pilot who specialized in anti-shipping missions was Werner Baumbach. Starting with the crippling of the heavy cruiser *Suffolk* and a hit on the battleship *Resolution* off Norway in 1940, he went on to score a string of successful dive-bombing attacks throughout the war. Here a stick of bombs falls across anchored Soviet submarines, destroyers and depot ships at the Black Sea port of Tuapse. (Author's collection)

► An attack on a British supply convoy to Malta in June 1942. LG 1 dive-bombers leave a large merchant ship ablaze and sinking during Operation 'Harpoon'. Note the two destroyers circling the wreck to pick up survivors. (Gerd Stamp)

Stuka, yet she made it back.

The balance sheet of "Stuka-slaughter of Thorney Island" was as follows: 12 aircraft would not be returning; the Gruppenkommandeur was missing (his corpse was later returned for burial in France). Eighteen of his fellow aircrews were dead, several more were seriously wounded. A further six Stukas crash-landed back on the coast, shot to pieces.

Goering was obliged to withdraw his hitherto victorious dive-bombers and there was widespread dejection among the aircrews with a marked reluctance to speak of their experiences. The Stuka never flew against England again.' [This latter statement is of course not true.] Poor Meisel's replacement was Hauptmann Helmut Bruck.[42]

After this the Stukas were concentrated in the Pas-de-Calais in readiness for the invasion itself, which of course never came. However they *did* fly against England again. Under Hauptmann Mahlke they made several highly successful attacks on British convoys in the Thames estuary in October and November. The final attack was, for the first and last time, controlled by the fighter commander who misdirected the dive-bombers over AA positions at Dover and away from his own fighters, which he kept well clear. As a result

several Ju 87s were shot down by British fighters unopposed. This ineffectual German fighter commander was later court-martialled for his part in this affair. Nor was that the end of the Stuka over England. As Horst Lippach was to remind us:

'My Stuka unit formed a special Staffel from Stukageschwader 1 in the autumn of 1940 and we conducted night attacks against shipping and against Dover and Margate. We flew at a height of 4,000m to avoid the Flak and night fighters. We operated on clear nights looking for ships' wakes in the Channel and the North Sea. We illuminated them and from 4,000m height we made many diving attacks.'[43]

The Thorney Island massacre was undoubtedly the Stukas' greatest defeat. There was no gainsaying its severity. However, when one stands back and compares it with other, Allied, defeats, one gains a truer perspective. The loss of twelve aircraft in one sortie was a ghastly casualty rate. Then one remembers the loss of 10 out of 22 Vickers Wellington bombers over the Heligoland Bight on 18 December 1939; the loss of 40 Fairey Battles out of 71 on 14 May 1940, flying vainly against the Maas bridges; of 60 Flying Fortresses on 14 October 1943, or 96 Avro Lancasters on

the night of 30 March 1944 for example. And these attacks had achieved very little in compensation. In taking out Poland, Norway, Holland, Belgium, France, Yugoslavia, Greece and Crete, the Stukas lost a total of 631 machines, only a typical two-month loss rate for the heavy bombers of the RAF Bomber Command and USAAF later in the war.

Dive-bombers *were* most certainly vulnerable to fighter attack when unescorted – but so equally were every other type of bomber. Nor did this episode mark the end of the Stuka which kept fighting to the very last day of the war. And nor did it mark the end of dive-bombing generally. The main war effort now moved down to the Mediterranean area.

The Picchiatelli off Tobruk

Early in 1941, the victorious British Army, which had driven back, the Italian invasion and had gone over to the offensive against them in Libya, received a setback with the arrival of a small German armoured and motorized formation known as the Afrika Korps, under Irwin Rommel. To give them air support, and to close the central Mediterranean to the Royal Navy, came the Stuka dive-bombers of I./St.G.1, commanded by Hauptmann Paul-Werner Hozzel and II./

St.G.2 led by Major Walter Enneccerus. They quickly wrecked the aircraft carrier *Illustrious*, sank the cruiser *Southampton* and damaged the cruisers *Gloucester* and *Perth*. This done, I.St.G.1 joined in the land battles which threw the British back from Agheila in a few short weeks. Tobruk held out, and to sustain the siege the Royal Navy had to run in a continuous stream of supplies, food ammunition and men. The supply ships soon became too vulnerable, so warships were used instead. The Stukas had a field day among these, and losses became severe on the 'Tobruk Run' as it became known. The German Stukas were aided in their endeavours at this time by the newly formed Italian Stuka squadrons, now getting into their stride after brief training in Germany.

The first Italian unit was 236 Squadrigilia, commanded by Tenente Fernando Malvezzi, part of 96 Gruppo B.a.Tuffo. (Capitano Ercolano Ercolani), which arrived at Castel Benito, Benghazi, during the afternoon of 1 February 1941. Next day they were joined by seven Ju 87s of No 237 Squadriglia, led by Capitano Giovanni Santinoni. The Picchiatelli (as the Italians dubbed their Stukas) of these two units were soon in action along the North African coastline and worked in conjunction with the German Junkers Ju 87s of the units which rotated in that zone, III./St.G.1, II./St.G.2 and the Stab/St.G.3.

One of the Italian Stuka pilots who flew against Tobruk and also against the British warships supplying it, was Major Ennio Tarantola. Now in his seventies, he clearly remembers his dive-bombing days and he kindly gave me much detailed information as well as his eyewitness accounts of these operations.

'I flew the Stuka in combat for about a year, which gave me ample time to consider both its merits and failings. I can sum up simply by stating, merits – a large number; defects – very few. I should also state that I speak as a former fighter pilot who served in bombers and dive-bombers before returning again to fighter aircraft, so I can speak from a broad knowledge and comparison base.

During my period flying dive-bombers I was fortunate in that my commander was one of the best in this field, Giuseppe Cenni, who was sadly killed in action much later in the war. We Italians named the Stuka the Picchiatelli in our reports, the word means 'Striker' and aptly portrayed our precision targeting role in the war.

The actual methods we employed were quite diverse, and depended really on the targets allocated to us. Against ship-ping there was initially the classic dive-bomber approach of diving at 90 degrees vertically in groups of two or three aircraft at a time. This was the system the Germans used so effectively and it was this way that they taught us when we trained with them. Their method was to thus attack the ships from ahead and therefore, no matter which way the target vessel put her helm over to avoid the leading Stuka, numbers two and three following her down could adjust their attacks and ensure that they scored hits. The German pilots extended their dive brakes and commenced their dives from about 4,000m, pushing on down vertically to around 700/800m before bomb release and letting their sirens scream on the way down to add effect. We too adopted this method most successfully.

However, later on, we Italian crews adopted a different system to compensate for our smaller number of aircraft. We circled the ship, keeping just off its left-hand flank to avoid the worst of the AA fire, and watched for its defensive turns. Once the ship was committed to an evasive turn we dropped down gently by banking without use of the dive brakes. This gave us greater final approach speed. We found the vertical dive at 90 degrees was accurate, but gave the

◄

A remarkable photograph taken aboard *Illustrious* as the splashes, spray and smoke of near-misses and direct hits soar upward and a signalman, helmetless despite the bomb splinters watches the AA fire peppering the sky as the Stukas continue their pulverizing attack upon the British carrier. (Imperial War Museum)

►

The Royal Navy auxiliary *Ulster Prince* photographed from the Junkers Ju 88 dive-bomber which sank her at Nauplia, Greece on 25 April 1941. (Gerd Stamp)

defences a nil-deflection shot at the leading aircraft. In our method the target was confused and the majority of the ships' guns were masked and thus made ineffective. We called this the 'Grazing' or 'Shaving' attack because we went in only a few metres above the sea.

The most favoured method finally used by we Italians was the now famous 'skip-bombing' attack. The Americans in the South-West Pacific claimed to have invented this method of hitting ships, but we were using it at least a year earlier, thanks largely to the passion of Cenni in developing and perfecting the technique. I myself participated in one of our first successes with this type of attack, which took place off Sollum as early as June 1941. As perfected, the Stukas approached at low-level and, still out of range of the ships' close-range weapons, we deliberately released our bombs by under-aiming when the target ship vanished beneath our propeller. If correctly done the bomb would strike the surface of the water and bounce twice (or skip) before striking the target's hull and detonating. This opened the ship's hull up on the waterline and let the sea in very effectively.'

Major Ennio Tarantola described two attacks in which he participated, one highly successful, the other less so for

him personally.

'The first action developed on 29 June 1941, with reports of enemy destroyers off the coast and we took off in conjunction with our German friends to make a combined attack, although we actually attacked in two separate waves and using our own different methods. There were ten German Stukas and we had seven machines and there was fighter cover also as I recall. The German unit flew direct to the target while we took a more diverse route. They made their dives on one of the ships and returned directly to their base.

We found the two destroyers off Sollum and commenced our assault. I was armed with a 500kg bomb and we took the second destroyer as our target. We made the conventional vertical dives on this ship and achieved very accurate bombing. As a result of very close misses alongside her, our target was disabled and brought to a halt. We later learnt that she was the Australian destroyer *Waterhen*. All the Stukas returned safely to base without any casualties.'

Their destroyer victim was taken in tow, but gradually her ancient hull leaked and the water rose until, next day, she went down. But not before she had survived another attempt to put her and her towing companion under as well.

'The ship remained afloat to start with and next day, 30 June, we were again sent off to attack her, but this time only we Italians were sent out. We adopted the usual system of attack. We were heavily fired on as we circled just outside effective range of their guns and then we went in. However, in the face of the heavy AA fire, we scored no hits only more near-misses. For myself I made my dive but, to my chagrin, my bomb 'hung-up' on me and did not release. I pulled out, went round and made a second dive on the target.

The second time I was alone and got all the return fire. I managed to drop my bomb but was immediately badly hit and my machine so damaged that I was forced to ditch in the sea some 50km offshore. I spent eighteen hours adrift on the open sea before I was eventually rescued by an air/sea rescue float-plane.'[44]

1▲   2▲ 3▼

1. The Italian Stuka ace, Nicola Patella (sitting atop the engine), with his aircraft. (Nicola Patella)

2. A formation of Italian Stukas over the Italian mainland. After purchasing these aircraft from Germany aircrews were sent to train there. The pilots were almost exclusively former fighter pilots, but the training courses were very rudimentary because of the need to get the squadrons formed and into action. (Nicola Patella)

3. Patella's Junkers Ju 87B airborne over the mountain ranges of the Albanian/Greek border regions. The bomb racks are empty indicating that they are on the way back from another mission during the brief and bloody Balkans campaign of 1941. (Nicola Patella)

4. An Italian dive-bombing attack on Eighth Army armoured personnel carriers in the Libyan desert. (Forte Perroni)

5. A good study of a close-formation Stuka duo as Sergeant Major pilot Tarantola Ennio follows his leader in Indian file after an attack on the Libyan front in 1941. (Ennio Tarantolo)

4▲ 5▼

3. The War in the Pacific, 1942–43

IN Europe the war expanded from June 1941 onwards with the German invasion of Soviet Russia where again the Stukas spearheaded the invasion that cut deep into the Russian heartland. But on 7 December of that year the conflict truly became world-wide with Japan's carrier attack on Pearl Harbor, Hawaii. Here the US Navy's main fleet was sunk at anchor by a combination of dive- and torpedo-bombing. Japanese dive-bombers were to the forefront also in their great sweep southwest, and the conquest of British, Dutch and American possessions from the Philippines, through Singapore to Sumatra and Java. The onrush also swept through British Burma and it was here that the Allies first fought back equipped with improvised dive-bombers of their own to stem the tide.

How a Tiger learnt to bite

Although many had declared that high-speed monoplane fighters would never be able to dive-bomb, time and time again during the war it was proven that they could. One of the first units to make this discovery, and then use it to good effect, were the famous 'Flying Tigers', the American Volunteer Fighter group flying for Chiang Kai-Shek's Chinese Nationalist forces in their long battle against the Japanese. One such was Colonel Robert L. Scott. He gave his view of Kittyhawk dive-bombing:

'Any pilot who actually fought the Axis enemies in the P-40 Tomahawks, Kitty-hawks or Warhawks will tell you they are tough and dependable. They will dive with the best of projectiles – including a bomb.'

He also graphically described one of his earliest dive-bombing missions undertaken in the dark days of 1942.

'My greatest bombing day came late in the month of May, when I dropped four 500lb bombs at Homalin, down on the Chindwin, where the Japs seemed to be concentrating. Early in the morning I headed south with the heavy yellow bomb, slowly climbing over the Naga Hills and through the overcast, topping out at 15,000 feet. As I continued south on the course to where the Uyu met the Chindwin River, the clouds lowered, but the overcast remained solid. In one hour, computing that I had made the 180 miles to Homalin, I let down through the overcast, hoping that the mountains were behind me. Luck was with me, as it usually was in my single-ship war, and I found the overcast barely a hundred feet thick. I couldn't see Homalin and my target area, but I kept right up against the cloud ceiling and circled warily. I knew that I was in luck: I could drop the bomb and then climb right back into the

◄

Pearl Harbor! One of the dive-bombers' most spectacular victories. Here a pair of Japanese Navy Aichi Val's are seen pulling-up over the exploding American battleship *Arizona* after one of their bombs had penetrated her magazines.

▲▼

The Commonwealth Wirraway was the North American Texan or British Havard, but built in specially constructed factories in Australia in order to give that nation a start in the business. For want of anything else they were hastily

pressed into service as makeshift dive-bombers in the Malayan débâcle in December 1941, but also served quite well in that role in the South Pacific war zone throughout the rest of the war. (Australian War Memorial)

overcast, no matter how many Jap fighters came to intercept.

Soon I saw my target – and sure enough, there were loaded barges coming out of the broad Chindwin and heading for the docks of Homalin. I continued circling against the clouds at 11,000 feet.

For I had a plan. From my practise bombings on the Brahmaputra, I had developed a rule of thumb: I would dive at some forty-five degrees; then, as the target in my gunsight passed under the nose of my ship, I would begin to pull out slowly and count – one count for every thousand feet of my elevation above the target. Then as the ship came almost level, if I was at two thousand feet when I reached the count of "two", I'd drop the bomb.

I let the four barges get almost to the makeshift wharf; then I dove from my cloud cover. As I got the middle two barges on my gunsight, I made a mental resolution not to be short – for even if I went over I'd hit the Japs in the town. As I passed three thousand feet the nearest barge went under me, and I began to pull out and count: "One-two-three-pull" putting in the extra count to insure me against being short. I felt the bomb let go as I jerked the belly-tank release, and I turned to get the wing out of the way so that I could see the bomb hit.

The five hundred pounds of TNT exploded either right beside the leading barge or between the barge closest to shore and the docks. As the black smoke cleared, I saw pieces of the barge splashing into the river a hundred yards from the explosion. I went down and strafed, but the black smoke was so thick that I could see very little to concentrate on; so I climbed to three thousand feet and waited for the smoke to clear. Then I dove for the two barges that were drifting down the river. I must have put two hundred rounds into each of them. I got one to burning, and from the black smoke it must have been loaded with gasoline. The other would not burn, but I'm sure I left enough holes in it to sink it. Coming back over the target again, I strafed the Japs in the water who were either floating dead or swimming towards shore.

On my second raid I dropped a 500lb bomb on the largest building in Homalin, which the British Intelligence reported the next day had been the police station. They said that two hundred Japanese were killed in that bombing, and that between six hundred and a thousand were killed in the series of bombings. Many bodies were picked up about thirty miles down the Chindwin at Tamu and Sittang. All four of my bombs had done some damage, and I was quite satisfied.'[45]

The wheel of dive-bombing had come full circle and the shades of Lieutenant Harry Brown must have been hovering around Colonel Scott on that historic day.

Right Places, Right Times, Wrong Aircraft

The US Army Air Force came late to the dive-bomber and they came reluctantly. However, for a brief period, a few units did operate some of the 168 A-24s delivered in 1941 following urgent orders the preceding year. Further orders followed and a total of 950 were eventually delivered to the Army, but these latter were never used in combat. Just prior to Pearl Harbor about one-third of these A-24s were hastily dispatched to the Philippines with the 27 Bombardment Group. Their fate reflected the sad fate of the A-24 in Army service.

The unit had been constituted as 27 Bombardment Group (Light) on 22 December 1939, and was activated on 1 February 1940 at Barksdale Field, flying B-18s before switching to A-20s the following March. It finally took delivery of its dive-bombers in August 1941 at Savannah, Georgia. They now became 27 Bombardment Group (Dive) and were at this time commanded by Lieutenant-Colonel W. Wright. This meant training in

◄◄

The standard USAAC fighter of the early war period was the Curtiss P-40. It was not an outstanding machine in this role, but was reliable and in production and equipped a wide variety of air forces. Later it was fitted with a drop-tank to extend its range. This led to the idea that a bomb could be carried in a similar manner and a make-shift dive-bomber was produced. (Smithsonian Institution)

◄

An impromptu conversion of a fighter to a dive-bomber was undertaken by the Flying Tigers in China in 1942 and proved very successful indeed. Although few in numbers they were able to place their bombs on highly selective and important targets, as at the Battle of the Salween Gorge. (RAF Museum)

a new technique with a new aircraft with which none of the personnel were familiar, and it was therefore done with very little enthusiasm. This is perhaps reflected in the squadrons' sarcastic dubbing of their new mounts as 'The Blue Rock Clay Pigeons'.[46]

The three squadrons, 15, 16 and 17, participated in the Army Manoeuvres at Lake Charles in September and were joined by Banshees from 91 Dive Bomber Squadron which was just forming. 'They turned in an enviable record in that they flew many more missions than the competing Groups stationed with them,' it was recorded of this period. The following month their assignment to the Philippines was announced and on 19 October officers and men began moving to San Francisco to embark aboard the transport *President Coolidge*, which sailed on 1 November. Their A-24s were destined to be flown to the West Coast, to be crated and then loaded aboard a separate vessel and to follow them out.

The *Coolidge* reached Hawaii on 6 November and, after a short stop, sailed on in company with the Army transport *Winfield S. Scott* with tanks and infantry embarked and with the heavy cruiser *Louisville* as escort. This convoy finally arrived at Manila Bay on 19 November. The squadron's personnel were quartered at Fort McKinley and were to stay

there until its aircraft caught up with it. But of course they never did.

Pearl Harbor arrived before their aircraft transport did and thus the ship was hastily diverted to the safer waters of Australia. The pilots and crews were turned into makeshift infantry, finally surrendering on 9 April and participating in the infamous Death March of Bataan. From the total strength of 87 Officers and 717 enlisted men, 47 officers were flown out to safety in Australia before the final collapse. Ninety per cent of the remaining officers subsequently died in prison ships on the way to Japan and only about three in ten of those who surrendered survived the camps.

Those aircrew that got out in time finally made contact with their Banshees again in Australia, just in time to meet the oncoming Japanese tide which surged towards the Dutch East Indies. Although they had not flown for months, 27 Bomb Group set up base at Malang in the east of Java, south of Surabaja and, on 19 February 91 Bombing Squadron was joined by the following seven Banshees:
41–15786 Major E. N. Backus/Pvt. F. H. Larronde
41–15757 Captain H. L. Galusha/Top Sgt. H. A. Hartman
41–15795 2nd Lieutenant H. H. Launder/Pvt. W. L. Kidds
41–15810 2nd Lieutenant R. Hambaugh/

Pvt. J. K. Bryning
41–15804 2nd Lieutenant J. Ferguson/Pvt. D. A. Simpson
41–15760 2nd Lieutenant D. B. Tubb/Cpl. I. A. Lencicka
41–15800 1st Lieutenant J. Summers/Pvt. D. S. Mackay

They were soon in action. The very next day these seven took off from Singosari strip to attack an enemy invasion convoy reported off the island of Bali to the east of Java. Each A-24 carried one 300kg and two 50kg bombs. Their target was the Japanese Eastern Task Force, 41 troop transports with the Japanese 48 Division embarked. This was the unit that had taken the Philippines and so 91 was finally to face the same foes as its comrades there had done. The troop convoy was escorted by the cruisers *Jintsu*, *Naka* and *Kinu* and two destroyer flotillas. A covering force, consisting of the heavy cruisers *Haguro* and *Nachi* and four destroyers, was also operating in the eastern part of the Java Sea. They were engaged in preliminary moves from Jolo to Balikpapan to embark 56 Regimental Combat Group of the Japanese Army.

It was against one of the escorting cruisers that 91 made its dive-bombing attacks that day. Major Backus led in the attack and claimed that all three of his bombs were direct hits on the vessel. Lieutenant Summers followed up against

the same target and claimed to have hit with two of his 50kg bombs on the cruiser's stern. More hits were claimed by both Captain Galusha and Lieutenant Hambaugh who each hit amidships with two 50kg bombs. Lieutenant Ferguson's bombs landed in a line some 150 yards to the right of his target. There was no air cover over the convoy, but Japanese gunners aboard the ships nailed Lieutenant Tubbs aircraft, and it was last seen diving into the water. Another Banshee took a cannon shell but got back safely. Lieutenant Launder's aircraft also failed to return to base after the mission and it was also feared lost, but happily both he and his gunner turned up safely the following day. He had indeed been hit and forced to make a crash-landing off Bali but survived it. He claimed to have sunk a transport.

The Japanese later reported that the cruiser *Kinu* and one transport were damaged in these attacks. Despite some post-war assertions that this one sortie marked the end of their combat duty, in fact 91 had two A-24s airborne on the 25th when Captain Galusha and Lieutenant Hambaugh took-off to attack enemy ships at Bali itself. No ships were seen and so they bombed the airfield instead, meeting no resistance from flak or fighters.

On 27 February three Banshees sortied with an escort of eleven P-40 fighters. They sighted the main invasion convoy, which they estimated at about 43 transports protected by 15 destroyers. Three or four of the destroyers seemed to be on fire, but in fact they were probably laying smoke to shield their charges from attacks by an Allied fleet. The American dive-bombers tipped over against this mass and claimed to have sunk one transport and damaged a second in this attack.

It was not enough. At sea, the Allied naval squadron had been wiped out by the Japanese fleet and there was little the few remaining American, Dutch or British aircraft could do to stem the inevitable. Java fell and 91 again pulled back to Australia. Here a second Banshee unit, 8 Bombardment Squadron, led by Captain Bob Ruegg, with Lieutenant Schwab and 'Buzz' Wagner (both later killed in action) had been set up at Higgins Field on the Cape York peninsular in northern Australia. From here they just about had the range to reach enemy targets on the north-eastern shoreline of New Guinea, after crossing the inhospitable Owen Stanley range of jungle-clad mountains. Among early missions, in April 1942, were three separate strikes against Japanese bases being established at Lae and Salamaua, respectively north and south of the Markham in the Huon Gulf.

As the Japanese pressed south, Allied reactions grew more desperate. With the Japanese landings on 21 July establishing a forward base still further down the northern coast at Buna, on the north side of Oro Bay, another series of air attack were called for. In attacks on 22 July the dive-bombers hit and damaged the 9,788-ton transport *Ayatosan Maru* and the destroyer *Uzuki*. Another strike followed on the 29th against the same beachhead. 8 Squadron fielded seven Banshees for this mission, but the result was catastrophic. They carried out their dives and succeeded in scoring hits which sank the 6,701-ton troop transport *Kotoku Maru*, but they did not survive long to mark this victory.

Almost immediately they were intercepted by Mitsubishi Zero-Sen fighters and the squadron was cut to ribbons. In a brief action, starkly similar to the Stuka massacre over the English Channel on 18 August 1940, the Zekes shot down six of the seven A-24s for no loss to themselves. After this tragedy the USAAF simply pulled all its remaining A-24s out of combat service.

It was a bitter experience but happily the USAAF was later to find the right aircraft for dive-bombing and to return to it with considerable skill and achievement. But that was destined to be in the European Theatre. Winning the Pacific

◄ ►
It was the 'Flying Tigers' of Chennault's American-crewed Chinese Air Force Pursuit Squadron that first utilized the P-40 for dive-bombing in the Salween Gorge attack. Problems arose when this concept was introduced, many of the Americans had only signed up to 'defend' China, not to carry out 'Attack' missions. Others, like 'Pappy' Boyington, thought the whole idea of dive-bombing in a P-40 was lunacy, and said so, forcefully. But some former US Navy dive-bomber pilots thought the job could be done and tried it. It proved a great success. (Smithsonian Institution)

War was therefore left to the dive-bombers of the US Navy and Marine Corps.

Strike from Rabaul – Operation 'A' – I-Go Sakusen

Although the Japanese Navy's splendid Kyukoka Bakugekiki (Dive Bomber) squadrons suffered heavy casualties at the naval battles of Coral Sea and Midway in May and June 1942, and in the wastage during the struggle for Guadalcanal, Admiral Yamamoto determined to throw them in to the offensive once more in the spring of 1943. The main landing-fields around their base at Rabaul began to fill up with carrier aircraft from 1 Koku Sentai (Aircraft Carrier Squadron) of the Third Fleet based at Truk. These new Aichi D3A2 Type 99 aircraft, the Carrier Dive-Bomber Model 11, were mainly crewed with fresh pilots and navigators straight from training schools in the home islands. They had a leavening of experienced and combat-hardened personnel to lead and stiffen them, but the fierce attrition of the second half of 1942 had watered-down the Val squadrons from the peak efficiency of a year before.

Yamamoto had seen all his pre-war forecasts come true, a flood of early victories and then the halt and steady reversal as the American industrial power-house churned out more and more men and machines at a rate Japan could not hope to match. His new offensive, using Rabaul as an unsinkable carrier, was a last-ditch chance for the air arm of the Navy, the arm he had done so much to build up and in which he believed in, to try and stem that Allied tide. The American advances up the Solomon Islands chain threatened Rabaul from one side. American and Australian probes along the north-east coast of New Guinea from Allied bases in the Milne Bay area, and overland from Port Moresby, were converging on Buna and threatening Rabaul from another. The pincers had to be halted and reversed Yamamoto was a realist and doubted if that could be achieved now, but he hoped an all-out air offensive would at least cause his enemy such heavy casualties and losses to the Allies' shipping and aircraft that the twin attacks would be slowed down. Time was now desperately required for Japan to consolidate her own defence line. Dreams of further glorious advances south and east to Samoa and beyond had now gone for good.

The Japanese plan was Operation 'A' (I-Go Sakusen) and called for a series of strikes against targets in both the Guadalcanal and New Guinea areas. Heavy air raids were to be launched on General Douglas MacArthur's main supply bases at Port Moresby, Oro Bay and Milne Bay in the extreme south-east of the island. Reinforced by several hundred carrier aircraft, the operation began with an attack in the Guadalcanal area on 7 April and was followed up by similar-strength attacks on Oro and Harvey Bays on the east coast on 11 April and the harbour and airfields at Port Moresby on 12 April.

The returning Japanese airmen reported great success and it was thought that they had sunk a cruiser, two destroyers and twenty-five merchant ships as well as destroying 134 Allied planes in air, many more on the ground and wrecked four airfields. Even if this had been true it would have been a very small dent in the vast Allied armada. But it was far from true. The Japanese flyers had inflicted remarkably little damage and had suffered heavy losses in return, at least 49 Japanese planes failing to return and others being damaged. Far from stopping the Allies, the attacks had crippled the Japanese Carrier Fleet until yet more recruits could be hastily trained up to replace the losses.

Strangely, for so normally astute a commander, Admiral Yamamoto was convinced his aircraft had scored a great victory, but they had not. He was to die in ignorance that his last battle was a

failure for a few days later his own aircraft was intercepted, destroyed and the Admiral himself killed. This last desperate gamble and the loss of Yamamoto himself marked the end of the line for Japan in the Pacific.

But if the operation had failed it was not due to any lack of skill or bravery on the part of the Japanese dive-bomber units involved. As Australian historian Bob Piper told me, 'They were very well handled.'[47] As a good example of how the Japanese Vals operated at this period of the war let us examine in detail the part they played in I-go's last raid on 14 April, against shipping in the harbour at Milne Bay.

The dive-bomber force which lifted off from Rabaul on 14 April 1943, consisted of 23 Aichi D3A2s. There were twelve dive-bombers commanded by Lieutenant Toshizo Ikeuchi from the carrier *Hito*, and eleven led by Lieutenant Tsuda, from the carrier *Junyo*. They were part of a strong force which included 36 Betty long-range bombers and an escort of 30 Zeke and Hap fighters. Their assigned targets were the shipping in the harbour.

First warning of the raid was received from the radar plot at 1127 hours, and this was followed at 1146 by a Preliminary Warning from Kitava '41 Bombers 20 fighters Heading West'. Finally, at 1233 hours, Dawson Island reported '45

to 50 Bombers heading West'.[48]

The Japanese formation split into two some 110 miles north of Milne Bay. While one went direct to the East Cape, the other went due south to Dawson Island, then turned west and rejoined the first wave at the mouth of the Bay. They then proceeded up the bay in successive waves, the dive-bombers then apparently breaking off to the south and executing a semi-circle, at the same time losing height.

The entire force arrived over Gili Gili, Milne Bay at about 1215, the twin-engined bombers in close formation followed by the dive-bombers with the fighters as top cover.

Defensive attempts were made by some 36 P-40 Kittyhawk fighters of Nos. 75 and 77 Squadrons RAAF. All were airborne and carried out interceptions at heights of 20,000 to 25,000 feet over the bay. Visibility was good at 20–30 miles. They reported the Japanese aircraft were camouflaged dark green and brown all over and that this was very effective. They claimed to have destroyed five of the Mitsubishis, one Val and one Zeke, and to have damaged two more Bettys and a fighter. Some American P-38 Lightnings from Dobodura base also intercepted this raid and claimed another Betty and another Zeke destroyed. More P-38s from Moresby

were too late to intercept. The Australians' own losses were one P-40 missing but the pilot was safe, and one pilot wounded from No. 75 Squadron and one P-40 with its pilot, Flying Officer Melrose, missing, with three more making crash-landings from both squadrons, as did one P-38, killing its pilot Lieutenant Sells, USAAF.

The Australian Intelligence report recorded: 'Their plan of attack was apparently to make a large-pattern high-level bombing attack on the harbour and follow this up with dive-bombers. There was no doubt whatsoever that the target was shipping.'[49]

The Betty started their high-level bombing at 1230 hours, dropping a half-mile-long pattern of about 100 bombs right across the anchorage, completely obliterating the harbour. However spectacular, Flying Officer A. M. Stewart of No. 71 Wing HQ noted that these 'dropped several sticks harmlessly in the bay and only thirty craters were found on land. Turnbull Strip received one direct hit. Then the Vals tipped over. Only the dive-bombers scored hits.' Strangely enough less than half the dive-bomber force was reported by the defenders in the first attack. But it provides a first-class account of the methods used.

'Ten Vals approached in line astern from WNW at 10,000 to 12,000 feet

◀
A Japanese D3A1 'Val' takes off from the deck of her home carrier, to the cheers of the ship's company, to strike at an Allied Task Force over the horizon. In the early months of 1942 the Navy dive-bombers created havoc from Pearl Harbor to Colombo and Darwin almost with impunity. (Author's collection)

◀◀
Scourge of the Eastern Seas. Aichi 'Val' dive-bombers warm up preparatory to launch from their carrier during the Indian Ocean sortie which cost the Royal Navy an aircraft carrier, two heavy cruisers and several smaller vessels as the dive-bombers of the Imperial Navy ran riot in April and May 1942. (Author's collection)

losing height to about 7,000 feet and made individual runs on shipping in the harbour. They then swung away and made second individual runs from between SW and SE (this may well have been the second half of the dive-bomber force). Dives started at approximately 7,000 feet pulling out at about mast-head height.'[50]

Many of the Kittyhawks followed the Aichis down in their dives and therefore had to run the gauntlet of the friendly AA fire. They were reported to have 'wiggled their wings' to show off their markings although it is doubtful whether the gunners would take their fingers off the triggers while under such concentrated assault.

The fire from the ships and ashore was intense. Initial firing was commenced up to heights of 20–27,000 feet and some 245 rounds of heavy shell were fired at the twin-engined bombers and 110 rounds of 40mm were fired off at the dive-bombers. The gunners ashore claimed to have destroyed one Val and one Zeke. The merchant ships Balik-papan and Gorgon and the mine-sweeper Kapunda claimed a further three Vals destroyed between them.

Three ships were hit by the Japanese dive-bombers, an Australian corvette and two Dutch cargo ships. The cargo ship was the Van Heemskerk which was

manouevring off Waga Waga. She took many direct hits and was strafed by the dive-bombers' cannon as well. This caused extensive damage and fires aboard her, but her crew were able to beach her in the vicinity of Waga Waga before abandoning ship. Casualties in this ship were high. The auxiliary vessel Moa Moa was strafed off Kanakope by one of the Vals as she made her getaway pull-out, but reported nil casualties.

The coaster was the Gorgon which was hit twice while zig-zagging off Lau Lau Island. There were a large number of casualties aboard this ship many of which were caused by a bomb entering her side right on the waterline. It went through her plating here at an angle of 45± and exploded on the cattle deck, where a great number of the Javanese and Chinese crew had taken shelter. The explosions caused a fire which was later brought under control and caused moderate damage to the ship. Gorgon herself claimed to have shot down one dive-bomber in this attack and to have contributed to the destruction of a second.

Another freighter, the Van Cutthorn, was secured at Lyell Wharf at the western end of the harbour, and was also subjected to dive-bombing attack, being hit once and near-missed three

times. The hit caused a fire and extensive damage as well as casualties.

The total Allied personnel losses were reported as one Australian NCO and ten merchant ships' crewmen killed, six ship's officers, two ratings and fourteen crewmen, plus 23 US Army shipping personnel and 25 crew wounded.

As the Japanese dive-bombers pulled out over the bay and started to re-assemble they were subjected to further fighter attacks. Lest it be thought that the Vals were mere sitting ducks (as is so often still falsely claimed about all dive-bombers), let the report of a Kittyhawk fighter pilot speak for itself about the defensive capabilities and methods used. The narrator is Flight Sergeant P. M. Sheahan of No. 75 Squadron, RAAF. At about midday Sheahan with Flying Officer Brown had been scrambled away as 'Purple One' and 'Purple Two', with instructions to join up with the rest of their squadron. They headed down Milne Bay, eastwards, climbing in line abreast at an interval of approximately 200 yards. They had levelled off at about 18,000 feet, and begun weaving over position 'B' as Fighter Sector reported enemy formations in the vicinity. They heard 'Bandits' were approaching base and turned, flying west along the north shore of the bay and witnessed bomb explosions in the anchorage.

'At that time, approximately 1220 hours, I sighted fighters doing a head-on attack on large bomber formations in position west of Turnbull Field. They were five or ten miles due west of me, and approximately 1,000 feet above my height. I sighted dive-bombers attacking the shipping. I saw at least a dozen in various stages of their attacks. They were attacking from south over Waga Waga, to the north side of bay; staying low down, the leading bombers seemed to be in broad vics of three and appeared to be doing about 300mph.

Flying Officer Brown said, "Will attack those Dive Bombers," whereupon he rolled over to the left. I was line abreast on his starboard before attacking, so I was left two hundred yards behind. At approximately 10,000 feet a Zero attempted to attack "Purple One". I gave him a short squirt at about fifty down to twenty yards range. They seemed to go in but I did not watch him.

At approximately 8,000 feet I saw tracers going past my port wing and underneath it. I opened up to full throttle and did a diving aileron turn and the firing stopped. I pulled out of the dive and headed for a dive-bomber. I had not got near any when I saw more tracers going past my port wing. I did a violent lurch and did a diving steep turn to the left. My speed was approximately 400-

mph and I was not troubled by whatever was on my tail after the original two-second burst.

Coming out of my turn I found dive-bombers in front of me, diving at the ships. They were Vals. I did not see dive brakes on them; they seemed to be strafing a big ship and scoring hits. I could see red flashes from a little ship which appeared to be firing at the dive-bombers with a small cannon. I saw no fire from the ships near me and the dive-bombers.

I headed for the nearest Val and about one hundred yards astern he appeared to see me and turned slightly, whereupon I opened with a short burst from almost line astern. I thought I'd hit him, because he turned on his side and almost touched the water before recovering. Whereupon I closed up to fifty yards line astern and he did violent steep turns, with some vapour trails. Except for one burst all my bursts fell short by about ten feet.

I chased him round for about three miles, when tracers started coming past my port side. I opened full throttle, skidded, put my wings in the vertical plane and made off in a northerly direction to the north shore of Milne Bay. There was a strong smell of glycol and I though I was hit in the cooling system. I could see nothing wrong up front so looked around and saw three dive-

bombers going east at low altitude fifty feet along the North shore of the bay. One was straggling so I came in and approached him from the stern. At one hundred yards I opened fire and got off two bursts when I noticed tracers and splashes in the water on my port side. A Zero was making an attack on me from vertically above. I cut my throttle and skidded to the left. The Zero pulled straight up above me in the start of a loop. I pulled up after him and opened my throttle wide and put a burst in his general direction. I then nosed down and jinked for the hills, but he did not follow me. I avoided Turnbull Field which was close and went to Gurney Field, where I heard the order to land. I landed wheels down. The aircraft had 30 large calibre holes in near port part of fuselage and one cannon hole in leading edge of port tailplane. A hydraulic line was severed by a .30 calibre bullet.

I now think that Vals can out-turn a Kittyhawk at three hundred miles per hour. I saw no return fire from the rear of the Vals.'[51]

The all-clear was sounded at 1307 hours. In fact the claims of the Allies to have destroyed at least six of the Japanese dive-bombers was 100 per cent error, for only three failed to return to Rabaul that afternoon, one Val from the Ikeuchi Unit and two from the Tsuda

The American aircraft carrier *Hornet* under attack at the Battle of Santa Cruz in 1942. Lieutenant Seki's Aichi Val dive-bomber can be seen making its final dive onto the carrier's vulnerable wooden flight deck. (Imperial War Museum)

Admiral William Martin in 1969 when C-in-C American 6th Fleet in the Mediterranean. As a young dive-bomber pilot, Bill Martin flew a Dauntless at the Battle of Midway and participated in many dive-bombing missions while aboard the USS *Enterprise*, including one mission when he was shot down over the target and survived to escape the next day. (Bill Martin)

Major Lofton Russell 'Joe' Henderson, United States Marine Corps. After a distinguished pre-war career Henderson led the Marine Air Group based on Midway Island to immortality during the great naval battle of June 1942, where he was killed while leading the attack. (United States Marine Corps Official)

unit. Once again they had demonstrated, for the *n*th time, the clear superiority of this method over altitude attacks.

Two brave men

Vice-Admiral William I. Martin commanded the US Sixth Fleet in the Mediterranean in 1967–69. A quarter of a century earlier he was young Lieutenant Bill Martin, the Executive Officer of VS-10 aboard the aircraft carrier *Enterprise*. At that time his outfit was equipped with the Douglas SBD Dauntless dive-bomber. The Navy certainly had no problems handling these machines, in fact they used them so well that the Dauntless became the leading weapon in the destruction of Japanese shipping in 1942. At the decisive battle of Midway in June of that year Martin led the *Enterprise* strike force in the attack which sank the *Kaga* even though a fault in his dive-bomber's electrical arming mechanism had prematurely dumped his 500lb bomb into the ocean soon after take-off. Rather than abort, Bill Martin kept going and led off the stack in the actual attack, strafing the huge carrier and diverting Flak away from his following companions, until his machine-guns jammed.

The results of this battle, when the American Dauntless squadrons sank four big Japanese carriers, turned the

tide of the Pacific War, but Martin kept on fighting all the way through it. As he told me:

'I had three consecutive combat deployments (averaging eleven months each). At first I was flying the SBD dive-bombers, then Grumman TBF Avengers, because they were the first with radar. In daylight and good weather, we dive-bombed with this machine, at night and in 'Instrument Weather', we did low-level "masthead" bombing! In the third deployment I flew as Commander Night Air Group and here I flew both Night Fighter (Grumman F6F-5N Hellcats) and Night Attack (Grumman TBF-1N) missions.'[52]

At the Battle of Santa Cruz in October 1942, Bill Martin had just thrown himself clear from the aircraft carrier *Hornet*'s island superstructure when an Aichi Val dive-bomber, heavily hit crashed full tilt into the spot where he had just been standing. That plane had been piloted by an equally brave dive-bomber pilot, Lieutenant-Commander Mamoru Seki, who had led *Shokaku*'s twenty-two Aichis in conjunction with Lieutenant Sadamu Takahashi's twenty dive-bombers from the aircraft carrier *Zuikaku*.

Seki had led his force off their carrier at 0755 on the morning of 26 October and flew against the US Task Force. En route to their target the Japanese dive-

bombers actually passed two formations of American dive-bombers heading towards their own fleet, their fighter cover breaking off to engage the second group and leaving Seiki's force with hardly any protection. This might have had dire consequence when they ran into the CAP (Combat Air Patrol) over their target, but luck was with the Japanese initially. The Vals were actually sighted at 0859 at a height of 17,000 feet by the defending US fighters, but they were themselves at too low a height to effectively intervene. Seki radioed at once 'All planes go in'.

All depended on the fleet's AA guns as the dive-bombers commenced their dives, most of them concentrating on the *Hornet*. Pressing on down through the Flak the Vals scored one direct hit on the carrier's flight deck at 0910. Then came Seki's gallant sacrifice. It was described by another Japanese pilot, Lieutenant Kazuo Yakushiji, who survived the attack:

'Lieutenant-Commander Seki's 'plane seemed to have taken several direct hits soon after he gave the order to attack. His aircraft was directly in front of mine as I went into my dive. I noticed the bomber enter the dive and suddenly begin to roll over on its back. Flame shot out of the bomber and, still inverted, it continued diving toward the enemy

A rare view of an Aichi 'Val' taking off from a jungle airstrip somewhere in the Solomon Islands in 1943. By now the Navy dive-bomber crews had suffered heavily in the great naval battles and fresh crews were being thrown in wholesale and taking losses out of all proportion to their successes. The tide had turned. (Kantosha)

▶

A new squadron of Vals undergoing training in the home islands *circa* 1942. Note bold markings of aircraft (the censor has been at work on the tail number). As the war progressed and losses increased, the period of training was more and more curtailed and the skill of the aircrew dropped dramatically with each great battle until by 1944 most of the veterans had been killed. (Robert and Misake Piper)

ship.'[53] The death dive of Lieutenant Seki has been immortalized in a classic photograph reproduced here. Bravery in dive-bomber pilots knew no nationality barriers.

An Aussie Anson

The claim for the least-likely candidate for a dive-bomber must surely go to Australia. They made good use of the purpose-built Vultee Vengeance, and excellent use of makeshift dive-bombers, the Commonwealth Boomerang and Wirraway, but the strangest conversion of all was, the sedate Avro Anson! Let former Flight Lieutenant James M. Swan, RAAF, tell the story:

'A fact probably not widely known was that in this country the Avro Anson was at one time groomed to act as a dive-bomber in its role as a maritime patrol aircraft. I was attached to 73(R) Squadron, RAAF, using Avro Ansons from late January 1943 until early February 1944. This squadron was based at Nowra, NSW, with a detached Flight at Camden (about 25 miles south-west of Sydney). In company with sister squadrons these units provided maritime reconnaissance and anti-submarine patrols for many convoys and ships which passed along the Australian coastline.

Now, for the first ten months of my tour, the accepted anti-sub patrol was

carried out at about 1,200 feet plus or minus a bit depending on weather, sea conditions, etc., the plan was that on sighting a sub at or above periscope depth the aircraft would carry out a shallow dive to cross the sub at an angle, dropping our two 250lb in stick by pilot judgement, usually from between 300–500 feet. As I remember it, the bombs were GP and the anticipated concussion was the limiting factor in the dropping height. With practise (the aircraft carried four 8lb practise bombs plus sea-markers, etc.), which was frequently carried out at the end on a patrol when homeward bound, the pilots became quite accurate and I feel sure would have inflicted damage to a sub, but possibly not destroy it. After some months the 250s were replaced by two 375lb depth-charges, a change which called for removal of our rear turrets and other weight-reducing devices as we were always overweight anyway and the extra was the final straw. However, there were two great advantages: the depth-charges were set to explode at depth and were therefore much more lethal to the subs, and because of the underwater explosion, there was no height restriction on the drop except for possible skip. This latter was possibly not a problem as the Anson was not going all that fast at any time. Again with practise, it became

accepted that the practise bombs could be dropped into the smudge of aluminium powder from a sea marker each time, possibly a maximum error of 20–30 feet, from a height of 50 feet.

Enter Graham Pockley of 'Pockley's Corner' fame, whose remarkable exploits in anti-submarine operations are well known. He was posted out from England and given the job of revamping our Anson operation. Well his first major change was to change patrol height from the 1,200 feet or so to 5,000 feet. The theory I believe was to extend visibility range, possibly see deeper into the water and not be so readily seen by a searching sub. On a sighting being made, the aircraft was to be positioned on track towards the sub at the usual angle to sub track and when at the appropriate position power pulled off and the aircraft 'bunted' into the steepest dive possible. Bomb release was made quite high, I can't remember at what height but seem to recall about the 1,000 feet mark to allow for recovery.

Well this may have worked with whatever type of aircraft Graham Pockley had worked on, but the success rate of our crews during practice was dismal — the most that could be said was that we hit the Pacific Ocean. To go from an accuracy of a few feet to such inaccuracy was a blow to the unit. There were many

problems with such attack plans, the Anson very rapidly reached its Vne and the angle of dive had to be reduced, this caused the pilot to lose sight of the target very early. The Cheetah had fixed pitch props and reached max RPM with no piston load, they fairly screamed! So if the pilot did not keep speed, angle of dive and engine revs in control, there was a fair chance he would ride a wingless dart towards the target; if he did keep things in control, he lost sight of the target anyway. Perhaps a roll-over dive, like the Stukas used, might have helped but was not used probably due to wing stress, from a handling viewpoint. I found during testing it did improve accuracy just slightly. A look through my log-book indicates some high-level dive-bombing practise in early November and quite a lot of bombing practise (unspecified) for about three weeks beforehand. As I was Second-in-Command, Camden Flight at that time I could well have been involved in assessment and practise but details escape me. It is also significant that after the beginning of December 1943 the description of completed operations changed from "Patrol" to "Search" except in very few cases. I seem to remember that the original form of patrol, which consisted of a creeping line ahead of the convoy with an occasional sweep down each side and around the rear, was replaced by a search which was really an area surveillance through which convoys would pass. This was considered more effective when combined with the 5,000 feet patrol height and the dive-bombing attack. Even after all these years I am not convinced!'[54]

Captain Ron Walesby of No. 67 Squadron gave me additional details of this brief but no doubt traumatic change in the Anson's otherwise staid career:

'. . . the procedure was because in level flight the target disappeared under the nose so Pockley's idea of dive-bombing was to keep the target in sight as long as possible and hopefully until bomb release. The other point was that the aircraft would obviously reach Vne far too soon if one just shoved the nose down.

So the procedure was to approach the target at 5,000 feet, then at an appropriate time (guesswork) pull off power and hold the nose up until the approach to a *stall* was noticeable and then bunt into a dive. This was supposed to result in the aircraft diving from 5,000 feet to (I think) 2,000 feet for bomb release at about Vne or when the Navigators knuckles went white, whichever occurred first! This then allowed the aircraft to pull-out before reaching danger height. It was found that our "Aggies" were well overloaded so perhaps the two bombs would have kept going anyway if not released at the end of the dive and before pulling-out. I don't think the system was ever used in anger because we changed to carrying depth-charges, just as well or there would have been a mutiny of NAVs and WAGs.'[55]

▲
The RAAF was another early customer for the Vultee when their original orders for the Brewster Bermuda had to be cancelled due to production problems and delays with that aircraft. The Vengeance equipped five RAAF squadrons who took them into combat most successfully in New Guinea where they operated from Nazdab airfield in support of Allied forces in New Guinea. This formation is from No. 23 Squadron near Merauke in 1944. (Frank Smith via Chris Shores)

▼
An Australian Vengeance kicks up a dust storm as it taxiis out on to its jungle airstrip in preparation for another sortie. Note the white tail distinctive of Allied aircraft operating in this theatre at this stage of the war. Australian Vengeance squadrons flying this American-built dive-bomber found it common for US warships to open fire on them and they were often intercepted by American fighters who took them for hostile aircraft! (Australian War Memorial)

Klavia Fumicheva, Pe-2 pilot and twice Heroine of the Soviet Union. (Soviet Official)

Katerina Fedotova. (Soviet Official)

14.
The European War, 1943–45

IN Europe the major struggle continued on the vast Eastern Front where the armies and air forces of the two opposing dictators were locked in mortal combat. In the summers of 1941 and 1942 the Stukas had led the great German victories which had taken Hitler's armies to the River Volga and to within sight of the Caspian Sea. But it was the Soviet Pe-2 dive-bomber which led the great Russian counter-attacks that ended at the door of the Reichstag itself.

Elsewhere, the British and Americans cleared the North African coast in 1943, invaded Sicily and Italy, landed in Normandy and the South of France and then closed the ring on Berlin from the west. The battles were smaller in scale, but here again dive-bombers and dive-bombing featured prominently on every land and sea front right up to the very last days.

Vertushka over the Steppe

The introduction of the highly advanced Petlyakov PE-2 Peshka into the Soviet Union air armoury was widely welcomed, but initially it caused a few headaches. In the first place it was both technically and aerodynamically far ahead of what had gone before. This meant difficulties in production, which the shift of the factories beyond the Urals for safety complicated even further, and in providing sufficiently skilled crews to do justice to the aircraft itself.

The formation of the Pikiruyuschchii Bombardirovshchik (Dive Bomber) Regiments began to take place early in 1941 and by the end of that year some 1,869 had been produced. Such was their success that a grand total of 11,426 were built by the end of the war and equipped 75 per cent of the Soviet twin-engined bomber squadrons in 1945. Initially however the skills and expertise required to crew the Peshka (pawn) were beyond the scope of the crews converted from slower types. Moreover, in common with other air arms lately converted to dive-bombing, the Russians had to develop and perfect their own techniques almost from scratch and then test them.

As usual, outstanding dive-bomber pilots were thrown up in the harsh testing ground of war. These pilots tended to be

◄

Katerina Fedotova in the cockpit of her Pe-2 dive-bomber with its Swallow motif. (Soviet Official)

►

Unique aerial photograph showing bombs bursting on a German airfield during an attack by a women's Pe-2 dive-bomber squadron in the winter of 1944/45 during the offensive which cleared Belorussia and took the Soviet armies to the Vistula, just a stone's throw from Berlin. (Author's collection)

►►

Soviet women pilots flew with great distinction in the war and many of the most famous flew as dive-bomber pilots with the 587th Dive-Bomber Regiment equipped with the Pe-2 and the Tamansk (Women's) Air Regiment. Typical of these heroines was Lieutenant Natasha Meklin, seen here in 1945, on the Second Belorussian Front, when she had 1,000 combat sorties to her credit. (Novosti Press Agency, Moscow)

◄

Marina Dolin with her Pe-2. (Soviet Official)

◄

Katerina Fedotova on return from a sortie with fellow air and groundcrew. (Soviet Official)

born dive-bomber experts and had the natural flair and feel for it. Like Egusa in Japan or Rudel in Germany, such pilots became legendary in their skill. On the Eastern Front such specially gifted pilots, of both sexes, became well known for their accuracy, and were known as 'Snipers' so precisely could they place their bombs on target. Such expertise was always valuable, but the war in Russia was of vast dimensions and there was also the necessity for mass coupled with accuracy. Traditional bombers could not deliver it and so the need was to train up the rapidly expanding dive-bomber regiments to a minimum standard of skill.

In the Soviet Union the challenge and potential of the Pe-2 dive-bomber brought to the fore people like Colonel (later Major-General) Ivan Polbin. It was he who took the Pe-2 to war and wrote tactics in the heat of battle. Later he was to be twice decorated as 'Hero of the Soviet Union', the latter posthumously due to his death in action at Breslau near the end of the war. It was Polbin who developed the famous Vertushska method of dive-bombing in this machine.

This method required the attacking squadrons to first locate their target and then form up in a large circular formation overhead, a 'carousel'. This continuously circling formation of aircraft tended to confuse the mobile Flak gunners which accompanied every German armoured and motorized column, not allowing them to 'home-in' on a pre-determined target until it was too late. Once the target had been properly identified the leading aircraft would peel-off from this circle and initiate the dive-bombing attack by diving at an angle of approximately 70 degrees. The rest of the formation would break formation in turn and follow the leading aircraft down to the target at intervals of between 1,500 to 2,000 feet. This ensured that as one aircraft delivered its bombs at least two others were on their way down and the gunners would have to continually switch targets approaching them at speed.

Another outstanding pilot, Colonel A. G. Federov, was directed by Colonel (later Lieutenant-General) N. I. Krolenko, Deputy Chief of Staff on the VVS (Voyenno-Vozdushnyye Sily or Air Force), to draw up an official working paper for the correct use of the dive-bomber units. This incorporated Polbin's work to date. Practical testing was con ducted by Fedorov on the bombing ranges, but the final test came in battle. Fedorov himself led a special Pe-2 squadron into action against German tanks and artillery in the area of Roslav. The first flight of three Peshki concentrated in 60-degree dives against the German Flak positions to keep them busy while the others formed the 'Merry-Go-Round'. The tactic worked and not until it was repeated a second time did the enemy cotton on. By then it was too late and accurate bombing was conducted. This set the seal on Polbin's Vertushka technique.

Valentina Kravchenko, a woman pilot with No. 587 Air Regiment, here gives several good examples of how this technique was put into combat practice at the front, and she also gives some fresh insights into Russian dive-bombing techniques. Here is one action early in 1943:

123

◄
Last mission of a dive-bomber legend. An illustration showing the dive-bomber attack by Pe-2s on a German strongpoint near Breslau in March 1945, when the outstanding ace, Ivan Polbin, lost his life leading the mission. (Author's collection)

►►
Soviet women dive-bomber crews. Despite the poor quality of these photographs, and their obvious posing for the camera, their rarity value demands their inclusion. They show a Russian all-women aircrew examining flight path maps for a Pe-2 mission, the return from a successful mission and a mixed crew paying homage to a dead comrade killed during an attack. (Author's collection)

'Under the wing of my aircraft, torn to pieces in smoke and fires, crippled by the January frosts, Stalingrad! The squadron flew in battle formation, approaching from the direction of the Upper Achtuba lakes. Our target is the Tractor Factory area of the city. And now, ahead of us, bombs are already exploding in this area and my heart is torn apart at the destruction by ourselves of this great works, symbol of the first 5-year-plan. But we cannot allow the enemy to occupy any part of our city. It was here that our regiment, flying its first operational sortie, started its long combat journey and joined the family of Soviet airmen and airwomen at the front.

July 1943. Western Front. At the forward airstrip of Ezovinia Yezovnia the crews received their battle orders. The flight maps were placed before us for study in detail. From the aircraft assembly points come the roar of engines as our mechanics prepare the aircraft for the sortie. The exact targets as received from HQ are carefully plotted on our maps by the *Shturman* (co-pilots or bombardiers). [It is clear from

Valentina's eye-witness descriptions that at this stage of the war the Pe-2s were flown to the target by the pilot, but that the co-pilot or bomb-aimer took over for the final, crucial dive and bomb attack.] The Shturman mark carefully the route, the target itself and calculate the time of flight. Meanwhile the pilots have already received their ground mechanics' reports on the state of readiness of their aircrafts' armament and radio-equipment. Everything checks out. The aircrew assist in the hanging on the racks of the 250- and 500-kilo bombs, both groups working in harmony to get the job done they both know so well. Thus Ania Artemova, Ira Zubova, Sonia Mosolova and others are competing to be the first of the crews ready for take-off. But the bombs are very heavy and the girls have to help each other to hang them under the aircraft and set up their detonators.

Within a few minutes, however, the aircrews are in their aircraft and these soon begin to roll heavily down the runway, wing-to-wing. The airfield is now filled with the roar of aero engines, the wet grass bending and swaying

under the wind from the propellers and then the first three dive-bombers begin to get airborne. Aloft, the trio almost appear to be tied to each other as they increase speed, simultaneously climbing, retracting their undercarriages and gaining height. After the first trio gets into the sky they are quickly followed by 2, 3 and 4 Groups. Such a group take-off requires from pilots a particular exactness and skill. Serious and full of concentration therefore are Sasha Egorova, Nalia Matuchina and Tonia Skoblikova. Easily and surely the sections come together to form a solid column, with the aircrew competing to form the most perfect formation with precise intervals between aircraft and distances between trios. Then the whole regiment steers the course to the target as assigned by HQ. Back on the ground they are confident that the mission will be accomplished and that all the bombs will fall exactly on the target.

I am flying with Timofeyeva, a squadron leader in command of nine aircraft. I loved Jennie Timofeyeva very much. I liked her because she believed in me as

a Shturman, and also because during the whole of the mission she constantly worried about everyone that she led and was responsible for, she even took my attention away from my observations and calculations from time to time, telling me to keep close watch on new crews behind us. Although this sometimes interfered with my work. I always obeyed her instructions in this respect with pleasure because these orders were given not through fear of her own safety but because of her great concern for her comrades-in-arms. I also respected the professional manner in which she held to her target course, despite frequent and strong enemy AA fire and continual attacks by enemy fighters. She always attempted to carry out to the letter her battle orders, no matter what the difficulties.

She also had a good co-ordination with our radio-operator and machine-gunner, Grishko, who was in charge of the whole regiment's communications. "Flak explosions behind to the right!," calls Grishko. "Yes, Right," replies Timofeyeva briefly, immediately making

the necessary manoeuvres of height, direction and speed to avoid the fire. "Explosions under, to the left!," "Yes," and a new swerve. And so until we reach out target.

From this point for a few seconds Timofeyeva comes under the full orders of her Shturman. You can hear only short, concise commands; To keep that way! Two degrees left, one more degree left. Well! Well!". I press the bomb-release and the bombs fall exactly on target. After the command "Unload" Jennie keeps her course, manoeuvring both height and speed and I take a series of photographs and give the last order. "Turn about." I leave my instruments and look at Jennie. On her nose and upper lips lie sweat. She is very tense and strained as we leave the target zone after the attack because this is the point that is almost always accompanied by enemy fighter attacks.She is concerned for the crews following us, especially those on the outside of the formation as they can be left behind during the turn-around manoeuvre and picked off.

Accordingly Jennie slows down as

much as possible at this time so that all our aircraft can close up for mutual support. As they do so the radio-operator gives us his observations of the dive. "Matinchina went down, but there was no fire from her machine. Kirillova is lagging behind," and so on. Only after crossing back over the front, when we are beyond the enemy fighter patrols and over our own territory, does Jennie relax and ask, "How did it go?" "Well bombed!," I reply, "Accurately." "The photos will show," Timofeyeva replies. She does not like being praised.

On the return flight, when the front line is comparatively far behind us, Jennie allows herself a little rest; she leans back against her bullet-proof armoured head-rest and flexes her tired and tense wrist muscles. Then she made out her reports about the fulfillment of the mission orders, the circumstances of the flight, which were all given in an extremely concise and clear manner.

October 1943. The airfield of Lenidova near Elna. In strict silence the aircrews stand in line while Commisar Lina Yeliseyeva speaks of our comrades who

◄

Rare Soviet paintings. Here a regiment of Pe-2 'Peshkas' en route to the target, are attacked by Me109s over the Eastern Front. (Author's collection)

▼◄◄

Graphic illustration of Pe-2s diving to bomb from high altitude German armoured formations caught in the bend of the River Don. (Author's collection)

▼◄

Twice Hero of the Soviet Union, Ivan Polbin (centre) briefing two of his young 'Peshka' aircrew prior to another mission. Polbin did much to perfect the technique, but died later in the war leading his regiment into action at Breslau. (Author's collection)

▶

Stukas on the southern front in Russia, in this case Charkov in May 1943. Here Radio-Operator Maahs receives the traditional garland to mark his 500th combat mission. On his left is Oberleutnant Haker the Staffelführer of 6.St.G.77. (Maahs)

only yesterday were our loving friends but who are now fallen in the battle for the liberty and independence of our Motherland. The heart does not want to reconcile itself with the hard fact that Liuba Gubina, Anna Tazevskaya and Lena Ponomareva will no long be flying with us. It is painful to look on Katia Batuchtina, the Shturman of Liuba Gubina. They were like sisters, took care of one another, trusted one another and now Katina suffers badly the loss of her friend and beloved superior. Liuba Gubina died trying to save her crew, staying in her machine after it had been hit, long enough for them to bale out to safety. But alas the machine had lost too much height when they came free and they were too low for the parachutes to open.

A rifle salute was fired and pilots, co-pilots, navigators, radio-operators and technicians all swore an oath over the graves of their dear friends to fight the enemy even harder and so avenge the deaths of their battle comrades. In the evening one could not hear the usual jokes and laughter. And only from the

farther corner, at first softly, and later more surely, could be heard the low controlled voice of Masha Kirllova singing the traditional pilot's death song:

"Black Raven, Black Raven,
  Why are you circling above me,
You will have no luck, Black Raven,
  I am not yet yours."

The girls begin to join in and with the singing their grief is eased and throats are not so dry. I sing along with them and love them all, these blue-eyed and brave patriots. One song follows another and again the crews begin preparing for fresh combats. Squadron-Leader Klavdia Fonickeva is making battle plans for tomorrow's attacks. Meanwhile Lina Yeliseyeva is bending over an oil-lamp, she is our Commisar and is writing mournful letters to the relatives of Liuba, Anna and Lena.

October 1943 still. The airfield at Leomidovo. Today is a significant day, everyone is proud and alert, full of life. At any moment now all the personnel of the regiment will be lined up. At a staff hut gathered representatives of divi-

sional headquarters, of the corps and of the political department of the army. At this assembly we proudly took stock of our military work up to that time. 587 Womens Regiment has made 4,419 combat sorties, shot down 38 enemy fighter aircraft and not a single enemy bomb has fallen on the area defended by our regiment. All our personnel received awards and medals of the Soviet Union.'[56]

An hour across the Garigliano

The A-36 Invader really made a lasting impression on the Italian campaign and the young dive-bomber pilots of the US Army proved themselves every bit as good at the job as their counterparts in other nations air services. They had the plane, they gave themselves the expertise. Their accuracy and results confirmed the deadliness of the combination. John Blair Watson, Jr., flew the A-36 with 86 Fighter Bomber Group, 525 Squadron, Twelfth Air Force, in Italy from October 1943 until August 1944. He had 85 missions in the A-36 plus eleven more in P-40s and ten Naples-to-Anzio liaison

◄

The relentless and tough fighting which eventually led to the conquest of Sevastopol in the Crimea, the most powerfully defended fortress in the world at that time, involved almost non-stop missions by the Stukas which often flew three or four sorties a day. Here a Kette returns after a strike on AA positions in the city. Note the wheel spats have been removed to cope with the atrocious Russian runways. (Archiv Sellhorn)

▼

The 7.Staffel St.G.77 after their last combat mission with the Junkers Ju 87B (Bertha) before it was replaced by the 87D (Dora) improved model. They are returning to their base at Sarabus-South in July 1942. (Böde)

►

Aircraft of 3.Staffel St.G.77 over the Charkov Tractor Works, strongpoint defended by the Soviets during the battle for that city in 1943. (Niermann)

missions in the C-78 (Cessna Bobcat). No. 525 was the last squadron to fly the A-36 in combat, in July 1944, as all the remaining serviceable A-36s had been turned over to the squadron. Blair kindly gave me a great deal of first-hand knowledge regarding this superb aircraft and also gives this graphic description of his very first mission:

'I flew one or two flights each day until October 24 when I was told I was going on my first mission beyond the enemy lines. On the 25th we took off with two flights, four aircraft in each flight. I was on the wing of the mission leader, Lieutenant S. C. Shortlidge. We took off to the west out over the Gulf of Salerno, then flew north over the Amalfi Peninsula and west of the Bay of Naples, finally coming near the mouth of the Garigliano River. Our target was not many miles inland, some gun emplacements on the north slope of some hills. There was a little Flak below as we crossed the coastline and again as we neared our target, making our attack seem more important. I was not able to tell whether the Flak was light, medium or heavy because I

was concentrating on flying a good position on my leader. Apparently it was not very accurate for no one reported being hit. We had reached 12,000 feet before we began our run to the target and dropped our noses to pick up speed so we would be making 270–280mph when we got over the target. The change in altitude and speed was our tactic to throw off the calculations of the German anti-aircraft gunners on the ground.

The formation slid into more of a trail in line with the leader and spread out some before he opened his dive brakes and rolled over. We maintained very strict radio silence. (During my combat tour it seemed to me that our radio discipline was much better than that of the other fighters we often heard on the air.) The signal to spread out was given by the leader with a galloping action of his aircraft caused by pumping the control stick back and forth a few times. Each pilot would then open his dive brakes when he saw the leader doing so. When the leader rolled over each pilot followed in sequence one or two seconds apart, trying not to lose sight of the one in

front. The effect was that of a very loose formation hurtling down through the air, almost as if they were dog-fighting with each other. (A description written by a P-40 fighter-bomber which I read years later said that he watched in awe as the A-36s seemed to hang over the targets they were bombing, making themselves excellent targets for the gunners below. We did not have the same point of view, objectively or spiritually! Possibly ignorance was bliss.) Each pilot in our flight tried to pick up the target in his gunsight, at the same time keeping his eyes open for the aircraft he was keyed on out in front and slightly off to one side. No guns were to be fired if it appeared some aircraft was going to cross in the line of fire.

You hoped you had a good bead on the target when the leader's bombs were released because you would toggle yours off immediately. He could be seen pulling out of his dive as he began to move up your windshield. As soon as the nose of the aircraft was a few degrees above the horizon the brakes would be closed, and full throttle was applied. This

During 1943 the Italian dive-bomber crews changed over to single-seater fighter adaptations for their missions. Here Tarantola poses in front of his Macchi MC 202 aircraft, which he named 'The Banana'. Note bomb in place under the fuselage, mottled paint scheme of this stage of the war and the Fascist emblem just in front of the cockpit. (Ennio Tarantola)

The custom-built A-36 Apache, three of which are seen stepped over the North African coast in 1943. The 'Apache' handle never stuck. When first used in the Mediterranean against the islands of Pantelleria and Sicily some pilots suggested the name 'Invader' as they were always used to support invasions, and in Italy at least, the name stuck for a while. (Hugh V. Morgan)

was the time to pick up as much speed as possible. The effect could be compared with that of a stone in a sling-shot. You felt as if some external force was kicking you forward.

Usually the flight would assemble after the attack at some rendezvous point designated during the pre-mission briefing session. This would likely be at a 4,000–6,000 feet level, depending on the nature of the terrain. The leader would circle the point, picked for its easy identifiability and probable remoteness from ground fire while the rest of the aircraft would fly up to and inside the circle. Normally, one or two circles by the leader would allow the four or eight aircraft to assemble. A twelve-ship mission, not used frequently, would take another circle or two to get together. The leader would attempt to count the number circling to make sure all were there, but an element leader might break radio silence if he detected his mate had not joined up. Fortunately, this did not happen often. Sometimes an element leader might be heard over the radio saying that he could not locate the

rendezvous and was proceeding home alone with his buddies.

The only time radios were likely to be used was in the case of someone being hit, someone getting separated from the attack or the rendezvous, or an infrequent attack by enemy fighters. We were a bit careless about the latter because the Allies had controlled the Italian skies for so long! So, "bogies" and "friendlies" in the sky were called out over the radio. Otherwise, it was a fairly silent hour or so on a mission. A pilot was little aware of his engine or propeller noise, the scream of his dive which got so much attention on the ground, the rat-a-tat of his guns, the boom of his or other's bombs exploding (he might see them), or the Flak blowing up in the vicinity. If it exploded very near he might never hear anything ever again. That kind of experience seldom got described!'[57]

Wrong Aircraft, Right Tactic, Right Result

Nobody could ever fall passionately in love with the Fairey Barracuda. It won the prize for the ugliest and most out-

landish aircraft of the war, and was a pig to get off a carrier deck. It had the elegance of a warthog and a temperament to match. But what it did have were the Fairey-Youngman flaps attached to the trailing edges of its great plank, shoulder-mounted wings. These flaps could be inclined to 30 degrees and, in theory (and, alas, in post-war reference books) were supposed to act as dive brakes and thus, in common with most Royal Navy practise during the war, enable this ungainly torpedo-bomber to be turned into a highly efficient dive-bomber. However, ex-Barracuda aircrew have informed me that in fact they were not so used, even for dive-bombing. Nor indeed were they much used for torpedo-bombing for it was a very rare thing for the Barracuda to carry a torpedo into combat. The earlier Barras had a nasty habit of not pulling-out of their practise dives, whether the flaps extended or not, and had to be treated with great care.

Despite such murderous handling characteristics, coupled with an indifferent performance from its Rolls-Royce

◄

Another A-36 on a North African desert air strip in 1943. Notice the stripe on the wing inboard of the national insignia, now a plain white star in a circle. (Hugh V. Morgan)

▶

The anti-personnel fragmentation bomb containers used by Italian and German Stukas from 1942 onward. This one is in position under the wing of the Stuka of the Italian pilot, Spezzoni. Note the warning signs are still in German. (Tarantola Ennio)

▶

Another Italian Stuka victim, a freighter caught and sunk off the island of Corfu during the brief Balkan campaign in April 1941. (Ennio Tarantola)

◄

'Dot' and her pilot. An A-37 of the 27th Fighter Group on a rough Sicilian airstrip in 1943. (Mark Savage)

◄

The North American A-24 Invader dive-bomber, a Mustang adaptation used by the USAAF in Italy and Burma with much success. This aircraft is 'Mary', which belonged to the 86th Fighter-Bomber Group. (J. E. Thompson)

◄

Other nations adopted the Vengeance, but all experienced a great many engine problems initially, the Cyclone proving most unreliable and heavy on oil fuel. Many machines were shipped out to the French air force when it reformed in North Africa in 1943. However unserviceability was very high and before all the problems could be ironed out, the French relegated them to second-line duties and replaced them with the older, smaller but more reliable SBD Dauntless. (SHAA, Paris)

▶

Towards the end of the war in Europe both the French Navy and Air Force employed the Douglas Dauntless SBC-5 dive-bomber to blast German garrisons from their formidable defences along the French Atlantic coast. This they did with great skill, and their many combat missions were made with minimum casualties despite all the dire predictions of earlier years. This trio are French Navy aircraft with their distinctive two-tone colour scheme. (ECP des Armées, Fort d'Ivry)

◄

Another most useful addition to the Tactical Air Forces' armoury in the last year of the war in Western Europe were the bomb-equipped Hawker Typhoon squadrons. Although not given the blaze of publicity of the rocket-firing missions, the dive-bombing exploits of the 'Bomphoons' were equally as devastating and accurately delivered. (RAF Museum)

◄

Even a pure thoroughbred of a fighter like the superb Supermarine Spitfire was found to be readily adaptable for dive-bombing, although the stress factors of the terminal dives did cause some problems on occasion. Here is Pilot Officer Denis Young of the 'Desert' Air Force, based near Rimini in Italy, with his Spitfire Mk 9 bombed-up with a 250-pounder under the fuselage in readiness for a rail-cut mission in 1944. (Denis Young)

▶

Another photograph of Commandant Mailfert who led the 2nd Vendee squadron in October 1944. (Musée de l'Air, Paris)

◄ ▲
Commandant Mailfert who flew the Dauntless on the Atlantic Front at the end of 1944. The brooms represent recce 'sweeps', the bombs dive-bombing sorties and his aircraft's name is also visible. (Musée de l'Air, Paris)

► ▲
The Fairey Barracuda was the typical British answer to the problem of producing a good carrier-borne strike aircraft. It was often said to have been designed by a committee and built in a madhouse. It was certainly one of the ugliest aircraft that ever flew! As a torpedo-bomber it was a disaster, but as a dive-bomber it carried out some spectacular missions, *without* resorting to its Fairey-Youngman flaps. (Fleet Air Arm Museum)

◄
The flag hoisted on the aerial denotes the Commander's machine on this Dauntless dive-bomber of GCB 1/18 in the winter of 1944–45. The unique 'cheese-grater' dive brakes are clearly visible as are an impressive number of sortie tallies under the cockpit. (Musée de l'Air, Paris)

30 or 32 Merlin engine, the Barracuda earned undying fame with its precision dive-bombing attacks which crippled the German battleship *Tirpitz* in her Norwegian achorage in 1944, scoring a record number of direct hits. As we have seen there was no hope of such attacks carrying large enough bombs to actually sink this monster, but they did cause heavy casualties on her exposed upper decks and helped keep her immobilized for a few more precious weeks.

When the Barracuda turned its attention to less well-armoured targets, results were forthcoming. The only trouble was that such targets were few and far between towards the latter part of the war. German convoys did not resemble the vast Allied groupings covering several square miles of ocean. They concentrated two or three vital ships, surrounded them with large numbers of small escorts and hugged the Norwegian coastline, with fighter cover on call. Inside the Inner 'Leads' they had islands to seaward of them and mountains inshore of them, making air approach both difficult and limited. The odds therefore

were firmly in the defenders' favour.

However, the young Fleet Air Arm aircrews took their fleeting opportunities as and when they could. Typical of such opportunism, and a good example of dive-bomber tactics as practised by the Royal Navy at this stage of the war, were strikes made on 6 May 1944. The hunting area was off the Norwegian coast in the waters off Kristiansund/North, which is located between Averoy and Smola Islands off the southern approaches to Trondheim Fjord (63±08° N; 7±43° E). The Task Force consisted of the fleet carrier *Furious*, and the escort carrier *Searcher*, escorted by the heavy cruiser *Berwick* and six destroyers. The escort carrier had Grumman Wildcat fighters embarked while *Furious* had Fairey Barracudas of No. 8 Wing (Nos. 827 and 830 Squadrons) and Supermarine Seafire fighters on her strength. It was one of the rare occasions that a few of the Barracuda used torpedoes, but the main strike was dive-bombing.

An excellent eye-witness account of these attacks was given to me by Allan H. Thomson, then a young TAG (Tele-

graphist/Air Gunner) with No. 830 Squadron. He also gives valuable information about the dive-bombing techniques employed:

'The attacking force consisted of the eighteen Barracudas of No. 8 Wing escorted by four Wildcats and 12 Seafires. It was timed to catch the two German convoys as they overlapped each other, or, as seemed likely, just after their tracks had passed. One convoy consisted of only two small ships of about 2,000 tons each, while the other was much larger and heavily escorted by Flak ships.

Our arrangement was that, if the targets were close enough, the strike force would operate as one unit; if not, then four Barracudas and four Wildcats were to attack the two lone ships. In all we had fourteen dive-bombing Barracudas and four carrying torpedoes. The smaller Barracuda force had three dive-bombers and one torpedo aircraft. The dive-bombers were armed with three 500lb medium case bombs.

The predicted position of the convoy was exactly as expected and I was in the

third dive-bombing Barracuda of the small force. Since dive-bombing at 87 degrees was extremely accurate, both ships were hit and one was left on fire and smoking heavily. They were so close together when last seen that a collision seemed almost certain. I had a photograph showing the position of these two vessels with a torpedo track running very close astern of them. So both ships were certainly badly damaged, if not sunk.

Our bombs were dropped from 1,500 feet and, as we pulled-up out of the dive, probably from a height of about 400 feet, I glimpsed an aircraft down in the water ahead of the ships. It looked like one of the Wildcats with square wingtips, but on checking the remaining aircraft we had only three Barracuda and the three Wildcats were still with us so it was obvious it was the torpedo Barracuda I had spotted. I only had a fleeting instant to observe it on the water as changing light patterns obscured it, or, more likely, it had sunk. Flotation time was about 40 seconds with full tanks, perhaps two minutes if empty. The crew was Jimmy A. Grant (Pilot), A. C. P. Walling (Observer)

and D. Bussey (TAG). For some reason only the latter two names appear on the FAA 'Missing in Action' Memorial at Lee-on-Solent.

The attack took place around midday. One of the three torpedo aircraft was lost in the other part of the action also, but no dive-bombers were lost that day. Barracudas were reckoned by we crews to be almost suicidal in dropping torpedoes. They could drop and bank away almost over the target or plough overhead at best 180 knots; either way presenting a point-blank target to the enemy. I believe lots were drawn before this attack to see who should be unfortunate enough to carry torpedoes. With two out of four lost and no dive-bombers lost on this occasion, I think Their Lordships at the Admiralty finally got the message and did not again use Barras for torpedo attack.

The only time I can recollect seeing a Barracuda using its Flaps/Dive Brakes in the full DIVE position was on a full-scale practise attack in the Clyde by the whole Wing (24 aircraft). The idea being to slow the aircraft sufficiently to reach a

safe dropping speed. Dive-bombing was always done *without* the use of flaps and we operated at 87-degrees dive until No. 8 Wing's last attack on *Tirpitz* with ten aircraft from *Furious* on 24 August 1944. Here the Barracuda carried out 60-degree Glide bombing. This was official policy that had been introduced due to metal fatigue problems on the Barra, but we in No. 8 Wing usually stuck to vertical dives as this was a safer and more precise attack approach.'[58]

On this mission the results were satisfactory for they sunk both the 7,913-ton tanker *Saarburg* and the 2,522-ton ore carrier *Almora*.

A Douglas SBD-5 Dauntless of the French Navy's 3rd Flotilla, of Groupement Aéonavale 2 under the overall command of Francis Laine, seen here in front of the devastated hangars at Cognac airfield in December 1944. From here they operated numberous highly successful dive-bombing missions against German fortresses and garrisons on the north Biscay coast around the Gironde estuary. (Admiral Francis Laine)

A fine study of a French Army Douglas Dauntless in 1944. (Musée de l'Air, Paris)

15 April 1945. The pilot, Capitaine de Frégate, Francis Laine (right) and his passenger, Minister of Marine M. Jacqurinot, after a reconnaissance sortie over the German-occupied sector of Royan. (Admiral Francis Laine)

15 April 1945. Another distinguished Dauntless crew return from observing Royan. From left to right: Vice-Admiral Lemounier, Chef d'Etat Major of the Navy, with his pilot, Lieutenant de Vaisseau, Ortolan, commander of the 3rd Dive Bomber Flotilla, Aéronavale. (Admiral Francis Laine)

15. Last actions in the Far East

AS the war in Europe drew to a conclusion, the carrier conflict in the Pacific reached a peak with the last dive-bomber duels of the naval war. After the Philippine Sea battle the Japanese carrier fleet was reduced to a handful of ships with hardly any aircraft. The final fighting was conducted by the US Navy and Marine Corps dive-bombers operating against these remnants, but mainly in support of the troops ashore, much as in Europe. In Burma the great Japanese offensives against India were blocked at Kochima and Imphal and the British and Indian dive-bombers were crucial to that success. The final British offensives were spearheaded by fighters used as dive-bombers, again as in Europe.

Providing the Vengeance's Sunday punch

Different targets required different ordnance. Armour-piercing bombs were essential in the great naval battles, although claims that modern battleship armour could be pierced by dive-bombers' weapons were an over-estimation of their capabilities.[59] Nevertheless, the dive-bomber could wreck the AA batteries of the heaviest warships, allowing in the torpedo-bombers to finish them off. Against more lightly armoured war-

ships like destroyers, or against unprotected merchant ships, the dive-bomber was indeed a deadly threat.

Against land targets however far different ordnance was required. In Burma, for example, the Japanese infantry became highly skilled at digging themselves in deep. Their bunkers were burrowed-out of the hills and covered with earth and tree trunks. Such refuges were invulnerable to anything other than a direct hit and even this would have to penetrate several feet before exploding in order to be effective. Only the dive-bomber could hit such a pin-point target in the boundless green expanse of the jungle, but unless it dropped the right weapon, fuzed in the right way and checked to explode as planned, a direct hit would be no more effective than the futile carpet bombing of the altitude bombers.

During the sieges of Imphal and Kohima on the border of India and Burma in the spring of 1944, the six British and Indian Vultee Vengeance squadrons operating in close support of Fourteenth Army, really came into their own. The Japanese surrounding the British bases dug themselves steadily closer to the perimeters, in much the same way as the Viet Minh were to infiltrate and destroy piecemeal the

An Aichi D3A1 'Val' heads off into the Pacific overcast bound for Guadalcanal. At first sorties were flown from Rabaul with little or no chance of the crews surviving, so great was the range involved. Later in the war whole carrier air groups operated from ashore and struck at targets in New Guinea and New Britain as well as at sea. (Author's collection)

Massed ranks! To bolster Rabaul's striking power for continuing attacks on the Allied advances that were steadily outflanking them, the Japanese Navy flew in batches of Aichi D3A2s to its airstrips with fresh crews and aircraft from its fleet carriers. These were thrown into battle and took heavy casualties, thus reducing the striking power of the fleet and ensuring that it went to battle at the Philippine Sea encounter with hardly any experienced aircrews available. (Author's collection)

French defences at Dien Bien Phu. That Kohima and Imphal did not go the same way owes much to the round-the-clock precision bombing of the Vengeance dive-bombers which earned high praise from the Army.

But to keep up such a high sortie rate meant an all-out effort by those keeping the aircraft serviced and ready. One of the foremost dive-bomber units in this rugged war of attrition was No. 84 Squadron, RAF. Tommy Thompson was an armourer with this squadron and he provides us with a detailed and fascinating personal account of the life and work of a dive-bomber squadron's back-up team deep in the jungle.

'In India I was posted to No. 84 Squadron and during all my previous service time and our intensive training time I had never fuzed a bomb for real.

The bombs used on the Vengeance were 250lb and 500lb. Instantaneous detonators were inserted into the nose of the bomb, and delay detonators in the tail end. Both the nose "pistol" and the tail "fuze" were armed in the same manner. When dropped, the rush of air rotated a vane which quickly "armed" the bomb. To prevent unwinding accidentally while still attached to the aircraft, a retaining fork was held in position against the vane. This fork was attached to the bomb rack by a short metal cable. Tail and nose selector switches were operated by the pilot, or bomb-aimer, so they could choose the type of explosion required. If the operator failed to select any switch and left it in the "off" position the bomb would drop with the retaining forks in place and no explosion would occur.

Nose-end pistols were simple in design and consisted of a "trigger" held in position within the body of the pistol by a soft metal shear-pin, and a threaded barrel, the end of which was fashioned as a vane. When the vane unwound this left only the shear-pin holding the trigger in place. The inertia on impact overcame the shear-pin and the trigger was impounded on to the detonator causing the bomb to explode.

The tail-end fuze operated in a similar manner, but when the vanes unwound the trigger was left suspended on a coiled spring. Again, on impact, the power of the spring was overcome and the trigger shot forward and exploded the detonator and the bomb.

Short delays were arranged by using pre-determined and coded detonators. Long delays (days or weeks) were of course more complicated and again used self-contained and pre-set delay times. This type of fuze, if my memory is correct, was known as No. 35a and was also fitted with an anti-handling device. Selector switching was still necessary, but on impact a glass vessel containing acid was smashed. The acid reacted on celluloid washers which when eaten away, allowed small ball-bearing retainers to fly back into slots and release a spring-powered trigger to detonate the bomb. The number of washers within the pistol determined the delay time.

This type of fuze (35a) was made with a weaker mid-section. The front part of the fuze had a thick rubber washer, which splayed out on being screwed into the bomb and held the fuze very tightly. Anyone attempting to defuze the bomb by unscrewing the fuze would be unaware that he was in fact only unscrewing the top half (the weak mid-section allowing the fuze to split in two). The ball-bearings would fly apart and the trigger would shoot into the detonator, exploding the bomb.

If an armourer cross-threaded the fuze, and it stuck, there was no way he could remove it and the bomb would be moved to a safe area and destroyed. By the way, I confirmed my belief, in fact, that the "old-timers" were stale, by pretending I had done just that, cross-threaded, and muttered aloud that I would have to unscrew it. The WO Armament, on a visit,

The rear twin .303in machine-guns of the Vultee Vengeance operated by the WOP/AG (Wireless Operator/Air Gunner). Note armoured plate, hand grips and sight. In RAF service the guns were later replaced by the more reliable .5in. (RAF Museum)

"to see how things were", instantly beat a very hasty retreat!

Usually both instantaneous detonators in the nose and delays in the tail were used on bombing missions. This allowed the pilot at the time of bombing (especially dive-bombing) to use his judgement whether due to changed circumstances, or alternative and unexpected targets, to choose the type of explosion required. By switching the selector tail end "on" he had a delayed explosion and by switching both selector switches "on" he had an instantaneous explosion. You will appreciate that the latter type of selection rendered the delay immaterial anyway.

When a pilot had no choice but to do exactly as briefed – delay explosion only or bring bombs back – the nose was not even allowed a detonator, and the nose ring was left in place.

This nose ring was used to transport bombs, and the quick method of loading a bomb trolley was to insert a phosphor-bronze rod in the nose ring and, with a man at the tail end, manhandle it on. On one occasion my tail-end man moved in his arc too quickly for me and the nose ring slid along the bar, pinched my hand and I let the bomb drop the short distance to the ground. Unfortunately it took the bar with it and gouged a two-inch-long and half-inch-deep cut in my calf. My only war wound was stitched up by the MO and I was back on duty in half an hour.

No. 84 Squadron, equipped with the Vultee Vengeance, was posted to Khumbergram to help in the defence of Imphal and Kohima. I was 22-years-old, only a LAC and virtually in charge of the bomb dump, fuzing all the bombs needed. Senior airmen to me had spent so much time overseas that fast and newer technology had passed them by. This is a fact. Why? I cannot explain but I know it to be true.

When the time came for our first bombing operation, and thus for me to fuze my very first bombs, I remember I did my job well and I was proud that my training had not let me down. It was only when the "kites" were airborne that overwhelming doubts flooded into my mind. I became scared I had done something wrong. Would the bombs explode? Would the pilot perform correctly? Would I be responsible for blowing up one of the aircraft – or the whole bloody squadron?

Everything went according to plan and the aircraft returned safely. I fuzed and de-fuzed many hundreds of bombs after that but nothing has matched that first exhilaration.'[60]

Right Tactic, Right Result, Wrong Target?

The clumsy Barracuda was phased out by the Royal Navy for the last part of the war and the British Pacific Fleet, built around the most modern ships and aircraft, was sent out to act as a fourth Task Group for the US Fleet's final drives on Japan by way of Okinawa. The Americans had newer, larger, faster, better-armed, better-equipped and supplied ships, more modern aircraft and plenty of them. None the less, pride dictated that the Royal Navy play a part, although a supporting role, in the final defeat of Japan. Certainly there was no lack of bravery or skill among the officers and men of the warships and aircraft sent out, although they were all, from Admiral Sir Bruce Fraser, the C-in-C, down to the FAA pilots and TAGS, very conscious of how far behind Britain's fleet had fallen in three short years. One manifestation of this was the utter reliance on American aircraft types. Although a few British planes, Seafires, Fireflies and the like, were used, they were markedly inferior to the Avengers, Corsairs and Wildcats embarked in the British carriers for the work in hand.

It was the Grumman Avenger that had replaced the Barracuda and the older biplane types like the Fairey Swordfish

▶

Having been on the wrong end of dive-bombing when his destroyer, HMS *Kelly*, was sunk by Stukas off Crete in May 1941, Admiral Mountbatten was an enthusiastic backer of this method of precision attack. Thwarted in the Middle East he was able to get his wish when he was appointed C-in-C in India. Here he inspects the officers of No. 84 Squadron, a Vultee Vengeance unit which distinguished itself on the Burma Front. To the immediate right of Mountbatten's back is Squadron Leader Arthur Murland Gill who built the squadron up into a formidable fighting unit which won the praise of General Wingate. (Arthur Gill)

▶

Unusual view of Vultees from No. 110 Squadron in India during 1943. Four RAF squadrons and two Indian Air Force squadrons were equipped with this aircraft and used it to good effect in the Arakan campaign, with Wingate's Chindits and in the Battle of the Boxes. (Donald Ritchie)

▶

A Canadian aircrew with their groundcrew. No. 110 Squadron in Burma was a crack unit with men from all over the Commonwealth knitting together as a team. Although conditions were primitive the groundcrew performed wonders and a high sortie rate was maintained. (Bud McInnes)

◄

Vengeances of No 24 Squadron RAAF off North Australia in 1943. The Vultees saw much action here and in New Guinea and flew some remarkable and accurate sorties during this time. (Australian War Memorial)

▶

Vengeance in a jungle revetment being prepared for another sortie. In addition to the fighting on the Indian-Burmese border, several Vengeance squadrons participated in the final breakthrough on the southern Arakan Front including the battles for Akyab Island in 1943–44. (RAF Museum)

and Albacore which had disgracefully lingered so long in front-line service in the fleet. Again, as torpedo targets were few and far between, the Royal Navy used this aircraft mainly in the shallow dive-bombing role, as indeed did the US Navy and Marine Corps in the Pacific. It served well in this role having a good range and carrying capacity.

The British dive-bomber pilots spent most of their days off Okinawa putting bomb holes into the runways of obscure little islands to prevent the Japanese staging aircraft through to the main battle. It was not very glamorous or rewarding work for these highly skilled aircrew, but the US Commander, Admiral 'Bull' Halsey, was determined to keep the British fleet well away from any more worthwhile targets which he regarded as his exclusive prey! No chance of a crack at the *Yamato* then for the Fleet Air Arm.

But, on their way out to the Pacific earlier, the young dive-bomber aircrews did take part in attacks on the Japanese controlled oil refineries at Pladjoe and Songei Garong near Palembang in Sumatra. These attacks were delivered with great panache and enthusiasm by the Avengers and they were rewarded with damage reports and photographs showing the oil tanks burning well and

covering the area with great black clouds of smoke. It all looked very satisfactory and technically it *had* been very well done. There was no question that the dive-bombers had conducted themselves well and, at first, little doubt about the results they had achieved. For example, the historian of the War at Sea, the late Captain Stephen Roskill, stated quite firmly that, 'according to Japanese reports, the output of the Pladjoe refinery was halved'. He added: 'These two raids were by far the most successful so far carried out in the theatre, and as late as the end of March 1945 the Palembang refineries were only working at one-third of their capacity.'[7]

Not until later were any doubts expressed or was it? There is firm evidence to suggest that reasoned and carefully thought-out opinions against this operation had been fully expressed *prior* to the attack. It seems clear that these had been overruled at a very high level indeed. J. R. Speirs kindly gave me this analysis of the situation as viewed from the sharp end at the time:

'It was my job to brief the pilots for this raid. I first attempted to persuade the powers that be, that the raid was a waste of time and resources for many reasons. Two of them will suffice for now.

In the first place it had been agreed, a

year before the raid, that, as between Borno, Sumatra and Burma, the Japanese would have all the oil they needed and plenty to spare. Where they *were* vulnerable was in tankers to transport the oil to where it was needed, i.e., Japan itself. At the time of the raid the Japanese had few tankers left to transport oil from Sumatra, i.e., they did not *need* this production.

In the second place we had experience of bombing refineries in Europe. Now, although the RAF record, when it came to hitting pin-point targets, was miserable, their failure was not quite 100 per cent. On the few occasions when a raid on a refinery was successful, every attempt was made to find out how long the refinery was out of commission. The average time was sixteen days. You will of course realize that the RAF over Germany could carry a much heavier bomb load than dive-bombers. It follows that even if the dive-bombers were completely successful it would be unlikely for these refineries, which were anyway surplus to requirements, to be out for as much as sixteen days. I was told that for political reasons the raid had to go ahead.

I then suggested that they should fly a recce to see if there were any tankers in the area. If there were they would make

an ideal target for dive-bombers. If there were not it would tend to confirm that the targets were not very important. The idea was turned down.

In briefing the pilots I told them to avoid bombing the oil tanks for the reason that if they fired the oil stocks they would find the whole target rapidly covered by an impenetrable smoke-screen. Furthermore, although burnt-out tanks might look derelict, in fact the lower twelve feet or so would be intact, even if the roof had collapsed, and the tank could be in use, with reduced capacity, almost immediately. In the event they did bomb the tanks. I told them to go for the stills, cracking plant and distillation columns.

At the time of the raid most of the Japanese tankers had been sunk. The Japanese economy was on the point of collapse. The atom bombs were not necessary. We failed to convince the Americans that this was so. To sum up, you should say, for the sake of posterity, that this was a classical case of the *misuse* of dive-bombers.'[61]

The only slight mitigation against this judgement would seem to be in its 'blooding' value for untried aircrew. When I interviewed Admiral Sir Michael Denny about this raid he told me: 'The Palembang attacks were of

immense value in increasing the efficiency of my young pilots in *Victorious*. I was always thankful for them because of the excellent training they provided. The real object of the creation of the carrier squadrons was for the final business of fighting the Japanese in their home waters, but it was fortunate that these earlier attacks took place when they did as the experience was first class and something we all needed.'[62]

Wirraway missions

The Australian Army and Air Force fighting the Japanese in the jungle-clad hills of Papua and New Guinea were making the best use of what aircraft they could find in the dive-bombing role. These turned out to be the Wirraway and the Boomerang and they continued to use these two stalwarts in this role even after the true dive-bombers, the Vultee Vengeance, had been withdrawn to Australia. Paul L. Muir, Major R. J. C. O'Loan and the men of No. 4 Squadron, RAAF, have provided a detailed account of this work, never before recorded in detail.

'On 6 October 1942, General Blamey, the Australian C-in-C, made a request for an Army Co-Operation squadron armed with comparatively slow aircraft. He quoted Walker as suggesting a

squadron consisting of Wirraways, Boomerangs and Tiger Moths. Next day he was informed that No. 4 (Army Co-Operation) Squadron would be sent to Port Moresby as soon as possible. This proposal met with some opposition at GHQ. The Wirraway, it was held, was obsolete and if intercepted by Japanese fighters, casualties would be high. Blamey agreed that the evidence indicated the unsuitability of the Wirraway, but said that this would be acceptable if no more suitable aircraft were available.

The first of three aircraft arrived at Port Moresby on 7 November 1942 and by 21 November the unit was established on the Berry strip outside Port Moresby, with eighteen Wirraways on its strength. Its tasks were aerial reconnaissance, photography, artillery-spotting, message and supply dropping, strafing and dive-bombing and the distribution of propaganda leaflets. To this "maid of all work" role was added weather reconnaissance. Supply dropping, so vital, to the Australian troops on the Kokoda track, was very largely dependent on favourable weather. The Wirraway pilots sortied in the Kokoda Gap — the true gap, which was an air route between the mountain peaks at an altitude of 7,500 feet instead of about 12,000 to 13,000 feet, the altitude needed to pass over the

◄
A wrecked Wirrway flown by Flight Lieutenant Cyril McPherson, RAAF, after a forced-landing on Howard Island in the Arafuara Sea on 25 February 1943. (Cyril McPherson)

◄
A Type 99 Mk 2 Val takes off from a dusty jungle airstrip in the southern Pacific war zone in 1943. Now the drab green paint for concealment indicates how things have changed, but the Japanese dive-bombers still proved capable of delivering telling blows against the Allied landing fleets during this period. (Kantosha)

▼
The USS *Franklin*, listing and heavily on fire after being dive-bombed by a Judy off Japan. (US National Archives)

Typical of pre-combat briefings the world over. Here a US Marine Corps Dauntless squadron based in the Marshal Islands in 1944, is briefed for its attack on yet another isolated Japanese-held atoll. Constant pounding of these by-passed garrisons proved the SBD's main role until the invasion of the Philippines brought their close-support role to the fore once more. (Elmer Glidden)

main range. Here they circled, signalling back to base and advising New Guinea Force HQ if weather conditions were such that air craft could land with safety at Kokoda.

On 24 November the squadron was given its first attack mission; two flights, each of three aircraft and each aircraft carrying two 250lb bombs and 1,200 rounds of .303in ammunition, strafed and dive-bombed targets in the Gona area.

My diary (strictly illegal) for 24 November reads: "The army needs some co-operation at Gona and the Wirra's are going over to do some dive-bombing. At 0700 the first flight took off. Each has 2 – 250lb bombs under its wings. (Later) Heard the Wirras had returned. The bombing was a success. Monday 7 December 1942. The Wirras are going out to dive-bomb the west end of Buna strip. The infantry are going in after this. The signal is a long burst of machine-gun fire into the water. The Wirras came back OK. They dropped nine out of sixteen bombs on the target. We do not know how the infantry got on yet. Wednesday 9 December 1942. Lieutenant Eaton went to NGF to see Sir Thomas Blamey so the Wirras could go and do some bombing. Friday 11 December 1942. Six of our kites are going over to bomb some

supply huts at Sanananda Point. Two kites failed to return from the raid. Saturday 12 December 1942. At 0700 three Wirras took off to bomb the same place as yesterday."

These entries in my diary are the only ones that appertain to any dive-bombing done by No. 4 Squadron during the Buna campaign. The squadron had had very little training on dive-bombing during its stay on the mainland. While waiting to go to New Guinea at Kingaroy in Queensland they received two Wirraways equipped with dive brakes. One was written-off in a prang and the other was taken back. When the squadron arrived in New Guinea no aircraft of the squadron was equipped with them, nor did they receive any.

It continued in operations continuously throughout the war and co-operated with all field units wherever operations were in progress. It was re-equipped with Boomerang aircraft in May and June 1943 and these carried out a lot of the tasks that the Wirraway had previously done. However the Wirraways were utilized to the utmost at all times on photo recces, supply drops, couriers to and from detached flights and sub-flights and also to take army personnel on familiarization flights over areas of operations in which they were actively involved. The

continuity of operations brought the pilots of the squadron a degree of skill on reconnaissance missions that caused reports to come from both the field and Headquarters that their reports on enemy movements in jungle terrain were such as would equal the skill of the American Indian. Working with both the American forces or with Australian forces, they had the tracking capacity of the Australian aborigines. They were uncanny in their ability to locate, read and decypher tracks and signs of Japanese movements. This led to a new field of endeavour. They could read the jungle from the air like it was the palm of their own hand. With the advent of the fighter-bomber it became obvious that the fighter pilots needed a guide to enable them to obtain the results that were needed from their missions. The Wirraway crews developed a method of lead-in strikes. They would indicate to the fighter-bomber pilots where they could get the best results by firing a burst of tracer into the target area and the fighters would then deliver their load where it did the most good.

At the beginning of 1945, No. 4 Squadron had flights at Gusap, Madang and Aitape in New Guinea and at Cape Hoskins and Cape Gloucester in New Britain. HQ at this time was at Nazdab in

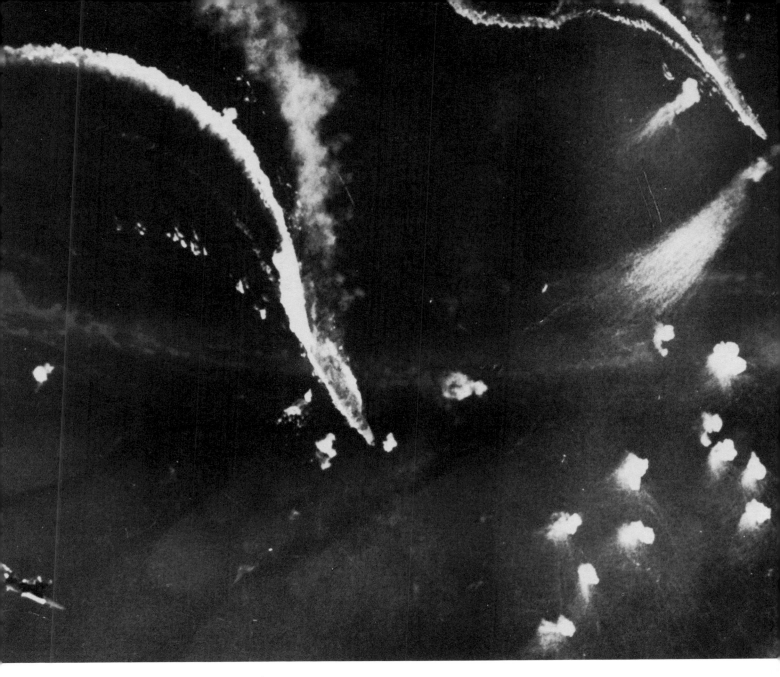

◀ US Navy Helldivers attacking the Japanese battleship *Musashi* during the Battle of Leyte Gulf, 24 October 1945. The lower photograph shows direct hits being scored. (U.S. National Archives)

▲ The pattern of the Pacific War. A Curtiss Helldiver can be seen (bottom left-hand corner) hurtling down through the Flak on to the wildly twisting and turning Japanese aircraft carriers *Zuikaku* and *Zuiho* during the great Battle of Leyte Gulf, on 25 October 1944. (US National Archives)

New Guinea. For the Borneo operations, HQ and A Flight were based at Labuan in British North Borneo, and B Flight was at Balikpapan in Dutch Borneo (now Indonesia).'[63]

James L. R. Flynn amplifies the above information with details from his Flying Log-book of his own operations in these aircraft during the final months of the war:

'The dive-bomb attack on 27 February 1945 on the 20/40mm gun emplacements at Dagua and But was carried out in a Wirraway. Dive-bombing with a Wirraway was fairly precise and I had a deal of such experience. Training in Southern Rhodesia on Havards was my first introduction, followed by Wirraway dive-bombing on our SACO range at Canberra while instructing there, and then some practise drops and operational drops with No. 4 squadron.

I used the standard techniques, positioning of target relative to wing root in straight and level flight, roll turn into steep dive, careful handling to avoid any deviation during dive before release of bombs effected at a safe height to allow for pull-out.

My log-book does not record any damage to my aircraft from this mission, but I noted that as I flew away at low level along the beach from the target a

Khaki-uniformed soldier slapped me a salute! I assumed he was a Jap!

My log-book shows I carried out some dive-bombing practise in a Boomerang on 25 January 1945. For that I utilized the standard techniques learned on the Harvard/Wirraways, but modified to recognize the higher dive speed and long pull-out radius of the Boomerang.'[64]

The last dive-bombing attacks

What must surely qualify for some of the last dive-bombing attacks of the war took place in Burma, on 9 August 1945. They were conducted by No. 8 Squadron, Indian Air Force, and they were flying Supermarine Spitfires. No. 8 Squadron had earlier been equipped with the Vultee Vengeance and had carried out numerous dive-bombing missions on the Mayu Peninsula during the successful final Arakan Campaign. Operating from Cox's Bazaar, this unit became the first Indian Air Force Squadron to re-equip with Spitfires, making its operating début with this aircraft on 3 June 1944, over the Akyab Islands.

Although the fighter aircraft supreme, the Spitfire, lacking aerial opposition, was frequently pressed into service as a dive-bomber, operating on the 'Cab Rank' system with 250lb bombs under

each wing. This technique had been pioneered in Italy by the Desert Air Force. It was found that the Spitfire could deliver the goods quite well in steep dives, although this aircraft had not of course been designed to stand up to such use and some curious wing-root configurations (the ripple effect) often resulted after a terminal-velocity dive and recovery.

On 28 January 1945, No. 8 IAF Squadron gave close air support to an Indian Brigade of 25 Division which, after taking Myebon Island, had thrust across the mainland to cut off the retreating enemy withdrawing down the Kaladan Valley. Working from Ramree Island they had also dive-bombed the enemy at An where they were making a final stand.

General Slim's land battles to clear Burma of the enemy had been a great success and Rangoon had fallen as early as 3 May 1945. But there were still many stubborn pockets of resistance holding out in the Sittang area south of the country until Japan's final surrender, and these had to be systematically mopped-up. These were the survivors from several large groups of fully combat-worthy Japanese troops, some 20,000 in all, who had earlier taken refuge in the Pegu Yomas hills north of Pegu itself. Here they bided their time to await a

◄
One little-known unit to use the Dauntless in the South Pacific with great success was the Royal New Zealand Air Force's Number 25 Squadron on Bougainville in 1944. (Meg Campbell)

►
The leader of the New Zealand dive-bomber force was Squadron Leader T. J. McLen de Lange. They co-operated with the US Marine Corps SBDs in first holding the bridgehead against Japanese assault and then in the pounding of the Rabaul airstrips. (Meg Campbell)

▼
With the arrival of overwhelming numbers of American fleet and light cruisers, equipped with hundreds of Grumman Hellcat fighters, and warships fitted with scores of automatic AA weapons from 20mm and 40mm up to 5-inch guns, the chances of conventional dive-bombing attacks getting through fell dramatically. Although such attacks continued to be mounted, increasingly the older dive-bombers were converted for use as suicide craft, the Kamikaze idea. Here D3A2 Vals, so converted to Special Attack units, are seen taking-off from an airbase in the vicinity of Manila on 22 November 1944, to attack the US invasion fleet offshore. (Tadashi Nozawa)

◄

When the British Pacific Fleet finally got to the Pacific they were eager to take on the Japanese Navy head-on to avenge earlier defeats at their hands, but they found that the Americans had already just about finished the job anyway. They had to be content with the more lowly role of putting bomb holes in island airfields to prevent the Japanese flying in reinforcements to the Okinawa battle. This task was tackled with dedication and skill, but was not very fulfilling. Here an Avenger of 848 Squadron is seen diving over yet another Kamikaze nest. (Fleet Air Arm Museum)

▶

Front-line Wirraway. This is the mount of Squadron Leader J. Hearn with 5 Squadron on Bougainville Island, 1945. The Wirraway was found to be ideal for accurately marking difficult precision targets with smoke-bombs so that the more powerfully armed Corsairs could make their follow-up strikes with confidence. But, from time to time, the Wirraways also got into the act with their own combat dive-bombing missions. (R. & P. Hourigan)

◄

On 24 January 1945, aircraft of the Fleet Air Arm attacked Palembang in Sumatra and inflicted damaged on the oil installations there. Grumman Avengers were utilized in the shallow dive-bombing role in this attack, diving through a balloon barrage and being attacked by Japanese fighter aircraft. They scored numerous direct hits on oil tanks and other facilities. Great play was made of the effect this had on the Japanese Fleet's ability to operate, but in fact production was not greatly curbed, nor for long, and Japan had few warships left to use the oil anyway. The attack was a great morale-raiser for the newly formed British Pacific Fleet before they took on the Kamikazes off Okinawa and the bombing was pressed home with great gallantry. (Imperial War Museum)

suitable opportunity to break out across the River Sittang and seek sanctuary across the border in Thailand. The move was made in July and resulted in a bloody slaughter with Allied ground, naval and air forces blocking their path, driving them into the swamps and pounding them continually. The Japanese lost 6,270 killed and 740 taken prisoner from their force. The survivors retreated back into the jungle and had to be carefully and patiently flushed out.

Accordingly, No. 8 Squadron (which since 12 March had become Royal Indian Air Force) was moved down from Baigachi to Mingaladon Field and carried out a series of intensive combat patrols over the Sitang region to locate and attack, in co-operation with the army, such Japanese groups as remained and eliminate them.

The success of these dive-bombing missions was reflected in the signals received from the Army. After a particularly potent attack against a concentration of Japanese trying to slip across the river on 3 August 1945, the following signal came in: 'Good Strike today. Many killed. Raft Concentration broken up. Japs screaming. 70 plus killed in suicide crossing after strikes.' And an attack the next day brought the signal: 'All bombs on target. Lovely sight.'

Such complimentary signals were known as 'strawberries' to distinguish them from the more well-known 'raspberry' when things went wrong. The Squadron report on this last sortie reads: 'In spite of obtaining excellent results (in the first attack), the Army called upon No. 8 Squadron to attack the same village with eight aircraft as it appears a large number of Japs were trying to escape.'[65]

And so, at 1440 on 9 August, the second dive-bombing attack of the day was made against enemy concentrations in a small village on the west bank of the river. This strike was led by Flight Lieutenant Foster. The other pilots who participated in this final attack were, Flight Lieutenant Curtis, Flying Officers Bouche, Chaves, Dhillon, Ridges, Singh and Sipurkar. It is noteworthy that due to the considerable expansion of the RIAF, many Commonwealth pilots from Canada, Australia and New Zealand were still flying with the Royal Indian Air Force at this time. The results were devastating.

'Out of eight bombs, six scored direct hits destroying 6 Bashas (native huts) out of eight. One bomb undershot and luckily struck something big as a large explosion followed with a thick column of black smoke. The bombing was

followed with sixteen strafing runs. Very little could be seen in the target area owing to the smoke. A 100 per cent result was obtained. We were quite satisfied that such good damage has been inflicted in this raid.

It is really satisfactory that within one week of operations we started receiving a number of "strawberries". Regarding this excellent result a word must be said which gives a credit to all our pilots, that none of them had any bombing experience at all. In spite of which such good results were obtained in a few days. Probably these good results can be attributed to the tradition of this squadron being originally a "Dive-Bomber" squadron – the spirit of the Vengeance still lingers!'[66]

Source Notes

1 Hans-Ulrich Rudel to the author, August 1974.

2 *Outline of the History of Dive-Bombing in Sweden;* prepared for the author by Colonel Nils Kindberg, *Flygvapnet.* Also, Squadron Leader Lennart Berns, Swedish Air Force, Swedish Aviation Historical Society told the author in February 1987 that: '. . . a lot of the development of the dive-bomber took place in Sweden during the early 1930s tie-ins with the Junkers K-47 — and the tests done by Swedish dive-bombing pioneer Bjorn Bjuggren. There has been a long debate in Sweden as to whether the Swedish-built K-47 was a predecessor to the Ju 87 and whether the tests by Bjorn Bjuggren had any influence. Bjorn Bjuggren — who ended his career as a Swedish Air Force General — had then acquired a couple of Hawker Harts for his tests, much to the horror of the manufacturer. The Germans took great interest in the Swedish trials and they may have contributed to the development of the Ju 87 Stuka.'

3 Extract from Official Rugen Test Centre Reports quoted by my old friend, Hanfried Schliephake, in his book *The Birth of the Luftwaffe,* Ian Allan, 1971.

4 Air Ministry: *Dive-Bombing,* RAF Official, London, 1940.

5 Jean Cuny to the author, September 1987.

6 Squadron Leader D. Lapraik: *Report – The German BZA-1 Dive Bombsight,* 12 September 1941 (AIR 40/36).

7 Squadron Leader R. Steele: *Report – Japan – Preliminary Report on Navy T99 Dive-Bomber,* 13 December 1941 (AIR 40/35).

8 Summary of the A-35 Airplane Project, USAAF Document No. 202, 1–3 September 1944.

9 Memorandum from General Brett, USAAF, dated 3 July 1940. Also Memorandum to Materials Division, Washington, DC, of Conference with General H. Arnold, Colonel Echols and Doctor Meads, 2 July 1940, Washington, DC (cf7).

10 US Director General of Military Requirements, quoted in *U.S. Naval Fighters of World War II,* Michael O'Leary, Blandford, 1986. See also: (1) Morris Wilson, Briny Signal 1924 dated 13 December 1940, to Lord Beaverbrook (MAP). (AIR19/498 71942) '. . . the position here is that the U.S. Army have no dive-bombers in stock or on order. They may order some of the Brewster dive-bombers which are now being designed and built to our order but Knudsen recognizes the incompetence of the Brewster organization and the certainty that they will not achieve the delivery programmes previously expected by the U.S. Army Department to be possible. Following a visit to the Brewster plant by Fairey, Phillip Young and Forrestal, the U.S. Administration took strong action against the management, but the organization of the firm is not yet strong enough to overcome the inertia of the past. The new management should give deliveries in the summer, but that is the best we can hope for.' (2) Extract from Briny Signal 5397, dated 8 June 1942 to Air Ministry (AIR20/4249 71989): 'Unfortunately the Bermuda still remains unsatisfactory and I am afraid that however efficient new control may be on paper, Brewsters are confronted with practical production and design difficulties that make it impossible to take an optimistic view of the future.'

11 Burton S. Block to the author, July 1987.

12 General Wolfe to Colonel Sassons. Recorded telephone conversations dated 1 September 1942, regarding Vultee and Curtiss dive-bomber procurement problems (cf7).

13 Summary of the A-35 Airplane Project, (USAF Document 202-1-3, dated September 1944). Made available to the author by USAF Historical Research Center, Research Division (RI), Maxwell AFB, 23 April 1985.

14 Stanley Worth to the author, September 1985.

15 Roland Tapp to the author, October 1986.

16 Robert Olds to the author, May 1987. See also Robert Olds, *Helldiver Squadron,* New York 1945.

17 Captain T. W. Harrington, RN Rtd, to the author, July 1986.

18 Lord Kilbracken, *Bring Back My Stringbag,* London, 1979.

19 Captain E. M. Brown, RN, to the author, June 1977.

20 L. F. Foster to the author, May 1986.

21 Flight Lieutenant H. Griffiths, *RAF in Russia,* London, 1942.

22 Squadron Leader D. Lapraik: Report – USSR PE-2 Twin-Engined Dive-Bomber, 11 September 1941 (AIR 40/35).

23 Meeting of Bombing Sub-Committee on proposed dive-bombers and proposed dive-bombing sight (AIR 20/4155). The Royal Navy's renewed interest in dive-bombing followed the visit of Lieutenant Commander St. J. Prentice to the USA in 1931. Despite the enthusiasm of both naval pilots and very senior officers, little progress was made. See Admiral Backhouse, Controller of the Navy, Memorandum, 7 May 1937 (ADM 116/4030). The wartime First Sea

Lord, Admiral Sir Dudley Pound, shared the same sentiments. See also Captain R. M. Ellis M/S on Naval Staff meeting on Day Two of the War, 4 September 1939 (ADM116/3720).

24 E. Christopher Deanesly to the author, May 1986.

25 R. A. E. Farnborough: Report on comparisons between actual German and Proposed British dive-bombing sights, 1 February 1940.

26 Wing Commander A. F. Blackadder, Air Fighting Development Unit, RAF Wittering: Report No. 149, Mustang Dive-Bombing, 10 October 1944 (AIR 24/605).

27 National Research Section (ADGB): Dive-Bombing Tactics – Analysis of two Bomphoon Attacks on Ground Targets in northern France, 14 March 1944 (AIR 2/1140).

28 Air Ministry: Dive-Bombing technique with high-speed aircraft of clean Aerodynamic design, 2 April 1936 (AIR 2/1655/5/36709).

29 Development of the A31/A35 dive-bomber. USAAF Official Report and Transcription of telephone conversation concerning same. Washington, DC, 1944.

30 Aviation Ordnance – Development. US Navy Bureau of Ordnance, Washington, DC, 1949.

31 Colonel Nils Kindberg, Dive-Bombing – Swedish principles and experiences. Memorandum presented to the author. Stockholm, 1978.

32 Erik A. Wilkenson, Doctor of Technology. How Sweden Developed a New Bomb Sight, SAAB, Stockholm, 1947. Also see Lennart Larsson, 'Svensk salde bombsikte till Pentagon!' ('Swede

sold bomb sights to the Pentagon!') in Flyghistoriskt Manadsblad, Stockholm, 1978.

33 Dr Erick A. Wilkenson to the author, March/April 1986.

34 Major Frank Neubert to the author, June 1986.

35 Admiral Francis Laine, French Navy, Rtd, to the author, March/May 1986.

36 Captain T. W. Harrington to the author, June 1986.

37 Captain S. W. Roskill, The War at Sea (4 vols), London, 1954–61.

38 War Cabinet Report: Experience with the U.P. Weapon at Dover, 4 August 1940 (WP (40) 303 Cab 66/10).

39 Len Deighton, Fighter, London, 1976.

40 Operations Record Book, RAF Hawkinge. 15 August 1940 (AIR 28/815).

41 Operations Record Book, RAF Tangmere, 16 August 1940 (AIR 28/815).

42 Flying Logbook of Heinz Sellhorn (on loan to the author) and Sellhorn interview, January 1986. See also Gunter Stiller, '30 Sekunden Zwischen Himmel und Holle' Interview with Heinz Sellhorn in Bild am Sonntag, Nr. 45, 5 November 1978.

43 Horst Lippach, Hanover: letter in Bild am Sonntag, Nr. 50, 10 December 1978.

44 Major Ennio Tarantola to the author, August 1977.

45 Colonel Robert L. Scott, God is my Co-pilot, New York, 1943.

46 27th Bombardment Group (Dive) USAAF, Squadron, Re-Union History. Dayton, Ohio, 4–5 June 1976.

47 Bob Piper to the author, September 1986.

48 RAAF: Confidential Report of Air Attack on Milne Bay, 15 April 1944. (RAAF Historical Section, (Department of Defence, Canberra A.C.T.) Also Sadao Seno to the author, November 1986.

49 Air Attack on Shipping at Milne Bay, Report of Lieutenant K. J. Bramley, RANR, Staff Officer, (Intelligence) Port Moresby, dated 22 April 1943, to Staff Officer (Intelligence), 9 Operation Group. (Confidential document P/12/1143/68) RAAF Historical Section, Canberra, ACT.

50 Report of Lieutenant K. J. Bramley, RANR, Staff Officer (Intelligence) P/12/1143/68, 22 April 1943 (ibid).

51 Report of Sgt P. M. Sheahan, No. 75 Squadron, RAAF, 14 April 1943 (ibid).

52 Admiral William I. Martin, USN, Rtd, to the author, June 1977.

53 Masatake Okumiya and Jiro Horikoshi, Zero!, London, 1957.

54 Flight Lieutenant James M. Swan, RAAF, Rtd, to the author, December 1986 and February 1987.

55 Ron Walesby to the author, February 1987.

56 M: Mol. gvardiia, V nebe frontovom, (2 vols), Moscow, 1962, 1971. (Memoirs of Soviet women pilots who distinguished themselves in the war) and see also: M. P. Chechneva, Letali devchata v gvardeiskom. (The Taman Aviation Regiment crewed by women, and their war exploits.) Also, Colonel N. Denisov, Boyevaia Slava Sovetskoi Aviatsii (Fighting Glory of Soviet Aviation), Military Publishing House, Ministry of Defence, Moscow, 1953, and I. V. Timokhevich, Operativnoe

Iskusstvo Sovetskikh VVS Velikoi Otechestvennoi Voine, Voenizdat, Moscow, 1976. The latter in particular provides a great depth of operational analysis, sortie rates, missions, army-air co-operation and such statistical data, as well as very clear and useful diagrams on Soviet dive-bombing techniques.

57 J. Blair Watson to the author, September 1986.

58 Allan H. Thomson to the author, July 1986.

59 Louis S. Casey, Naval Aircraft 1914–1939 and 1939–1945, London, 1975, in which he talks of dive-bombers carrying bombs powerful enough 'to crack open a battleship'.

60 Tommy Thompson to the author, September 1986.

61 J. R. Spiers to the author, March 1987.

62 Admiral Sir Michael Denny to the author, April 1968 (See also Peter C. Smith Task Force 57: The British Pacific Fleet 1944–45, London, 1969.)

63 Paul L. Muir and Major R. J. C. O'Loan to the author, May 1987, and Memorandum, 'The Role of the Wirraway as a Dive-Bomber', prepared for the author by ex-officers and men of No. 4 Squadron, RAAF.

64 James L. R. Flynn to the author, June 1987; Charles Dallow to the author, January 1987.

65 Operations Record Books of Nos. 7 and 8 Squadrons, Indian Air Force, 1945 (AIR 27/123).

66 No. 8 Squadron Squadron Diary and Signal Logs, July/August 1945 (AIR 27/123).

▶
One of the only two Vultee Vengeance dive-bombers to escape the scrapyard lies in a small Australian Museum hangar where it was lovingly restored by a serving member of the present-day RAAF. (Wayne Brown)

▶▶
'Margie H' as she is preserved today in full working trim with dive brakes down and dummy bombs, kills and missions all marked up. And in front of her, her old pilot, Larry Dye. (L. W. Dye)

Bibliography

This book has been written mainly from first-hand sources – interviews and correspondence with air and groundcrew of dive-bomber forces from many nations, supplemented by documentary sources, many hitherto little examined. Printed sources were not called on other than for the broader outline, but the books listed below should prove a useful starting point for further research into the subject.

Documents
Admiralty: Meeting of Bombing Sub-Committee on proposed dive-bombers and proposed dive-bombing sight (AIR 20/4155).

Air Ministry: Dive-Bombing technique with high-speed aircraft of clean Aerodynamic design, 2 April 1936 (AIR 2/1655/5/36709).

Air Ministry: Briny Signal 5397, dated 8 June 1942, to Air Ministry (AIR 20/4249 71989).

Air Ministry: Dive-Bombing, RAF Official, London, 1940.

Air Ministry: Operations Record Book, RAF Hawkinge, 15 August 1940 (AIR 28/815).

Air Ministry: Operations Record Book, RAF Tangmere, 16 August 1940 (AIR 28/815).

Air Ministry: Operations Record Books, Nos. 7 and 8 Squadrons, Indian Air Force, 1945 (AIR 27/123).

Air Ministry: No 8 Squadron Squadron Diary and Signal Logs, July/August 1945 (AIR 27/123).

Blackadder, Wing Commander A. F., Air Fighting Development Unit – RAF Wittering: Report No. 149, Mustang Dive-Bombing, 10 October 1944 (AIR 24/605).

Bramley, Lieutenant K. J., RANR, Staff Officer (Intelligence). Report dated 22 April 1943 (P/12/1143/69).

Kindberg, Colonel Nils: Dive-Bombing – Swedish principles and experiences. Memorandum presented to the author, Stockholm, 1978.

Kindberg, Colonel Nils, Outline of the History of Dive-Bombing in Sweden; prepared for the author by Flygvapnet, Stockholm.

Lapraik, Squadron Leader D., Report: USSR PE-2 Twin-Engined Dive-Bomber, 11 September 1941 (AIR 40/35).

Lapraik, Squadron Leader D., Report: The German BZA-1 Dive-Bombsight, 12 September 1941 (AIR 40/36).

Larsson, Lennart: 'Svensk salde bombsikte till Pentagon! ('Swede sold bomb sight to the Pentagon!') – Article in Flyghistoriskt Mandasblad, Stockholm, 1978.

Memorandum, The Role of the Wirraway as a Dive-Bomber prepared for the author by ex-officers and men of No. 4 Squadron, RAAF, 1987.

National Research Section (ADGB): Dive-Bombing Tactics – Analysis of two Bomphoon Attacks on Ground Targets in northern France, 14 March 1944 (AIR 2/1140).

Privately published – 27th Bombardment Group (Dive) USAAF, Squadron, *Re-Union History*. Dayton, Ohio. 4–5 June 1976.

RAAF: Confidential Report of Air Attack on Milne Bay, 15 April 1944. (RAAF Historical Section, Department of Defence, Canberra ACT).

RAAF: Air Attack on Shipping at Milne Bay, Report of Lieutenant K. J. Bramley, RANR, Staff Officer, (Intelligence) Port Moresby, dated 22 April 1943, to Staff Officer (Intelligence), 9 Operation Group. (Confidential document P/12/1143/68) RAAF Historical Section, Canberra ACT.

R.A.E. Farnborough: Report on comparisons between actual German and Proposed British dive-bombing sights, 1 February 1940.

Riviere, Pierre, 'Les Forces Aériennes de L'Atlantique, 1944/45, in *Le Fana d'Aviation*, Paris, 1983.

Sellhorn, Heinz, Flying Logbook (on loan to the author), and Sellhorn interview, January 1986.

Sheahan, Sergeant P.M., No. 75 Squadron, RAAF, Report dated 14 April 1943.

Stiller, Gunter, '30 Sekunden Zwischen Himmel und Holle', Interview with Heinz Sellhorn in *Bild am Sonntag*, Nr. 45, 5 November 1978.

Steele, Squadron Leader R., Report – Japan – Preliminary Report on Navy T99 Dive-Bomber, 13 December 1941 (AIR 40/35).

USAAF: Summary of the A-35 Airplane Project, USAAF Document No. 202 1-3, Washington, DC, September 1944.

USAAF: Summary of the A-35 Airplane Project, USAAF Document 202-1-3, dated September 1944. Made available to the author by USAF Historical Research Center, Research Division (RI), Maxwell AFB, 23 April 1985.

USAAF: Development of the A31/A35 dive-bomber. USAAF Official Report and Transcription of telephone conversations concerning same. Washington, DC, 1944.

US Navy: Aviation Ordnance – Development. US Navy Bureau of Ordnance, Washington DC, 1949.

War Cabinet: Experience with the U.P. Weapon at Dover – Report. 4 August 1940 (WP (40) 303 Cab 66/10).

Wilkenson, Erick A. Doctor of Technology. *How Sweden Developed a New Bomb Sight*, SAAB, Stockholm, 1947.

Wilson, Morris: Briny Signal 1924 dated 13 December 1940, to Lord Beaverbrook (MAP) (AIR 19/498 71942).

Books

Baumbach, Werner. *Broken Swastika*. London, 1960

Casey, Louis S. *Naval Aircraft 1914–1939* and *1939–1945*. London, 1975

Chechneva, M. P. *Letali devchata v gvardeiskom . . .* Moscow, 1967

Clostermann, Pierre. *Flames in the Sky*. London, 1953

Deighton, Len. *Fighter*. London, 1976

Denisov, Colonel N. *Boyevaia Slava Sovetskoi Aviatsii* (Fighting Glory of Soviet Aviation). Military Publishing House, Ministry of Defence, Moscow, 1953

Edmonds, Walter D. *They Fought With What They Had*. (2nd ed.) – Washington, DC, 1983

Griffiths, Flight Lieutenant H. *RAF in Russia*. London, 1942

Haight, John McVickar, Jnr. *American Aid to France*. New York, 1970

Irving, David. *Hitler's War*. London, 1977

Kilbracken, Lord. *Bring Back My Stringbag*. London, 1979

Mol. M. gvardiia, *V nebe frontovom*, (2 vols). Moscow, 1962, 1971

Niepold, Gerd. *Battle for White Russia*. London, 1987

Obermaier, Ernst. *Die Ritterkreuztrager der Luftwaffe; Stuka- und Schlachtflieger, 1939–1945*. Mainz, 1976

Okumiya, Masatake, and Horikoshi, Jio. *Zero!*. London, 1957

Olds, Robert. *Helldiver Squadron*. New York, 1945

O'Leary, Michael. *U.S. Naval Fighters of World War II*. Poole, 1986

Roskill, Captain S. W. *The War at Sea* (4 vols). London, 1954–61

Schliephake, Hanfried. *The Birth of the Luftwaffe*. Ian Allan, 1971

Scott, Colonel Robert L. *God is my Co-pilot*. New York, 1943

Smith, Peter C. *Task Force 57; The British Pacific Fleet, 1944–45*. London, 1969

— *Vengeance!; The Vultee Vengeance Dive Bomber*. Shrewsbury, 1986

— *Jungle Dive Bombers at War*. London, 1987

— *Dive Bomber!* Ashbourne, 1982

Timokhevich, I. V. *Operativnoe Iskusstvo Sovetskikh VVS Velikoi Otechestvennoi Voine*. Voenizdat, Moscow, 1976.

Index